JEFFREY ANDERSON

fifth edition

MANAGEMENT

Kendall Hunt
publishing company

Cover photo © Shutterstock.com

Kendall Hunt
publishing company

www.kendallhunt.com
Send all inquiries to:
4050 Westmark Drive
Dubuque, IA 52004-1840

Copyright © 2016, 2017, 2018, 2019 by Kendall Hunt Publishing Company

PAK ISBN: 978-1-5249-8053-5
Text Alone ISBN: 978-1-5249-8054-2

Printed in the United States of America

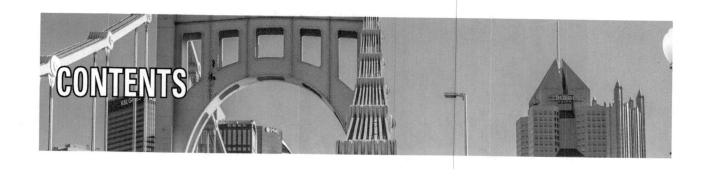

CONTENTS

CONTENTS

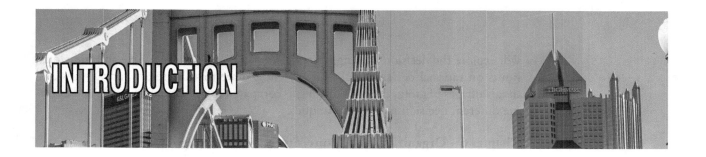

Chapter 1 – Introduction to Management

Management is all about working with people in organizations. Few meaningful outcomes in the workplace happen as a result of the effort of one person. Rather, most accomplishments are the product of a group of people working together in an organization. Regardless of your occupation, it is likely that you will work with others in your career. In this chapter, you will be introduced to the study of management and the roles that managers perform in organizations.

Chapter 2 – The Environments of Management

In this chapter, we explore the multiple environments within which organizations operate. These environments provide significant influences on an organization's operations and overall effectiveness. To be successful, an organization must align its strategy to fit factors such as economic conditions, political and legal concerns, technological developments, and trends in society. The complex environment creates uncertainty on how to make important organizational decisions. Managers must serve multiple stakeholders including owners, employees, and customers. Ethics, standards of right and wrong that influence our behavior, play an important role in helping managers make complex decisions that deal with competing stakeholder interests.

Chapter 3 – The Global Environment of Management

Globalization is an increasing trend that impacts managers. Individual country markets are now replaced by global ones. In this chapter, we will explore the reasons why organizations conduct business internationally. We will examine methods to do business internationally, and we will also examine how organizations do business and manage people in spite of cultural differences that are a part of the global business environment.

Chapter 4 – Planning and Strategy

Planning is the first step in the management process. Strategic plans are long term in nature and determine the overall direction for the organization. In this chapter, we will explore the planning process from the perspective of strategic management, starting with the organization's mission and outlining strategic management tools. We will discuss grand strategies and outline steps for analyzing an industry and reducing environmental uncertainty.

Chapter 5 – Making Decisions

As we discussed in Chapter One, managers perform in four different decisional roles; resource allocator, disturbance-handler, entrepreneur and negotiator. In this chapter, we will explore the decision making process. We will discuss the cognitive and individual limits on rational decision making. We will explore the differences, advantages and disadvantages of group decision making as compared to individual decisions and examine different decision making techniques.

Chapter 6 – Organizations, Culture, Structure and Design

In this chapter, we consider the management function of organizing. Organizing is about arranging tasks and people to accomplish the goals of the organization. We will start with division of labor, breaking a job down into discrete parts. Next we will examine various ways that organizations group people and tasks. We will conclude the chapter by discussing the dimensions of organizational culture and the ways to develop a positive culture in the organization.

Chapter 7 – Human Resource Management

This chapter is all about how organizations manage their people. For many organizations, people are their most valuable resources. We will explore the set of processes that organizations use to attract, develop, and retain qualified people. First, we will explore the legal environment of human resource management. Then, we will examine the ways that organizations recruit and select people. Next, we will look at ways that organizations develop and retain employees. Finally, we will examine the unique set of circumstances that comprise organizations with union employees.

Chapter 8 – Managing Diverse Individuals

In this chapter, we explore managing individuals. While some managers may direct many followers, each follower is an individual with different personalities, beliefs and attitudes. We will explore the perception process and outline personality types and dimensions. We will discuss individual attitudes and the relationship between attitude and job satisfaction.

Chapter 9 – Motivation

In their role as leaders, managers must motivate individuals to perform those actions that are necessary for the organization to reach its goals. In this chapter, we will explore three different perspectives on motivation. First, we will examine needs theoris that includes Maslow's hierarchy of needs and McClelland's learned needs theory. Next, we will discuss how reinforcement theory is used as a tool to modify behavior. Finally, we will examine cognitive motivation theories including expectancy theory, equity theory, and integrative approaches to motivating employees.

Chapter 10 – Managing Teams

Much of what is accomplished today in organizations is not the result of individual work, but rather work performed by teams. In this chapter, we will examine the various characteristics of effective teams. We will outline the team development process and discuss team roles and norms and the effects of teams on individual behavior.

Chapter 11 – Leadership

In previous chapters in this book, we have discussed the management functions of planning and organizing. In this chapter, we explore the leadership function. Leadership is about influencing others to take those actions that are necessary for the organization to achieve its goals. In this chapter, we will discuss power, the ability to influence others. We will compare leaders to managers and explore traits of effective leaders. We will explore leader behaviors, situational leadership and strategies for improving leadership.

Chapter 12 – Information, Communication, and Technology

Managers use information, communication, and technology daily. They monitor, collect, and process data that provide them with information to make better decisions. They communicate with others both inside and outside their organization, and managers use technology to improve their efficiency and effectiveness.

In this chapter, we'll explore the different types of information systems that managers use to process data. We'll outline the communication process and affirm the importance of communication. Finally, we'll look at ways that organizations can achieve a competitive advantage by organizing and interpreting vast amounts of data.

Chapter 13 – Controlling

In chapter one, we introduced the management process. The process begins with planning and closes with controlling. Planning and controlling are inextricably linked. We don't know the outcomes of our plans without the controlling function. Past performance, as evaluated by the controlling function, in term provides valuable information for future planning. In this chapter we will explore the management controlling function and its purpose. We will examine various control mechanisms including financial measurements that managers use to monitor performance, compare that performance to planned goals, and take corrective action as needed.

CHAPTER 1 INTRODUCTION TO MANAGEMENT

Key Terms

Administrative management
Bureaucracy
Conceptual skills
Contingency approach
Controlling
Decisional roles
Effectiveness
Efficiency
First-line manager
Functional managers
General manager

Hawthorne effect
Human relations approach
Informational roles
Interpersonal roles
Interpersonal skills
Leading
Manager
Managerial roles
Middle manager
Operations management
Organization

Organizing
Planning
Quantitative approach
Scientific management
Systems theory
Technical skills
Theory X
Theory Y
Top managers

Introduction

Management is all about working with people in organizations. Few things in the work world happen as a result of the effort of one person but rather the work of an organization. Regardless of your occupation, it is likely that you will work with other people in organizations. In this chapter, you will be introduced to the study of management and the role of managers in organizations.

© Shutterstock.com

Learning Outcomes

After reading this chapter, you should be able to:

❏ **Explain** the role of managers in organizations
❏ **Remember** and **understand** different types of managers
❏ **Describe** a manager's job functions and roles
❏ **Remember** and understand the various skills required of managers
❏ **Explain** the evolution of the study of management

What Is an Organization?

An organization is a group of people who work together in a structured and coordinated way to achieve a set of goals.[1] Examples of organizations include for-profit

Organization A group of people who work together in a structured and coordinated way to achieve a set of goals

businesses like Apple and Nike as well as not-for-profit organizations like the Red Cross, government agencies, and many others. All organizations have a purpose, expressed in goals. That goal may be to earn a return on the investment of the owners in the case of for-profit organizations or to serve a need in society in the case of not-for-profit organizations.

What Is Management?

Simply stated, management is what managers do. More specifically, management is the set of activities directed at achieving organizational goals. Management is the process of getting things done through people[2], a process we will explore throughout this chapter.

Who Are Managers?

Manager
Someone who coordinates the work of others to achieve organizational goals.

Efficiency
Getting the most output from the least amount of resources.

Effectiveness
Doing the right things that will result in achieving organizational goals.

Top managers
A manager who makes long-term decisions about the overall direction of the organization.

A manager is someone who coordinates the work of others to accomplish organizational goals.[3] Managers work in organizations, collections of people who work together for a common purpose.[4] A manager's job is to work with and through people in an organization to make that goal a reality. In their pursuit of organizational goals, managers must use organizational resources, things like people, money, and equipment, effectively and efficiently.

Working efficiently, in a management context, refers to getting the most output from the least amount of resources.[5] As part of the management process, managers coordinate resources like people's time and effort, and money. As these resources are limited, managers need to use those resources wisely and efficiently. It's not enough to be efficient though, organizations need to reach goals. A manager works effectively, when he or she does those things that will result in achieving goals.[6]

What Are Different Types of Managers?

One way to classify different types of managers is according to their position on the organizational hierarchy. In a traditionally structured organization, managers fall into one of three levels; top, middle and first line.[7] This hierarchy is outlined in Figure 1.

Top managers are a relatively small group of executives who manage the entire organization.[8] Top managers make long-term decisions about the overall direction of the organization. They establish the organization's objectives and strategies and policies to reach those objectives.[9] Top managers have titles like president, vice president, chief executive officer (CEO), chief operating officer (COO), or managing director.[10] Top managers set the strategy and lead the organization according to its mission or purpose. They pay particular attention to the organization's external environment and stay alert for long-term problems and opportunities.

FIGURE 1 THE MANAGEMENT HIERARCHY. COURTESY OF JEFFREY ANDERSON.

Top
manage the entire
organization

Middle
implement the plans of top
managers and coordinate the
activities of first line managers

First Line
coordinate the activities of non-managers

Middle managers are a larger group of managers; their titles include plant manager, division manager, district manager, regional manager, and operations manager.[11] Middle managers are responsible for relatively large divisions or departments within the organization. They are responsible for implementing policies and strategies developed by top managers and coordinating the activities of first-line managers. Middle managers are typically responsible for a specific division of the organization and they supervise multiple first-line managers.

First-line managers direct the daily activities of operating employees or non-managers. They are the only managers who don't supervise other managers. Some common titles of first-line managers include supervisor, coordinator, and office manager.[12] First-line managers make daily operating decisions and focus on short-term objectives of the organization.

Another way to classify managers is horizontally across the organization. Functional managers are responsible for groups of employees who perform a single job function, like sales, production, advertising, and accounting. General managers are responsible for employees with multiple job functions. A general manager is typically responsible for different departments in an organization. A store manager or plant manager are examples of general managers.[13]

Middle manager
A manager who implements the policies and strategies developed by top managers and coordinates the work of front-line managers.

First-line manager
A manager who directs the daily activities of non-managers and focuses on short-term daily objectives of the organization.

Functional managers
A manager who is responsible for one job function

General manager
A manager who is responsible for multiple job functions.

What Do Managers Do?

Management Functions

© Shutterstock.com

We can categorize the activities of managers by using the functional approach. In the early twentieth century, French mining executive and management theorist Henri Fayol classified a manager's job into five functions. Over time, these functions have been streamlined into the four; planning, organizing, leading, and controlling.[14] Ultimately, the critical function of a manager's job is to achieve high performance by making the best use of organizational resources through these four functions of management known as the management process.[15] The management process is illustrated in Figure 2.

Planning is the process of setting objectives and determining how those objectives will be met.[16] Through planning, managers identify goals, either for the organization or their area of responsibility, and determine methods to achieve those goals. Planning is the logical starting place when describing management functions. All managers set goals and determine a means to achieve these goals. Planning includes analyzing current situations, anticipating future events, determining objectives, and deciding on courses of action and resources needed to reach the organization's goals.[17]

Planning
The process of setting goals and determining a means to achieve those goals.

Organizing is arranging people, tasks, and resources to accomplish organizational goals.[18] In the organizing function, managers assemble and coordinate the human, financial, physical, informational, and other resources required to reach goals. In the organizing function, managers put plans into action by defining jobs and tasks, assigning those tasks to individuals or groups, and providing support in terms of technology and other resources. Organizing includes attracting people to the organization, outlining job responsibilities, grouping jobs into work units, and allocating resources to achieve success.[19]

Organizing
Arranging tasks, people, and other resources to accomplish organizational goals.

Leading is directing, motivating, and influencing employees to work toward reaching organizational goals.[20] At its core, leading is about influencing others to take those steps necessary for organizational success. Sergio Marcioni, CEO of Chrysler Group, spends half of his time in Michigan, meeting with executives to motivate people to reach his ambitious goals. A manager doesn't have to be a top manager to be a leader though and many managers provide strong leadership at all levels of an organization.[21] Managers lead by building commitment, and encouraging activities that support goal attainment.

Leading
Directing, motivating, and influencing people to work toward organizational goals.

Finally, in the controlling function, managers monitor the performance of their group and compare that performance to goals, taking corrective action when needed. Managers exercise control by gathering and interpreting performance data and using that information to make changes to plans and methods if needed.[22] Control is a critical management function as work often doesn't go as planned and plans must be adjusted to fit circumstances. Control closes the loop on the management process by ensuring that work performance is directed at reaching organizational goals.

Controlling
Monitoring performance, comparing to goals, and taking corrective action if necessary.

Managerial Roles

Managerial roles
Specific actions or behaviors of managers.

In the 1960s, management researcher Henry Mintzberg studied managers at work. He found that managers worked at a hectic pace, they communicated frequently with others

FIGURE 2 THE MANAGEMENT PROCESS. COURTESY OF JEFFREY ANDERSON.

FIGURE 3 MINTZBERG'S MANAGERIAL ROLES. COURTESY OF JEFFREY ANDERSON.

Interpersonal Roles	Informational Roles	Decisional Roles
• Leader • Liaison • Figurehead	• Monitor • Disseminator • Spokesperson	• Entrepreneur • Disturbance handler • Resource allocator • Negotiator

and worked on many different tasks. As a way to better understand the complex nature of a manager's job, Mintzberg identified a set of roles filled by managers. From his observations, he concluded that managers perform three broad roles or sets of behavior; interpersonal, and decisional informational, and decisional.[23] He further divided these three roles into 10 key subgroups as outlined in Figure 3.

Interpersonal Roles

Interpersonal roles include those roles and behaviors where managers interact with others both inside and outside the organization.

- ❏ As a **figurehead**, managers perform ceremonial and symbolic duties such as greeting visitors and signing legal documents.
- ❏ In the **leader** role, managers direct and motivate, train, counsel, and communicate with others.
- ❏ Working as a **liaison**, managers work inside and outside the organization to represent the interests of their group.

Interpersonal roles
Those roles and behaviors where managers interact with others both inside and outside the organization.

Informational Roles

Informational roles
Those roles and behaviors where managers collect and share information with others both inside and outside the organization

Informational roles include those roles and behaviors where managers collect and share information with others both inside and outside the organization.

- ❏ As a **monitor**, managers scan for information via the internet, periodicals, reports, and personal contacts.
- ❏ In the **disseminator** role, managers share information internally to other organization members through reports, phone calls, memos, and e-mail.
- ❏ As a spokesperson, managers share information outside the organization through speeches and reports.

Decisional Roles

Decisional roles
Those roles and behaviors where managers make decisions to solve problems or take advantage of opportunities.

Decisional roles include those roles and behaviors where managers make decisions to solve problems or take advantage of opportunities.

- ❏ In the **entrepreneur** role, managers initiate improvements and identify new ideas to make the organization successful.
- ❏ As a **disturbance handler**, managers correct problems, respond to crises, and resolve disputes.
- ❏ Managers make decisions as a **negotiator**, representing their unit's interests to other groups and negotiating budgets, contracts, and purchases.
- ❏ As a **resource allocator**, managers make decision on budgets, priorities, and who gets to use resources.[24]

What Do Managers Need to Know?

Managers need to master a range of skills. Robert Katz proposed that managers need to master three critical skills to be an effective manager; technical, human, and conceptual.[25]

Technical skills
Job specific knowledge and expertise needed to do well at work tasks.

Technical skills are the job specific knowledge and expertise needed to do well at work tasks. Technical skills are the ability to use special proficiency or expertise to perform job related tasks. Accountants, engineers, consultants, market researchers, financial planners, and system analysts are all examples of jobs that require technical skills and special expertise.[26] These skills are critically important for first-line managers as they manage employees who produce the organization's goods or services.

Interpersonal skills
The ability to work well with others, individually or in groups

Interpersonal skills involve the ability to work well with others, individually, or in groups. These are "soft" skills and include the ability to collaborate, communicate, motivate, and contribute to a team.[27] These skills are equally important at all levels of management as all managers work with others to achieve results.

Conceptual skills
The ability to think analytically and analyze abstract and complex situations

Finally, conceptual skills are the skills managers use to think analytically and analyze abstract and complex situations. Conceptual skills involve the capacity to break problems into smaller parts and see the relationship between the parts. This is also known as critical thinking.[28] Conceptual skills allow managers to diagnose complex circumstances and see how things fit together to facilitate good decision-making.[29] Conceptual skills are especially important for top managers so that they can see the organization as a whole, understand the relationship between subunits, and understand how the organization fits into its broader environment. Figure 4 shows the relative importance of skills for top and first-line managers.

The Evolution of the Study of Management

In this section, we will examine the historical and contemporary perspectives of management. Understanding the past helps us understand the present and allows us to prevent the mistakes of the past. Managers can benefit from integrating the best parts of historic management theories into their management practice.

The Classical Approach

The classic approach to management was born at the beginning of the last century. This viewpoint had two branches, scientific management and administrative management.[30]

Administrative management
An approach to management which describes what managers do and what constitutes good management practice

FIGURE 4 THE IMPORTANCE OF SKILLS AT DIFFERENT MANAGEMENT LEVELS. COURTESY OF JEFFREY ANDERSON.

Important Skills for First-line Managers

Important Skills for Top Managers

■ Conceptual skills ■ Interpersonal skills ■ Technical skills ■

Scientific Management

In the early years of the twentieth century, productivity emerged as a significant business problem. As businesses expanded labor was in short supply and management needed to find ways to use labor more efficiently.[31] In 1911, Frederick Taylor published *The Principles of Scientific Management*. Taylor's goal was to improve the efficiency and productivity of workers by providing a consistent approach to work that minimized wasted motions.[32] Taylor came to many of his conclusions during his career at Midvale Steel Company where he conducted time and motion studies of jobs and developed a list of procedures, tools and equipment needed for each job. Taylor's called his approach, scientific management, where the scientific method is used to find the "one best way to perform a job."[33] The results? Through Taylor's scientific approach both productivity and employee wages increased.[34] Taylor's principles of scientific management are outlined in Table 1 below.

© Shutterstock.com

Taylor has been described as the "father" of scientific management and his work influenced others to adopt scientific management principles. Frank and Lillian Gilbreth, a husband and wife team, were two of his most significant followers.[35] The Gilbreth's pioneered the use of motion studies as a management tool. In a famous study of bricklayers, Frank Gilbreth developed a set of procedures for doing the job more efficiently, reducing the number of motions from 18 to 5 and increasing worker output by about 200 percent. Lillian Gilbreth made significant contributions to the field of industrial psychology and personnel management.[36]

Scientific management
Uses the scientific method to find the "one best way" to perform a job

Scientific management has had lasting influence. Scientific management principles are still used to prescribe work methods at organizations that require lots of human motions, like the United Parcel Service and Taco Bell.[37]

Administrative Management

In 1916, around the same time of Taylor's work, French industrialist Henri Fayol published *Administration Industrielle et Generale* in which he focused on the activities of all managers,

TABLE 1 FREDERICK TAYLOR'S PRINCIPLES OF SCIENTIFIC MANAGEMENT

1	Develop a science for each element of a person's work, replacing the old rule-of-thumb methods.
2	Scientifically select, train, teach, and develop the worker.
3	Heartily cooperate with workers to ensure work is done in accordance with prescribed scientific principles.
4	Divide work responsibly and equally between managers and workers, rather than throwing all responsibility to the workers.

Adapted from Taylor, F., Principles of Scientific Management, 1911, Harper, New York, NY.

not just first-line managers as was the case for Taylor and the Gilbreths.[38] Fayol was the first to identify the management functions of planning, leading, organizing, and controlling as the core of the management process. Most contemporary management books still agree that these functions are a critical part of a manager's job.[39] Fayol described the practice of management from his perspective as a mining director and developed 14 principles of management, outlined in Table 2 below.

Max Weber was a German sociologist who studied organizations in the early 1900s. Weber developed a theory of the ideal organization based on authority structures and relationships in a model he called bureaucracy.[40] At the core of Weber's thinking was an efficient form of organization based on principles of logic, order, and legitimate authority. Weber's elements of bureaucracy are outlined in Table 3.

© Shutterstock.com

Bureaucracy
An organization on authority structures and relationships

TABLE 2 FAYOL'S FOURTEEN PRINCIPLES OF MANAGEMENT

1	**Division of Work**—Specialization increases output by making employees more efficient.
2	**Authority**—Authority gives managers the right to give orders.
3	**Discipline**—Employees must respect and obey the rules of the organization.
4	**Unity of Command**—Every employee must receive from only one supervisor.
5	**Unity of Direction**—The organization should have a single plan of action to guide managers and workers.
6	**Subordination of Individual Interests to the General Interest**—The interests of any employee or group of employees should not take precedence over the interests of the organization.
7	**Remuneration**—Workers must be paid fair wages for their services.
8	**Centralization**—Centralization refers to the degree to which subordinates are involved in decision-making. Centralized or decentralized decision-making is a matter of proportion and the task is to find the optimum degree of centralization for each situation.
9	**Scalar Chain**—The scalar chain represents the line of authority from top management to the lowest ranks in the chain.
10	**Order**—People and materials need to be at the right place at the right time.
11	**Equity**—Managers should treat their subordinates fairly and kindly.
12	**Stability of Tenure of Personnel**—Management should provide orderly planning to ensure that replacements are available to fill vacancies.
13	**Initiative**—When employees are allowed to originate and carry-out plans they will exert higher levels of effort.
14	**Esprit de corps**—Promoting team spirit and harmony will build unity and harmony in the organization.

Adapted from Henri Fayol's 1916 Principles of Management, *Administration Industrielle et General;*

TABLE 3 ELEMENTS OF THE BUREAUCRATIC ORGANIZATION

Qualifications-Based Hiring—Employees should be hired on the basis of their educational background or technical training.

Merit-Based Promotion—Promotion should be based on experience or achievement and decided by managers, not owners.

Chain of Command—Each position is part of a hierarchy, and each position is accountable to a higher position.

Division of Labor—Tasks, responsibilities, and authority are clearly defined and divided.

Impersonal Application of Rules and Procedures—Rules, policies, and procedures apply to everyone in the organization impartially, regardless of one's position or status.

Recorded in Writing—All administrative rules, acts, and decisions will be recorded in writing.

Separation of Owners and Managers—The owners of the organization should not manage or supervise its operations.

Adapted from Weber, M. (1915) *The Theory of Social and Economic Organization*, translated by Henderson, A. & Parsons, T., 1947, The Free Press, New York, NY. Pp. 329–334.

Human relations approach
A management perspective that emphasizes the importance of understanding human behavior and motivation

A flaw with the classical approach to management is that it is too mechanistic and views human as cogs in a bigger machine.[41] The Human relations approach, described in the next section, addressed this problem.

The Human Relations Approach

The human relations approach emphasized the importance of understanding human behavior and motivating employees. The human relations approach developed over three phases; early behaviorism, the human relations approach, and behavioral science.[42]

Early Behaviorism: Mary Parker Follett and the Hawthorne Studies

Mary Parker Follett (1868–1933) was a social worker, who in her fifties, began lecturing on and writing about management. She worked extensively as a consultant for business and government leaders in both the United States and Europe.[43] Follett taught respect for worker's experience and perspective cautioned against too much hierarchy. She thought of organizations as communities where managers and workers should work together in harmony with collective responsibility. Her emphasis on groups and human cooperation are still relevant today and her influence is seen in employee ownership, profit sharing, and gain-sharing programs.[44]

© Shutterstock.com

The Hawthorne studies was a series of studies that began to study the effects of workplace lighting on productivity at the Western Electric Hawthorne plant in Chicago where they made telephones for the Bell system. Sponsored by General Electric, lighting in the plant was increased in stages. With each increase in the level of lighting, productivity in the plant increased. As a control measure, lighting levels where decreased in phases. Researchers expected productivity to drop with lighting levels but curiously productivity continued to increase.[45] Obviously, lighting was not the only factor in productivity. Researchers, led by Elton Mayo, concluded that workers worked harder because they received added attention from management, a phenomenon they called the Hawthorne effect. While the Hawthorne studies were later criticized for poorly designed research, they drew attention to the human factor in the workplace which led to the human relations movement in the 1950s and 1960s.[46]

Hawthorne effect
A phenomena where workers worked harder because they received added attention from management

The Human Relations Movement

Abraham Maslow and Douglas McGregor were two theorists that made significant contributions to the human relations movement. They proposed that better human relations could increase worker productivity.[47]

Abraham Maslow was one of the earliest researchers to study motivation. He proposed a hierarchy of needs; physiological, safety, love, esteem, and self-actualization. Maslow believed that these needs must be satisfied in a linear fashion and that higher level needs are not motivators until lower level needs are met.[48] We will explore Maslow's theory later in Chapter 9.

© Shutterstock.com

Theory X
Managers who believe that workers dislike work, have little ambition, resist change, and prefer to be led.

Theory Y
Managers who believe that employees enjoy work, accept responsibility, and are capable of self-control and self-direction.

Quantitative approach
An approach uses quantitative tools to improve managerial decision-making.

Operations management
A management approach that is concerned with helping the organization produce its product or service more quickly and efficiently.

Douglass McGregor suggested that it wasn't enough for managers to be liked but they also needed to be aware of their attitudes toward employees. In his 1960 book, *The Human Side of Enterprise,* McGregor described two types of manager assumptions of human behavior; Theory X and Theory Y.

Theory X managers have a pessimistic assumption of human behavior. These managers believe that workers dislike work, have little ambition, resist change, and prefer to be led. Theory Y managers have a more optimistic attitude. Theory Y managers believe that employees enjoy work, accept responsibility, and are capable of self-control and self-direction.

McGregor believed that these assumptions created self-fulfilling prophecies. When managers behave in ways that are consistent with these assumptions, they create an environment that encourages employees to conform to the manager's expectations.[49]

The Quantitative Approach

The quantitative approach to management was developed in the 1940s. This approach used quantitative tools to improve managerial decision-making. This includes mathematical and statistical solutions developed to solve problems for the military during World War II.[50] The quantitative approach emphasizes the use of rational, science-based, mathematical models and techniques to improve decision making and strategic planning.[51]

Operations Management

Operations management is less mathematically oriented than the quantitative approach and can be applied more directly to management situations. Operations management

techniques are concerned with helping the organization produce its product or service more quickly and efficiently and can be applied to a variety of problems.[52] Operations management is concerned with work scheduling, production planning, inventory levels, and facility design and location. Operations management ensures that the organization manages resources and distributes products or services more efficiently and effectively through rational approaches.[53]

Systems Theory

Systems theory views the organization as a set of interrelated parts that work together to achieve a common purpose. Systems theory considers the organization as a set of subsystems making up the entire system.[54] As shown in Figure 5, we can describe a system in terms of four parts; inputs, transformational processes, outputs, and feedback. Inputs are organizational resources like human, financial, material and information resources. These resources are transformed through organizational processes process creating outputs like products and services, profits or losses, information, employee learning and behavior, and others. The environment reacts to these outputs and provides feedback to the system.[55]

Systems theory
An approach that views the organization as a system with inputs, transformational process, outputs, and feedback.

The Contingency Approach

The classical, behavioral, and quantitative approaches all try to identify the one best way to manage. By contrast, the contingency approach suggests that universal theories cannot be applied to all situations as each situation is unique.[56] The contingency approach emphasizes that organizations, employees, and situations are all different and require different ways of managing. That is, a manager's approach should be contingent on the individual and environmental situation. The contingency approach can be described as "if . . . then", if this is the situation, then this is the best way to manage this situation.[57]

Contingency approach
A management approach that managerial situations are unique and require different methods depending on the situation.

Twenty-first-Century Management Skills

Robert Katz's research on management skills dates back to the mid-1970s.[58] While Katz's research is still relevant today, additional skills are required for management success in the twenty-first century.

FIGURE 5 THE ORGANIZATION AS A SYSTEM. COURTESY OF JEFFREY ANDERSON.

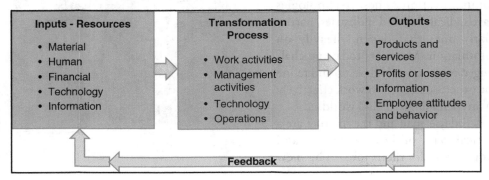

Customer Centeredness

Organizations need customers to survive. But customer service has traditionally thought to be the responsibility of marketing personnel.[59] Today, the majority of employees in developed countries work in service jobs. Examples of service jobs include food services, computer repair technicians, front desk clerks, consultants, financial planners, and bank tellers. In today's highly competitive marketplace, managers must recognize that consistent, high-quality customer service is critical to the organization's service. Twenty-first century managers need to create customer-centered organizations where employees are friendly to customers and willing to give extra effort to keep customers happy.[60]

Cultural Fluency

In his 2005 book, *The World Is Flat*, Thomas Friedman described the twenty-first century phenomenon of globalization where globalization has flattened the world, leveling

the competitive playing field between industrial and emerging market countries.[61] Managers today need cultural awareness and sensitivity to deal with an increasingly diverse global marketplace. With this cultural fluency, managers can make adjustments that are appropriate to deal with new business partners.[62]

Cultural fluency isn't limited to international business though. By 2050, the mix of American ethnic and racial groups will change significantly. Racial and ethnic minorities will make up more than half of the population.[63] Managers must be able to maximize the contributions of diverse groups of employees to succeed in the twenty-first century.

Digital Fluency

Twenty-first century managers work in an increasingly digital world due to the internet, e-commerce, and electronic communication. These technologies have radically altered industries, particularly ones that depend heavily on information. Managers today are challenged to continually develop and refine the expertise needed to work effectively in an increasingly digital world.

Today e-mail and the internet are a critical part of how managers and employees do their jobs. The new

frontier of the modern workplace is social media. In these forms of electronic communication, users create online communities to share information, ideas, messages, and other content. Social media platforms include Twitter, Facebook, YouTube, LinkedIn, and others. Many organizations are using social media not just to connect with their customers but also as a way to reach employees and manage human resources.[64] Whether they're interacting with employees on social media, checking inventory on enterprise systems or teleconferencing with business partners, managers need to develop a digital fluency, the ability to use technology as well as keeping up-to-date as technology continues to evolve.[65]

Summary of Learning Outcomes and Key Points

❑ **Explain** the role of managers in organizations

Managers work in organizations, a deliberate arrangement of people with a common purpose expressed in goals. Managers work with and through people, effectively and efficiently to achieve those organizational goals.

❑ **Remember** and **understand** different types of managers

Managers can be categorized into a hierarchy of top, middle, and first-line managers. Top managers make long-term decisions on the overall direction and strategy of the organization. Middle managers implement the policies of top managers and coordinate the activities of first-line managers. First-line managers direct the work of non-managers and make short-term daily operational decisions.

Managers can also be classified in terms of their job functions. Functional managers are responsible for one job function. General managers are responsible for multiple job functions.

❑ **Describe** a manager's job functions and roles

A manager's activities can be described in terms of functions and roles. A manager performs four management functions. (1) Planning involves setting organizational goals and developing a means to achieve those goals. (2) Organizing is concerned with arranging tasks, people, and other resources to accomplish those goals. (3) Leading is influencing and motivating people to work to achieve organizational goals. (4) Controlling is monitoring performance, comparing to goals, and taking corrective action if needed.

Another way to describe a manager's activities is in terms of the roles and behaviors they perform. Managers perform in three broad role categories where they interact with others, gather and share information and make decisions to solve problems, or take advantage of opportunities.

❑ **Remember** and understand the various skills required of managers

Traditional management skills include interpersonal, technical, and conceptual skills. Interpersonal skills are a manager's ability to work with individuals and groups. Technical skills consist of the job specific knowledge needed to perform a job effectively. Conceptual skills are the ability to think analytically and solve complex problems.

Managers need additional skills to work effectively in the twenty-first century. A manager needs to be customer centered; creating an environment that emphasizes customer service. Modern managers need to be culturally fluent, an ability to work in an increasingly global and diverse workplace. Finally, managers need digital fluency, the ability to use digital tools to gather information, make decisions, and communicate with internal and external audiences.

❏ **Explain** the evolution of the study of management

The study of management began with the classic approach which included scientific management and administrative management. Scientific management used management science to determine the one best way to perform a job. Administrative management was concerned with a manager's duties and performance.

The classic approach was followed by the human relations approach. First, during the Hawthorne studies and later with the work of Maslow and McGregor, managers were concerned with the importance of understanding human behavior as a way to improve management effectiveness.

The study of management further evolved with the quantitative approach, a method of using mathematical and statistical models to make decisions. The operations approach focuses on improving the efficiency of producing the organization's products and services. The systems approach views the organization as a system that includes inputs, transformational processes, outputs, and feedback. Finally, the contingency approach emphasizes that management situations are not universal and the appropriate management method depends on the situation.

Questions for Review

1. What are the three basic levels of management?
2. Describe the four management functions.
3. Identify several of the important skills for managers and how the importance of those skills vary by management level
4. Describe the goals of the scientific and administrative approaches to management.
5. Discuss the goals of the human relations approach to management. To what extent are these approaches still valuable today?

End Notes

1. Griffin, R. (2016). *Fundamentals of Management* (8th ed.). Boston, MA, p. 3.
2. Robbins, R., Decenzo, D., & Coulter, M. (2015). *Fundamentals of Management* (9th ed.). Pearson, Upper Saddle River, NJ, p. 8.
3. Robbins, S. & Coulter, M. (2016). *Management* (13th ed.). Pearson, Upper Saddle River, NJ, p. 5.
4. Kinicki, A. & Williams, C. (2013). *Management: A Practical Approach* (6th ed.) New York, NY, p. 5.
5. Robbins, S. & Coulter, M. p. 8.
6. Ibid.
7. Ibid, p. 5.
8. Griffin, R. (2016). *Fundamentals of Management* (8th ed.). Boston, MA, p. 5.
9. Kinicki, p. 19.
10. Robbins, p. 6.
11. Griffin, pp. 4–5.
12. Ibid, p. 5.
13. Daft, R. (2016). *Management* (11th ed.). Cengage, Boston, MA, p. 18.
14. Neck, C., Lattimer, C., & Houghton, J. (2014). *Management* Wiley, Hoboken, NJ, p. 10.
15. Schermerhorn, p. 16.
16. Lussier, R. (2017). *Management Fundamentals: Concepts, Applications and Skill Development* (7th ed). Sage, Los Angeles, CA, p. 6.
17. Bateman, T., & Snell, S. (2013). *Management* (3rd ed.). McGraw-Hill, New York, NY, p. 5.
18. Kinicki, p. 16.
19. Bateman, p.6.
20. Kinicki, p. 16.
21. Daft, p. 9.
22. Bateman, p. 9.
23. Kinicki, pp. 21–23.
24. Adapted from Mintzberg. (1973). *The Nature of Management Work* Harper & Row, pp. 92–93.
25. Robbins, p. 11.
26. Schermerhorn, J. p. 20.
27. Schermerhorn, p. 20.
28. Schermerhorn, p. 22.
29. Robbins, DeCenzo, & Coulter, p. 11.
30. Kinicki, p. 42.
31. Griffin, p. 12.

32. Schermerhorn, J. & Bachrach, D. (2015) *Management* (13th ed.). Wiley, New York, NY, pp. 30–31.

33. Robins & Coulter, p. 28.

34. Robins & Coulter, p. 28.

35. Robbins, p. 29.

36. Griffin, p. 13.

37. Schermerhorn, p. 31.

38. Schermerhorn, p. 31.

39. Griffin, p. 13.

40. Robbins & Coulter, p. 30.

41. Kinicki, p. 45.

42. Kinicki, p. 46.

43. Williams, C. (2016). *MGMT Principles of Management* (8th ed.). Cengage, Boston, MA, p. 33.

44. Schermerhorn, p. 34.

45. Robbins & Coulter, p. 29.

46. Kinicki, pp. 47–48.

47. Kinicki, p. 48.

48. Kinicki, p. 48.

49. Schermerhorn, p. 37.

50. Griffin, p. 16.

51. Kinicki, p. 50.

52. Griffin, p. 18.

53. Kinicki, p. 52.

54. Kinikcki, p. 53.

55. Griffin, p. 19.

56. Griffin, p. 20.

57. Robbins & Coulter, p. 32.

58. Kinicki, p. 29.

59. Robbins, DeCenzo, & Coulter, p. 15.

60. Robbins & Coulter, p. 15.

61. Friedman, T. (2005). *The World Is Flat: A Brief History of the Twenty-first Century* Farrar, Straus and Giroux, New York

62. Molinsky, A., Davenport, T., Iyer, B., & Davidson, C. (n.d.). Three Skills Every 21st Century Manager Needs. *Harvard Business Review.* Retrieved February 26, 2016, from https://hbr.org/2012/01/three-skills-every-21st-century-manager-needs

63. Kinicki, p. 11.

64. Robbins, DeCenzo & Coulter, p. 17.

65. Schermerhorn, p. 6.

CHAPTER 2 THE ENVIRONMENTS OF MANAGEMENT

Key Terms

Board of directors
Economic forces
Employees
Ethical dilemma
Ethics
General environment
Government regulators
Instrumental values

Internal environment
Managerial ethics
Owners
Political or legal forces
Sarbanes-Oxley Act of 2002
Sociocultural forces
Special interest groups
Specific environment

Stakeholders
Strategic allies
Technological forces
Terminal values
Values

Introduction

In this chapter, we explore the multiple environments within which organizations operate. These environments provide significant influences on an organization's operations and overall effectiveness. To be successful, an organization must align its strategy to fit factors like economic conditions, political and legal concerns, technological developments, and trends in society. Further, organizations are influenced by a number of factors specific to their industry, factors such as competition, changing consumer preferences, the employment market, and government regulations. Managers must constantly monitor these forces as they regularly change. A manager's ability to adapt to changing conditions can mark the difference between success and failure.

As you will see in this chapter, organizations operate in a complex environment. This complex can provide managers with uncertainty on how to make important organizational decisions. Managers must serve multiple stakeholders including owners, employees, and customers. At times, these stakeholders may be affected positively or negatively by a manager's decisions. Ethics, standards of right and wrong that influence our behavior, play an important role in helping managers make complex decisions that deal with competing stakeholder interests.

Learning Outcomes

After reading this chapter, you should be able to:

- ❏ **Describe** the general environmental forces that impact an organization
- ❏ **Remember** and **understand** the different stakeholders in the organization's specific environment
- ❏ **Explain** the importance of ethics in a manager's job
- ❏ **Remember** and understand the tools that managers might use to solve ethical dilemmas

The General Environment

General environment
Also known as the macro environment, external forces that create opportunities or threats.

The general environment includes political or legal, economic, sociocultural, and technological forces that indirectly affect all organizations. Changes in these forces eventually affect most organizations. For example, when the Federal Reserve lowers the prime lending rate, most businesses benefit because banks charge lower interest rates for loans. Consumers benefit when they can borrow money to make increased consumer purchases.[1] These environmental forces are summarized in Figure 1.

Political and legal forces
Forces in the general environment regarding laws and the political climate.

Political and Legal Forces

Forces in the political and legal environment include changes in how politics shapes laws. Dominant political views may determine how government handles antitrust issues where one company tends to create a monopoly in a particular industry.[2] These forces reflect current and proposed legislation, government policies and the philosophies and objectives of political parties. Managers monitor trends in issues like the minimum wage,

FIGURE 1 GENERAL ENVIRONMENTAL FORCES. COURTESY OF JEFFREY ANDERSON.

Political/Legal Forces
Government regulations and the relationship between business and government

Economic Forces
The overall health and vitality of the economy

Sociocultural Forces
The general behavior, attitudes, beliefs and demographic characteristics of society

Technological Forces
The methods available for converting resources into products or services

immigration reform, education reform, tax reform, and health care reform to determine their effect on government regulation, oversight, and the competitive nature of their business.[3]

Economic Forces

The economic environment consists of the overall health and vitality of the economy. Forces in this environment include factors such as economic growth, interest rates, inflation, and unemployment. The U.S. economy fell into a steep recession in 2008 causing and economic growth to slow dramatically. During the recession, prices on energy jumped and unemployment increased as businesses made workforce cuts.[4]

Economic forces
General environmental forces concerning the economy including interest rates, inflation, consumer spending, and numerous other economic indicators.

Sociocultural forces
General environmental forces related to society's values, characteristics, and trends in society.

Sociocultural Forces

Sociocultural forces in the general environment include the general behavior, attitudes, beliefs, and demographic characteristics of society. Social values and shifting trends affect how organizations focus on employment practices, advertising messages, internal policies, and even product offerings.[5] Sociocultural factors include demographic characteristics of a population such as age, gender, ethnic origin, level of education, and other factors.[6]

Technological Forces

Technological forces include developments in methods for transforming resources into goods or services.[7] Changes in knowledge, tools, and techniques

Technological forces
General environmental forces surrounding new developments in transforming resources into goods or services.

can provide organizations efficiencies, quicker time to market and new product and service offerings. Changes in computer and communications technologies, particularly the internet have transformed industries. New research into biotechnology may well transform medicine in the coming decades.[8]

The Specific Environment

Changes in the general environment will eventually affect most organizations. Organizations also operate in a specific or task environment unique to their industry.[9] The specific environment includes the organization's external stakeholders. Stakeholders are people or groups whose interests are affected by an organization's activities.[10] While an organization's task environment can be quite complex, it often provides more useful information than the general environment as managers can identify environmental factors specific to the organization rather than dealing with the more abstract nature of the general environment.[11] This next section outlines various stakeholders in the specific or task environment.

Competitors

Competitors are other companies that operate in the same industry and sell similar products or services to customers. Ford, Honda, Nissan, General Motors, and Mazda all compete for automobile customers. Similarly, McDonald's, KFC, Wendy's, and Burger King compete with one another for fast food customers.[12]

Customers

Customers are individuals and groups that pay for an organization's products or services. Customers may be individuals, or organizations like schools, hospitals, government agencies, wholesalers, retailers, and manufacturers.[13]

© Shutterstock.com

Suppliers

Suppliers are people or organizations that provide raw materials, services, equipment, labor or energy to other organizations.[14] For example, McDonald's buys soft-drink products from Coca-Cola and ketchup, salt and pepper, and paper supplies from other vendors. In addition to material resources, businesses also rely on suppliers for information, labor, and capital. Some organizations avoid depending on exclusive suppliers while others find it beneficial to build strong relationships with a single supplier.[15]

In recent years, supply chain management has become an increasingly important issue to competitiveness and profitability. Supply chain management is the managing of the entire network of facilities and people that obtain raw materials, transform them into products or services, and distribute them to customers. The goal of supply chain management is to have the right product in the right quantity available at the right price.[16]

Distributors

Distributors are organizations that support other organizations by helping them sell their product or service. Package delivery companies like UPS, FedEx, and the U.S. Postal service have become important distributors for items sold online. Another example would be Walmart, the giant retail distributor that sells consumer products from companies like Procter & Gamble, Unilever, and Colgate. Changes in distributors or methods of distribution can cause opportunities or threats for organizations. If distributors become so large and powerful that they can control customer's access to products and services, they can threaten the organization by demanding lower wholesale prices.[17]

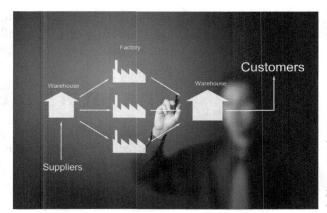
© Shutterstock.com

Government Regulators

Government regulators are bodies that have the potential to control, legislate, and otherwise influence an organization's operations and policies. The government creates regulatory agencies to protect the public from certain business practices or to protect organizations from one another. Government regulators like the Environmental Protection Agency (EPA), the Securities and Exchange Committee (SEC), the Food and Drug Administration (FDA), the Equal Employment Opportunity Commission (EEOC), and others exert powerful influence on how organizations operate. The FDA for example, protects the public from food contaminants and has a powerful influence on companies in the food service industry.[18]

Government regulators
Government bodies that have the potential to control, legislate, and otherwise influence an organization's operations and policies.

Strategic Allies

Strategic allies are companies that join together to gain a strategic advantage. The resulting relationship gives organizations advantages that neither can achieve independently.[19] For example, hotel chains such as Hyatt, Marriott, and Hilton partner with American Airlines, Delta, and others to creating synergies to attract more business travelers through shared loyalty programs. McDonald's has long partnered with Disney, promoting their movies in their stores in exchange for opening restaurants at Disney theme parks.[20]

Strategic allies
Companies that join together to gain a strategic advantage.

Local Communities

Local communities are an important stakeholder in the task environment. Schools and local governments rely on the tax base created when organizations operate in their community. Families depend on organizations for their paychecks. Often, communities provide tax incentives for major organizations to open new locations in their area because of the larger economic benefit to the local economy.[21]

Special Interest Groups

Special interest groups are groups whose members try to exert influence on particular issues. These groups include organizations like PETA, Mothers Against Drunk Driving,

Special interest groups
Are groups whose members try to exert influence on particular issues.

the National Rifle Association, and the National Organization of Women. Special interest groups may exert their influence through political contributions. They may picket and boycott an organization, withholding their patronage of certain companies.[22]

The Internal Environment

Internal environment
Those stakeholder groups that are directly impacted by an organization, includes owners, employees, and the board of directors.

An organization's internal environment consists of stakeholders that are directly impacted by the organization. These internal stakeholders are employees, owners, and the board of directors.[23]

Owners

Owners People or institutions that have legal ownership of an organization.

Owners are people or institutions that have legal ownership of an organization. Ownership may take the form of a sole proprietorship, an organization with one owner. Some organizations, like W.L. Gore & Associates and Publix Supermarkets are more than half owned by their employees through Employee Stock Ownership Plans (ESOP). Publicly-traded companies like General Motors and Apple have thousands of owners who hold shares of stock in the organization.[24]

© Shutterstock.com

Board of Directors

Board of directors
A group whose members are elected by the stockholders (owners) of the organization to represent their interests.

The board of directors is a group whose members are elected by the stockholders (owners) of the organization to represent their interests. Typically boards of directors set the organization's overall direction and strategy as well as approve the major decisions and compensation of top managers.[25]

Employees

Employees
People who make the organization's products or services.

Employees are the people who make an organization's products and services. Their role in the organization is critical and many forward-thinking organizations consider employees to be "talent", their most important resource.[26]

FIGURE 2 THE ORGANIZATION ENVIRONMENT.

© Courtesy of Jeffrey Anderson.

The General Environment			Macro level
Political/Legal forces Economic forces Sociocultural forces Technological forces	**The Specific/Task Environment**		Industry level
	Customers Competitors Suppliers Distributors Regulators	**The Internal Environment** Employees Owners Board of Directors	Organizational level

The Ethical Environment

What Are Ethics and Ethical Dilemmas?

© Shutterstock.com

Ethics are the moral code of principles that guide standards of right and wrong that influence individual behavior. Ethics help guide people to make moral choices and encourage ethical behavior.[27] Managerial ethics are those standards of right and wrong that guide managers in the workplace. One important consideration of managerial ethics is how managers treat employees. Issues like hiring, firing, wages, working conditions, respect, and employee privacy all have ethical implications.[28]

Values are the underlying, relatively permanent beliefs and attitudes that help influence an individual's behavior. Terminal values are preferences about desired end states, for example self-respect, family security, and happiness. Instrumental values are preferences on how those ends are accomplished. Instrumental values include ambition, honesty, creativity, self-discipline, and perseverance.[29]

Ethics Standards of right and wrong that guide human decisions and behavior.

Managerial ethics Standards of right and wrong that guide managers decisions and behavior in the workplace.

Values Underlying, relatively permanent, beliefs and attitudes that influence human behavior.

Terminal values Desired end states such as self-respect, family security, and others.

Instrumental values Preferences on how to reach desired ends, such as ambition and self-discipline.

Ethical Dilemmas

Values guide people's decisions on ethical dilemmas. Ethical dilemmas are situations where values are in conflict.[30] Often these situations involve complex choices with competing conceptions of right and wrong. Ethical dilemmas may arise when a person has to choose between different courses of action, knowing that whichever course he or she chooses, some stakeholders will be harmed while others will benefit.[31]

Ethical dilemmas A complex decision that involves a choice between competing values or stakeholders.

What are Alternative Views of Ethics?

Here are four viewpoints, summarized in Figure 3, which may serve as guidelines to solve ethical dilemmas.

The **utilitarian** view considers ethical behavior as that which delivers the greatest good to the greatest number of people. This is an end-based approach to making decisions following the work of the nineteenth century philosopher John Steward Mills.[32] Managers might perform a cost-benefit analysis using financial performance as a measurement of the greatest good.[33]

In the **individual** view, ethical behavior is guided by the outcome which will result in everyone's best long-term interest. The individual view assumes that people will be ethical in the short term to avoid being harmed in the long term.[34] The individual view assumes that people are self-regulating but not everyone has the same capacity for self-control and individuals driven by short-term greed may take advantage of situations to satisfy their self-interests.[35]

© Shutterstock.com

According to the **moral-rights** view, behavior is ethical when it is guided by respect for people's fundamental rights. Traditional human rights have included life, liberty, and fair treatment under the law. Today, these rights include employee rights such as privacy, free speech, safe-working conditions, and honesty.[36] The moral-rights view is a means-based approach that views ethical choices that respect individual's rights.

In the **justice** view, ethical choices are those that respect standards of fairness and equity. For example, a manager would be using the justice view when deciding to pay the same wages to individuals with similar backgrounds, responsibilities, skills, and performance, rather than arbitrary differences like gender, personality, or other factors.[37]

Managers are concerned with three types of justice. **Distributive justice,** requires that people are not treated differently because of arbitrary characteristics. The example of equal pay for men and women above is consistent with distributive justice. **Procedural justice**, requires that rules be administered in a consistent fashion. Rules must be clearly stated and impartially and consistently enforced. Finally, **compensatory justice** argues that individuals should be compensated for injuries by the party responsible for that injury.[38]

How Do People Learn Ethics?

An individual's behavior and decisions may vary based on their moral development. Psychologist Laurence Kohlberg proposed three levels of personal moral development; preconventional, conventional, and postconventional.[39] These three levels are outlined in Table 1. In the **preconventional level (Level 1)**, individual behavior is guided by following rules to avoid unpleasant outcomes like punishment. In the **conventional level (Level 2)**, individuals look outside themselves to conform to the expectations of others and decisions follow social norms. Finally, at the **postconventional level (Level 3)**, individuals follow their own internal standards and values when making decisions.[40]

Kohlberg believed that individuals progress sequentially these stages as they become more educated and mature, yet only 20 percent of adults reach the postconventional

FIGURE 3 FOUR ALTERNATIVE VIEWS ON ETHICS. COURTESY OF JEFFREY ANDERSON.

Utilitarian	Moral Rights
Ethical choices are theories that do the most good for the greatest amount of people	Respect fundamental human rights in the decision making process

Four Alternative Views on Ethics

Individual	Justice
Individuals make decisions to support their long-term best interests.	Ethical decisions are guided by fairness and equity.

TABLE 1 KOHLBERG'S LEVELS OF MORAL DEVELOPMENT.

Level 1— Preconventional	Level 2— Conventional	Level 3— Postconventional
Follows rules to avoid punishment. Acts in own self-interest. Obedience for its own sake.	Lives up to the expectations of others. Fulfills duties and obligations of the social system. Upholds laws.	Follows self-chosen principles of justice and morality. Aware that people hold different values and seeks innovative solutions to ethical dilemmas. Balances concern for the individual with concern for the common good.
Self-interest	Societal expectations	Internal Values

level where they are guided by internal principles. The postconventional level is the highest stage of moral development and only about 20 percent of managers reach that level. Most adults are in the conventional stage of moral development and look externally for guidance on ethical issues. That is to say, most people need leadership when it comes to making ethical choices.[41]

Today, it's common for most organizations to have a **code of ethics**, a formal statement of the organization's values and ethical standards. A code of ethics sets expectations for behavior and addresses issues like organizational citizenship, and relationships with co-workers, customers, suppliers, and others. Often codes of ethics offer guidelines for issues like bribes and confidentiality of organizational information.[42]

As a means of encouraging ethical behavior, employees should be protected from retaliation from whistle-blowing. **Whistle-blowing** occurs when employees expose what they consider unethical behavior on the part of their fellow employees.[43] Individuals who report organizational misdeeds often do so at great personal risk, and many have been fired in retaliation. While laws such as the Whistleblower Protection Act of 1989 offer some protection, these laws are regularly tested in court and viewed by many as inadequate.[44]

© Shutterstock.com

In recent years, the unethical actions of high-profile executives such as Mark Hurd (Hewlett Packard), Dennis Kozlowski (Tyco), Kenneth Lay (Enron), and Allen Stanford (Stanford Financial Group) have brought increased scrutiny on all executives. As a result, leaders are expected to establish norms and a culture that reinforces standards of ethical behavior. To support this view, Congress passed the Sarbanes-Oxley Act of 2002. This act, also known as SarbOx or SOx, requires CEO's and CFO's to personally vouch for the truthfulness of their organization's financial disclosures. The law imposes new strenuous measures to deter and punish accounting fraud and corruption.[45]

Sarbanes-Oxley Act of 2002 Also known as SarBox or Sox, provisions of this act require CEO's and CFO's to personally verify financial disclosers.

Summary of Learning Outcomes and Key Points

☐ **Describe** the general environmental forces that impact an organization

Organizations operate in complex environments. These environments provide a broad set of forces in an organization's surroundings and determine the overall context within which an origination operates. Political or Legal, economic, sociocultural, and technological forces provide opportunities for organizations to exploit and threats which might negatively impact organizational effectiveness. The impact of these forces is broad in nature and influences multiple organizations across multiple industries. Managers must monitor conditions in the environment and align their organization's strategies and practices to take advantage of opportunities and minimize threats.

☐ **Remember** and **understand** the different stakeholders in the organization's task environment

Stakeholders are important groups in the organization's task environment. This task environment is specific to the industry within which an organization operates. Stakeholders in this task environment are impacted by the organization and have an interest, or "stake" in the organization's operations. These stakeholders include customers, competitors, suppliers, distributors, special interest groups, local communities, and government regulators.

☐ **Explain** the importance of ethics in a manager's job

Ethics are the standards of right and wrong that influence human behavior. Managerial ethics are those standards of right and wrong that influence managerial behavior in the workplace. How a manager treats employees is an important part of managerial ethics. Values are underlying beliefs and attitudes that influence human behavior. Terminal values are desired end states while instrumental values guide decisions toward those end states.

☐ **Remember** and understand the tools that managers might use to solve ethical dilemmas

Ethical dilemmas are complex situations where managers have to choose between competing values. In an ethical dilemma there is no clear right or wrong choice. There are four ethical theories that individuals may use to help guide decisions when faced with ethical dilemmas. In the utilitarian approach, managers are guided to make the decision choice that creates the greatest good for the greatest number of people. In the moral rights approach, managers respect human fundamental rights as a guide to the correct decision choice. In the individual approach, individuals are guided by their own long-term self-interest and finally, the justice approach considers equal treatment across individuals when making decisions.

Questions for Review

1. Describe the forces in an organization's general environment.
2. List the stakeholders in an organization's specific environment.
3. Distinguish between ethics and values.
4. Compare the four ethical theories a manager can use when faced with an ethical dilemma.

End Notes

1. Williams. C. (2016). *MGMT Principles of Management* (8th ed.). Cengage, Boston, MA, p. 48.

2. Kinicki, p. 77.

3. Schermerhorn, p. 79.

4. Griffin, p. 37.

5. Schermerhorn, p. 8.

6. Kinicki, p. 77.

7. Griffin, p. 37.

8. Schermerhorn, p. 76.

9. Williams, p. 52.

10. Kinicki, p. 69.

11. Griffin, p. 39.

12. Williams, p. 53.

13. Griffin, p. 39.

14. Kinicki, p. 72.

15. Griffin, p. 40.

16. Bateman, T. & Snell, S. (2015). *Management* (11th ed.). McGraw-Hill, New York, NY, p. 55.

17. Jones, G. & George, J. (2014). *Contemporary Management* (8th ed.). McGraw-Hill, New York, NY, p. 171.

18. Griffin, p. 40.

19. Kinicki (6th ed.). p. 72

20. Griffin, p. 40.

21. Kinicki (7th ed.). p. 73.

22. Kinicki (7th ed.). p. 80.

23. Kinicki, A. & Williams, B. (2016). *Management* (7th ed.). McGraw-Hill, New York, NY, p. 74.

24. Kinicki (7th ed.). p. 74.

25. Kinicki (7th ed.). p. 75.

26. Kinicki (7th ed.). p. 75.

27. Schermerhorn (13th ed.). p. 52.

28. Griffin (8th ed.). p. 43.

29. Schermerhorn, p. 53.

30. Daft, R. & Marcic, D. (2015) *Understanding Management* (9th ed.). Cengage, Stamford, CT, p. 147.

31. Jones, G. & George, J. (2015) *Essentials of Contemporary Management* (6th ed.). McGraw-Hill, New York, NY, p. 81.

32. Schermerhorn, p. 54.

33. Kinicki, p. 79.

34. Kinicki, p. 79.

35. Schermerhorn, p. 55.

36. Schermerhorn, p. 55.

37. Robbins, DeCenzo & Coulter. *Fundamentals of Management* (9th ed.). p. 67.

38. Daft & Marcic, p. 148.

39. Kinicki, p. 81.

40. Kinicki, p. 81.

41. Williams, (8th ed.). p. 74.

42. Schermerhorn, p. 62.

43. Lussier. (2016) *Management Fundamentals* (7th ed.). Thousand Oaks, CA, p. 50.

44. Schermerhorn, p. 63.

45. Griffin, pp. 45–46.

CHAPTER 3 THE GLOBAL ENVIRONMENT OF MANAGEMENT

Key Terms

Contract manufacturing
Culture shock
Embargo
Ethnocentrism
Euro
European Union (EU)
Exporting
Foreign subsidiary
Franchising
Geocentric managers
Global mindset

Global sourcing
Globalization
Greenfield venture
High-context culture
Importing
Joint venture
Licensing
Low-context culture
Monochromic cultures
Multinational corporations
Non-tariff barriers

North American Free Trade
   Agreement (NAFTA)
Political risk
Polycentric managers
Polychromic cultures
Quotas
Subsidies
Tariff barriers
World Trade Organization (WTO)

Introduction

Globalization is an increasing trend that impacts managers. Individual country markets are now replaced by global markets. In this chapter, we will explore the reasons why organizations do business internationally. We will examine methods companies use to do business internationally and we will also examine cultural differences that impact how organizations do business and manage people.

The Hungarian Parliament in Budapest photo courtesy of Jeffrey Anderson

Learning Outcomes After reading this chapter, you should be able to:

☐ Realize how globalization is creating a world marketplace
☐ Remember and understand why and how organizations do business internationally
☐ Recognize barriers to trade and global trade agreements
☐ Appreciate manager views on culture and differences in national culture

Linked by the internet and affordable air travel, the world has become a figuratively smaller place.

Globalization

Globalization refers to the extent to which trade, investments, information, cultural and social ideas, and political cooperation flow between countries. Through globalization, the world is becoming a more interdependent system as reflected in the term "global village."[1]

During the 1950s and 1960s, communication philosopher Marshall McLuhan posed the notion of a "global village," the shrinking of time and space by air travel and electronic media. As a result of technology developments, the world has become a smaller place.

The global economy refers to the increasing trend of economies of the world to interact with each other as one single global market instead of

Globalization Refers to the extent to which trade, investments, information, cultural and social ideas, and political cooperation flow between countries

many different national markets.[2] Globalization is the extent to which trade and investments, information, social and cultural ideas, and political cooperation flow between countries. Globalization has been increasing rapidly since the 1970s, and most industrialized nations have a high degree of globalization today. The KOF Swiss Economic Institute measures economic, social, and political aspects of globalization and ranks countries on an index. According to the index, the ten most globalized countries are Belgium, Ireland, the Netherlands, Austria, Singapore, Sweden, Denmark, Hungary, Portugal, and Switzerland.[3]

> Today, after more than a century of electronic technology, we have extended our central nervous system itself in a global embrace, abolishing both space and time as far as our planet is concerned.
>
> Marshall McLuhan, Understanding Media, 1964

One way to see how globalization has become so widespread is to consider the country of origin for some familiar consumer products. You might be surprised to find that many products you thought were made by U.S. companies are actually owned by foreign companies. The Tetley Tea and 8 O'Clock Coffee brands are owned by the Tata Group, a giant Indian conglomerate. The Mexican beers Dos Equis and Tecate are owned by Dutch beer maker Heineken. Tombstone and Digiorno frozen pizzas and Lean Cuisine frozen meals are owned by the giant Swiss multinational Nestle.[4]

Many clothing manufacturers make their clothes outside the United States in countries like Vietnam to take advantage of lower labor costs.

Why Companies Go Global

Why do companies expand globally? There are many reasons. Here are just a few:[5]

- **It's cheaper.** Often it's cheaper to do business internationally because companies can reduce production costs and pay employees in some countries' lower wages. Apple outsources the bulk of its iPhone production to Asia for this reason.

- **Tax savings.** Many companies expand internationally for the tax benefits that international trade provides. The United States is the only country that offers double taxation. For some companies, it's better to set up operations internationally and operate in the Unites States as an international company for tax reasons.

- **Economies of scale.** Expanding to new international markets allows companies to produce more units, which lowers per unit costs and increases profit margins.

Even Coca-Cola, which is distributed in more than 200 countries, has room for international growth. Currently 80% of Coke sales come from its 16 largest markets.

- **Flat domestic sales.** For some companies, the domestic market is saturated. International markets can present better opportunities for companies to expand sales and extend the product life cycle for their product or service.

- **It's easy.** The Internet has made it easy for companies to do business around the world. Now you don't have to have a physical presence in a foreign country to do business. Teleconference software makes it easy to stay connected at all times.

How Companies Go Global

The means of pursuing a global business strategy are outlined in Figure 1. Most companies pursue global sourcing, importing/exporting, and licensing/franchising as a market-entry strategy. These strategies don't require a significant investment. Joint ventures and foreign subsidiaries are direct investment strategies that typically require a major investment but provide ownership rights and control over operations in the foreign location.[6]

FIGURE 1 GLOBAL BUSINESS STRATEGIES. COURTESY OF JEFFREY ANDERSON.

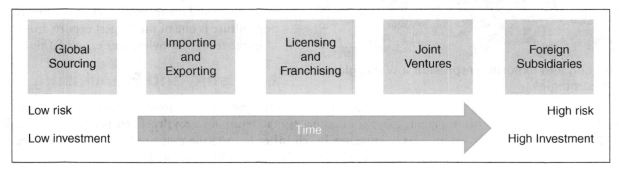

Global Sourcing

Global sourcing is a low-risk and low-investment strategy for going global. Global sourcing or offshoring, is the practice of purchasing materials or labor from around the world. Global sourcing is an early step for organizations that want to enter global markets. The goal of global sourcing is to take advantage of lower costs to be more competitive.[7]

Global sourcing is a common practice for many companies. Even the iconic American motorcycle brand Harley-Davidson outsources parts from around the world, using foreign made components to keep the prices of their motorcycles lower.[8]

Harley Davidson sources parts from around the world for its street 750 cycle.

Global sourcing Also known as offshoring, is the practice of purchasing materials or labor from around the world

Contract manufacturing A situation where a company has another company manufacture its products

Importing Acquiring products made overseas and selling them domestically

> Globalization has changed us into a company that searches the world, not just to sell or to source, but to find intellectual capital—the world's best talents and greatest ideas.
>
> Jack Welch, former CEO General Electric

Contract manufacturing is an extension of global sourcing. In contract manufacturing, a company has another company manufacture its products. This is easily adapted to an international context. Nike focuses on product design and marketing but doesn't own any manufacturing facilities, instead contracting with foreign companies to produce virtually all of its products.[9]

Importing and Exporting

Importing and exporting (or both) is typically a company's next step in international business. With importing, a company buys goods from outside the country and sells them domestically or uses them as inputs for other goods. Many of the products we use are imported, whether it's Heineken beer from the Netherlands or Honda motorcycles from Japan.[10]

Exporting involves making a product domestically and selling it to an international customer for delivery and use in another country. American pop culture is one of the biggest exports from the U in the form of movies, music, and fashion.[11]

Licensing and Franchising

Exporting Making products domestically and selling them abroad

Licensing is an arrangement where a company allows another company to use its brand name, patent, copyright or other asset in return for a royalty. These royalties are typically based on sales.[12] Anheuser-Busch InBev licenses the rights to brew and sell Budweiser to companies such as Labatt's in Canada and Kirin in Japan.[13]

Importing and exporting represent low risk global entry strategies.

Franchising is a form of licensing where a company allows a foreign company to use its brand name and operating methods for a fee. Companies such as McDonald's, Wendy's, and Subway franchise their facility designs, product recipes, and operating methods to foreign investors.[14]

Licensing is an approach typically used by manufacturers that make or sell another company's products. Franchising is generally used by service companies that want to use another company's brand and methods.[15]

During the 1970s and 1980s, Kentucky Fried Chicken (now KFC) expanded their global presence. KFC now has restaurants in China, Taiwan, Cambodia, Singapore, Vietnam, Thailand, and other Asian countries as well as other locations around the world. Most of these locations are franchises although some are joint ventures with Yum! International, KFC's parent country.[16]

KFC has expanded its presence around the world through a strategy of franchising and joint ventures.

Joint Ventures

An international **joint venture** is a type of strategic alliance where a company partners with another company in a foreign location to form a separate independent company.[17] Together, these two companies share the risks and rewards of operating together in a foreign country. SABMiller and Molson Coors Brewing formed a joint venture to better compete against Anheuser-Busch InBev in the United States. Starbucks entered into a joint venture with the Tata group to form Tata Starbucks in India.[18]

Sometimes a joint venture is the only way a U.S. company can have a presence in a foreign country. Laws in China forbid foreigners from full ownership of local companies so car manufacturers form joint ventures with those companies to sell cars in China.[19]

Foreign Subsidiaries

Joint ventures pose some potential business risks as some partners may have different goals. In addition, the loss of trade secrets is a potential threat. One way around the risks associated with joint ventures is full or partial ownership of a foreign operation. A **foreign subsidiary** is a local operation that is partially or completely owned and controlled by a foreign company. These subsidiaries can be established through acquisitions, or they can be built from the ground up as a **greenfield venture**. A foreign subsidiary is the deepest level of involvement in international operations but can be very profitable.[20]

In 1977, Japanese car manufacturer Honda reached an agreement with the State of Ohio to build a plant in Marysville, Ohio as a greenfield venture. Today, Honda operations include four state-of-the-art plants in Ohio, employing nearly 9,500 people. This

John Deere is a multinational corporation with subsidiaries in more than 30 countries.

Honda has been manufacturing cars in Marysville, Ohio since 1982.

Licensing An organization authorizes another organization the right to make or sell its products

Franchising A form of licensing where a company allows a foreign company to use its brand name and operating methods for a fee

Multinational corporations Businesses with extensive international operations in multiple foreign countries

gives them a local presence in a strong market and also gives them the ability to deal with American customers as a local employer rather than a foreign company.[21]

Multinational Corporations

International business isn't something new. Companies such as DuPont, Ford, and H.J. Heinz have been doing business internationally for decades. But it wasn't until the mid-1960s when awareness of international trade grew. Today, only few companies don't do some business internationally.[22]

Global corporations, also called multinational corporations are businesses with extensive international operations in multiple foreign countries.[23] Each year, Forbes magazine lists the world's biggest global corporations. For 2016, the world's three biggest public companies where located in China. U.S. companies Berkshire Hathaway, JP Morgan Chase, Wells Fargo, Apple, and Exxon Mobile are in the top ten of the world's largest public companies.[24]

Wal-Mart has over 11,500 retail stores in 28 countries, employing over 2.3 million people internationally. There are some distinct advantages to establishing international operations. A presence in a foreign country allows a company to simplify business operations in a foreign country, reducing some of the complexities of managing from a distance. Corporations tend to establish operations in markets where the cost of capital or wages are the lowest. By producing the same quality of goods at lower costs, multinationals reduce prices and increase purchasing power of consumers around the world.[25]

© Shutterstock.com

Wal-Mart is a multinational corporation with nearly 11,500 stores in 32 countries.

Joint venture A type of strategic alliance where a company partners with another company in a foreign location to form a separate independent company

Foreign subsidiary It is a local operation that is partially or completely owned and controlled by a foreign company

Greenfield venture Establishing a new wholly owned subsidiary in a foreign country by building its facilities from the start

The Legal and Political Environment

Laws and regulations vary across borders. This makes doing business challenging for international firms. Host governments may have a myriad of laws concerning consumer protection, libel, information and labeling, employment, safety, and wages. International managers must learn these regulations. Additionally, they must deal with unfamiliar political systems and added government supervision and regulation. Governments and the public may view foreign companies as outsiders and can be suspicious of losing economic and political independence.

Political risk is the risk of loss of assets, earning power, or managerial control due to political events or actions of a host country. While many countries welcome foreign investment, political risk is a major concern for international companies. Political risk includes government takeovers of property and acts of violence directed against a firm's property or employees.

> Think global, act local.
>
> Akio Morita, co-founder Sony Corporation

Another problem in this environment is political instability which includes riots, revolutions, civil disorders, and changes in governments. The Arab Spring of 2010 caused significant concern for multinational corporations operating in Tunisia, Egypt, Libya, Syria, Yemen, and Bahrain.[26]

Barriers to Trade

Trade barriers are measures that governments take to make imported goods or services less competitive than those produced domestically. A trade barrier may be tied directly to a product or service or can be of an administrative nature, for example, rules and procedures in connection with the transaction.[27]

Trade barriers can make trade more difficult and expensive in the case of tariffs or prevent trade completely as in the case of embargos.[28] The following are examples of trade barriers:

Tariff barriers: Taxes on certain imports which raise the price of goods making imports less competitive.

Non-tariff barriers: These are rules and regulations which make trade more difficult. For example, complex manufacturing laws make it more difficult for foreign companies to trade. Foreign regulations on environmental health and safety can also restrict imports.

Quotas: These are limits placed on the number of imports.

Figure 2 Tarrits, Embargos and Quotas restrain trade

Subsidies: This is when government gives a domestic company a subsidy, creating a competitive advantage for that company.

Embargo: A complete ban on imports from a particular country, for example, the United States embargo with Cuba.

Promoting International Trade

GATT and the WTO

The General Agreement on Tariffs and Trade (GATT) is a trade agreement intended to promote international trade by reducing trade barriers, making it easier for all nations to compete in international markets. The GATT was first negotiated following World War II to avoid trade wars that would harm poor nations. By 1994, 117 countries had signed the agreement.[29]

Established in 1995, the World Trade Organization (WTO) grew out of GATT. The WTO represents the maturation of GATT into a global institution that monitors international trade and arbitrates disputes on some 400 trade issues. As of 2013, 159 countries were members of the WTO. The WTO brings greater trade liberalization, stronger enforcement of trade rules, and the power to resolve trade disputes.[30].

Euro a single European currency

North American Free Trade Agreement (NAFTA) An agreement between the Mexican, Canadian, and U.S. governments that eliminates trade barriers

International Trade Alliances

A trading bloc, also known as an economic community, is a group of nations generally within a specific geographic region that have agreed to remove trade barriers between one another. Some of the major trading blocs include countries who have agreed to NAFTA, the European Union, APEC, and the TPP.[31]

The North American Free Trade Agreement is more than 20 years old but still an often debated political issue.

European Union (EU) An agreement between 27 European countries to create a unified trade and economic entity

North American Free Trade Agreement

In 1994, the North American Free Trade Agreement (NAFTA) merged the United States, Canada, and Mexico into one single market. NAFTA was intended to spur economic growth, increase exports and create new jobs in all three nations by eliminating tariffs and trade restrictions. By 2008, virtually all U.S. industrial exports to Mexico and Canada became duty free.[32]

Many U.S. firms have taken advantage of NAFTA by moving production facilities to Mexico, mostly to benefit from lower wages paid to Mexican workers. NAFTA remains a controversial topic in political debates with detractors pointing to U.S. job losses to Mexico, lower wages to American workers, and increased trade deficits. NAFTA supporters argue that greater productivity in U.S. plants and greater cross-border trade has come as a result of the agreement. The Boston Consulting Group estimates that Mexico offers a 30 percent labor cost advantage as compared to China.[33]

The European Union is the world's largest free market.

The European Union

In 1957, the European Economic Community began as a way to improve economic and social conditions amongst member nations. This alliance has expanded into the 28 member European Union or EU. Current EU member countries are listed in Table 1. The biggest expansion had come in 2004 when the European Union joined with ten new members from central and Eastern Europe.[34]

The EU has virtually eliminated all internal trade barriers between member nations. The EU is a single market of borderless neighbors and the world's largest free market. Most members share a common currency, the Euro.[35]

TABLE 1 EUROPEAN *UNION MEMBER COUNTRIES.*

Current European Union Members with (year of entry)		
❑ Austria (1995)	❑ France (1958)	❑ Malta (2004)
❑ Belgium (1958)	❑ Germany (1958)	❑ Netherlands (1958)
❑ Bulgaria (2007)	❑ Greece (1981)	❑ Poland (2004)
❑ Croatia (2013)	❑ Hungary (2004)	❑ Portugal (1986)
❑ Cyprus (2004)	❑ Ireland (1973)	❑ Romania (2007)
❑ Czech Republic (2004)	❑ Italy (1958)	❑ Slovakia (2004)
❑ Denmark (1973)	❑ Latvia (2004)	❑ Slovenia (2004)
❑ Estonia (2004)	❑ Lithuania (2004)	❑ Spain (1986)
❑ Finland (1995)	❑ Luxembourg (1958)	❑ Sweden (1995)
		❑ United Kingdom (1973)

Source: https://europa.eu/european-union/about-eu/countries_en (retrieved 8/26/16)

In 2016, United Kingdom citizens voted in a referendum to exit the European Union. The term "Brexit," evolved as shorthand way to merge the terms Britain and exit.[36] Nothing will happen immediately as it will take years of negotiation to extract Britain from the EU. Nonetheless, world markets reacted strongly to the Brexit vote, the British pound plunged by nearly 20 percent against the dollar and as much as 13 percent against the yen, reaching 30 year lows.[37]

Asia Pacific Economic Cooperation

In Asia and the Pacific-rim, 21 countries established the Asia Pacific Economic Cooperation (APEC) to promote free trade and investment in the Pacific region. APEC countries include some of the world's fastest growing economies such as China, Indonesia, Russia, the Republic of Korea, and Australia. These countries present a potential market of nearly three billion consumers, far exceeding the EU and NAFTA.[38]

The goal of APEC is to ensure that goods, services, investment, and people move easily across borders. Members can facilitate trade through faster customs procedures at borders, more favorable business climates, and the alignment of regulations and standards across the region. One of APEC's initiatives is to synchronize regulatory systems across the Asia-Pacific economy so that a product can be more easily exported with just one set of common standards across all economies.[39]

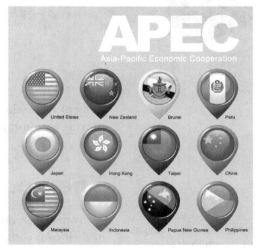

Twenty-one Asian and Pacific-rim countries form the Asia Pacific Economic Cooperation (APEC).

© Shutterstock.com

Trans-Pacific Partnership

The Trans-Pacific Partnership or TPP is a proposed trade agreement between 12 countries: the United States, Japan, Malaysia, Vietnam, Singapore, Brunei, Australia, New Zealand, Canada, Mexico, Chile, and Peru. The agreement aims to strengthen economic ties between those countries by slashing tariffs and fostering trade to boost growth. Member countries also hope to foster a closer relationship based on economic policies and regulation. In total, roughly 18,000 tariffs are affected. The agreement could create a new single market similar to the European Union.[40]

The Trans-Pacific Partnership (TPP) is a proposed trade agreement between 12 countries in Asia and the Americas.

Most Favored Nation Status

In addition to trading blocs, countries may also extend special "most favored nation" status to another country. This status includes trading privileges such as the reduction of import duties. The purpose is to promote more stable political ties between nations.[41] The United States has granted "most favored nation" status to a number of countries.

Ethical Challenges

Corruption occurs when people practice illegal or unethical activities to further their personal interests. Corruption is a source of controversy and often makes for headline news stories in international business. Corruption poses significant challenges for international managers.[42]

The Foreign Corrupt Practices Act of 1977 was enacted for the purpose of making it unlawful for certain entities to make certain payments to foreign government officials to make payments to foreign government officials to assist in obtaining or retaining business. Specifically, the anti-bribery provisions of the act make it unlawful to make a payment, promise of a payment or provide anything of value while knowing that such payments will be offered to directly or indirectly provide an improper advantage to obtain or retain business.[43]

The Sociocultural Environment

Ethnocentrism A natural tendency of people to regard their own native country, culture, language, and behavior as superior to all others

Many managers don't realize that the values and behaviors that govern business operations in their own country don't always translate to other parts of the world. Ethnocentrism refers to the natural tendency of people to regard their own native country, culture, language, and behavior as superior to all others. Ethnocentrism can be found in any country and strong ethnocentric attitudes in a country provide challenges for foreign firms to

FIGURE 2 SUMMARIZES THE THREE DIFFERENT MANAGER VIEWPOINTS REGARDING CULTURE AND PRACTICE.

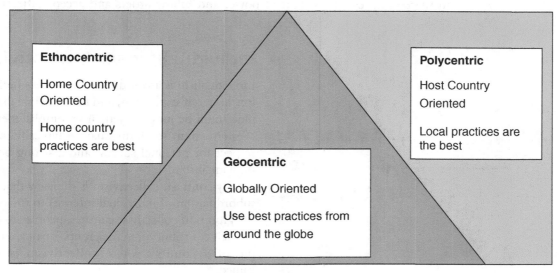

Ethnocentric

Home Country Oriented

Home country practices are best

Geocentric

Globally Oriented

Use best practices from around the globe

Polycentric

Host Country Oriented

Local practices are the best

Source: Figure 2 Manager Attitudes Regarding Culture. Courtesy of Jeffrey Anderson.

operate there.[44] The ethnocentric approach involves filling top management positions with people from the home country. These managers are known as expatriates.[45]

Polycentric managers believe that native managers best understand local personnel and practices. Organizations with this belief take a hands-off approach, leaving many decisions to native managers.

Geocentric managers fall between the ethnocentric and polycentric approaches. Geocentric manager believe that there are differences and similarities between domestic and foreign practices and that managers should use the techniques that are the most effective.[46]

Geocentric companies don't make a significant geographic distinction with their management. They reflect a transnational or borderless approach. Ford Motor Company is pursuing a "One Ford" approach to integrate its operations around the world. Another company, Thomson SA, legally based in France, has eight major locations around the world. "We don't want people to say that we're based anywhere," says their CEO.[47]

Polycentric managers They believe that native managers best understands local personnel and practices

Geocentric managers A believe that there are differences and similarities between domestic and foreign practices and that managers should use the techniques that are the most effective

Hofstede's Model of National Culture

Researchers have spent much time identifying differences and similarities in the values and norms of people from different countries. Dutch social psychologist Geert Hofstede developed one of the most widely recognized approaches to understanding cultural differences. His original research found four initial dimensions of national culture. He later added a fifth dimension.[48] These dimensions, with some country cultures as examples, are presented in Figure 3.

Power Distance

Power distance refers to the degree to which people accept or reject unequal power distribution among institutions, organizations, and people. Low power distance means that people in a culture expect power to be distributed equally. In cultures with high power distance, we see great respect for age, status, and position. People in these cultures are tolerant of power and follow orders and accept differences in rank.[49]

Individualism vs. Collectivism

Individualism is a world view that values individual freedom, self-expression, and the principle that people should be judged by their accomplishments. In Western countries, individualism typically includes respect for personal success and a strong belief in individual rights.

By contrast, collectivism is the view that values subordination of individual interests to the goals of the group. In collectivist cultures, people are judged by their contribution to the group. Japan is an example of a country where collectivism is highly valued.[50]

Some cultures value individual accomplishments while others value collective efforts.

Uncertainty Avoidance

Cultures that are high in uncertainty avoidance prefer structure and security. In these cultures, people are less likely to take risks. These cultures are more rigid and skeptical about people whose behavior differs from their own norms. Cultures with low uncertainty avoidance are more easygoing, value diversity, and tolerate differences in beliefs and actions.[51]

Masculinity vs. Femininity

Masculinity vs. femininity refers to the degree to which a culture values assertiveness and materialism vs. feelings, relationships and quality of life. This can be thought of as the tendency for members of a culture to show stereotypical traits of masculinity or femininity. In Hofstede's research, Japan had the highest score for masculinity. Visitors to Japan may observe how restricted career opportunities may be for women, ranging from outright sexism to attitudes about division of labor.[52]

Countries that are high in uncertainty avoidance are uncomfortable with risk and unknown outcomes.

Long-Term vs. Short-Term Orientation

Cultures that score high in long-term orientation look to the future and value saving and thrift. Cultures that are short-term oriented focus on the past and present and seek immediate gratifications. Americans have a tendency toward impatience and a desire for instant gratification. Many Asian cultures are future oriented and value thrift, whereas short-term oriented countries such as the United States focus on the past and present and seek immediate gratification.[53]

The GLOBE Project

The Global Leadership and Organizational Behavior Effectiveness (GLOBE) program is an ongoing research study that extends Hofstede's work by exploring cross-cultural leader behaviors. Using data from more than 18,000 managers in 62 countries, the GLOBE team identified nine dimensions cultural dimensions. Of those, power distance and uncertainty avoidance align directly with Hofstede's model.

The emphasis on short-term vs. long-term accomplishments is another dimension of culture

Four dimensions; assertiveness, future orientation, human orientation, and institutional collectivism are similar to Hofstede's original dimensions. Three new dimensions; gender differentiation, in-group collectivism, and performance orientation, offer additional insights into cultural differences.[54] Table 3 describes each of the GLOBE cultural dimensions and identifies countries that score high or low for each dimension.

Global Management and National Culture

The differences between national cultures can have important implications for managers. Management practices that are effective in one country may not work in another. Consider General Electric's purchase and subsequent management of Tungsram, a Hungarian lighting company. GE was attracted to Tungsram because it was one of Hungary's best companies and because of Hungary's relatively low wage rate. GE planned on using Hungary as a base to export products throughout Europe.

After the purchase, GE soon found out that the former communist-run company would not convert easily to American-style business practices. American managers faced employees who were used to a bureaucratic system where the workers didn't communicate with managers. A company where employees seemed to have a laid-back attitude toward their work and customers. American managers thought the Hungarians were lazy.

Tungsram employees considered the American managers uncomfortably aggressive. The Americans were risk takers while the Hungarians were reluctant to change. The Hungarians were unfamiliar with teams and team decisions. They had no motivation to produce quality products and customer satisfaction wasn't a priority. Tungsram employees expected to be paid at Western wage levels.

Despite underestimating the cultural challenges in Hungary, GE was able to turn Tungsram around. Through consolidation of operations, listening to employees and increasing wages, GE was able to take the formerly underproductive company and transform it into a key part of their European strategy.[55]

General Electric encountered cultural differences when it bought the Hungarian light manufacturer Tungsram.

Culture shock Feelings of disorientation experienced by someone who is suddenly subjected to an unfamiliar culture, way of life, or set of attitudes

Culture Shock

According to Hofstede, culture is "the collective programming of the mind distinguishing the members of one group or category of people from others."[56] Culture reveals the differences in social structures, language, religion, and the historical backgrounds of different countries. Culture shock occurs when a person has difficulty adjusting to a new culture with different norms, customers, and expectations.[57] Because familiar signs and symbols are no longer present in a new culture, disorientation along with physical

FIGURE 3 HOFSTEDE'S DIMENSIONS OF NATIONAL CULTURE

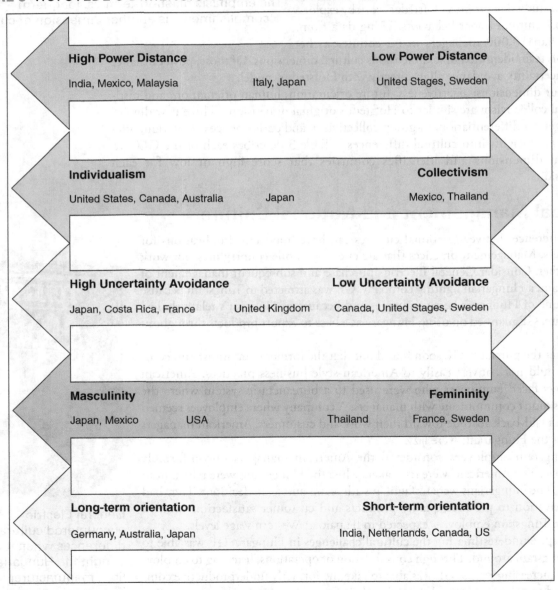

| **High Power Distance** | | **Low Power Distance** |
| India, Mexico, Malaysia | Italy, Japan | United Stages, Sweden |

| **Individualism** | | **Collectivism** |
| United States, Canada, Australia | Japan | Mexico, Thailand |

| **High Uncertainty Avoidance** | | **Low Uncertainty Avoidance** |
| Japan, Costa Rica, France | United Kingdom | Canada, United Stages, Sweden |

| **Masculinity** | | | **Femininity** |
| Japan, Mexico | USA | Thailand | France, Sweden |

| **Long-term orientation** | **Short-term orientation** |
| Germany, Australia, Japan | India, Netherlands, Canada, US |

Source: Hofstede, Geert, Culture's Consequences, International Differences in Work-Related Values, 1980, Sage Publications, New York.

and emotional discomforts are often common with people who go to other nations to live, work, or study.[58]

Communication Differences

People from some cultures pay more attention to social context, nonverbal messages and social status of their communication than others. In a low-context culture, most communication takes place through the written or spoken word. The United States, Canada, and Germany are all low-context cultures. In a high-context culture, the written and spoken word may only convey a part of the

Sometimes cultural differences can cause anxiety known as culture shock.

© Shutterstock.com

TABLE 3 COUNTRIES RANKING HIGHEST AND LOWEST ON GLOBE CULTURAL DIMENSIONS

ASSERTIVENESS		HUMANE ORIENTATION		IN-GROUP COLLECTIVISM	
How confrontational and dominant should individuals be in social relationships?		How much does society encourage and reward people for being kind, generous, friendly, and fair?		How much pride and loyalty do people have for their family or organization?	
Highest	**Lowest**	**Highest**	**Lowest**	**Highest**	**Lowest**
Germany	Denmark	Malaysia	Germany	Iran	Denmark
United States	Netherlands	Philippines	Spain	India	Netherlands
Austria	Japan	Ireland	France	China	Sweden
Sweden	New Zealand	Egypt	Singapore	Egypt	Finland
PERFORMANCE ORIENTATION		**INSTITUTIONAL COLLECTIVISM**		**POWER DISTANCE**	
How much are individuals rewarded for improvement and excellence?		How much do leaders encourage and reward loyalty to the social unit?		How much unequal power distribution should there be in an organization or society?	
Highest	**Lowest**	**Highest**	**Lowest**	**Highest**	**Lowest**
Singapore	Russia	Sweden	Greece	Russia	Denmark
Hong Kong	Argentina,	South Korea	Italy	Thailand	Sweden
New Zealand	Greece	Japan	Argentina	Spain	Netherlands
United States	Italy	Denmark	Hungary	Argentina	Israel
GENDER EGALITARIANISM		**UNCERTAINTY AVOIDANCE**		**FUTURE ORIENTATION**	
How much does a culture maximize gender role differences?		How much do people rely on norms and rules to avoid uncertainty?		How much do people delay gratification by planning and saving for the future?	
Highest	**Lowest**	**Highest**	**Lowest**	**Highest**	**Lowest**
Hungary	South Korea	Switzerland	Russia	Singapore	Russia
Poland	Egypt	Sweden	Greece	Switzerland	Argentina
Denmark	China	Austria	Venezuela	Netherlands	Poland
Slovenia		Germany	Bolivia	Canada	Italy

adapted from Javidan and House, "Cultural Acumen for the Global Manager," *Organizational Dynamics*, Spring 2001, pp. 289–305

TABLE 4 HIGH- AND LOW-CONTEXT CULTURES. IMAGES © SHUTTERSTOCK.COM

Japan	Vietnam	Greece	Italy	United States	Switzerland	Germany
High Context					Low Context	

Source: University of Louisville Institute for International Communications

Low-context culture A culture where most communication takes place through the written or spoken word

message. In these cultures, part of the message is contained in the nonverbal signals such as body language, facial expressions, and the social context of the communication. Thailand and Malaysia are high-context cultures.[59] Table 4 outlines some other high- and low-context cultures.

© Shutterstock.com

High-context culture A culture where the written and spoken word may only convey a part of the message

Monochromic cultures A culture where time is perceived as being limited, precisely segmented, and driven by schedules

Time Differences

Edward T. Hall (1914–2009) was an anthropologist who pioneered the study of nonverbal communication and interactions between members of different ethnic groups.[60] He described two types of ways that cultures deal with time.

In monochronic cultures, people often do one specific thing at a time. In this culture, time is perceived as being limited, precisely segmented, and driven by schedules. This is the standard practice in American business culture. In this type of culture, when you schedule a meeting with an individual, you would give him or her your undivided attention during that time.

In polychronic cultures, time is viewed as being more flexible and multi-dimensional. These cultures have a preference for doing more than one thing at a time. Mediterranean, Latin American, and particularly Arab cultures prefer polychronic time. A monochronic American visitor to a polychronic Egyptian client may be frustrated as he or she waits for meetings to begin then finds the meeting regularly interrupted.[61]

Differences in Space

People of different cultures have varying views on what is acceptable in terms of interpersonal space. Hall described these preferences in terms of proxemics, the study of how people use space to communicate. For example, people in North American and Europe generally conduct business conversations at a range of 3–4 feet. In Latin American and Asian cultures, the range is about 1 foot. For Arab cultures it's even closer.

According to Hall, "Arabs tend to get very close and breathe on you. The American on the receiving end can't identify all the sources of his or her discomfort but feels that the Arab is pushy. The Arab comes close, the American backs up. The Arab follows because he or she can only interact at certain distances." Once the American understands that this is how Arabs handle interpersonal space the situation can sometimes be redefined to make the American feel more comfortable.[62]

Polychromic cultures A culture where time is viewed as being more flexible and multi-dimensional

The Challenges of Global Management

To succeed at a global level, managers and organizations must develop a global mindset. Managers can help their organizations develop a global perspective and managers with global experience are in high demand. As managers find themselves working in international locations, they must develop an approach to navigate through ambiguities and complex situations that exceed their prior experiences. A global mindset is the ability of managers to appreciate and influence individuals, groups, organizations and systems that include different social, cultural, political, intellectual, and psychological characteristics.[63]

Some argue that the global mindset has two key components: (1) intellectual intelligence, including business acumen and (2) global emotional intelligence, which includes self-awareness, cross-cultural awareness, and the ability to make cultural adjustments. Development of a global mindset is one of the key challenges that confront global leaders and highlights what's important about global leadership.[64]

Global mindset The ability of managers to appreciate and influence individuals, groups, organizations, and systems that include different social, cultural, political, intellectual, and psychological characteristics

Summary of Learning Outcomes and Key Points

❏ **Realize how globalization is creating a world marketplace**

Globalization refers to the extent to which trade, investments, information, cultural and social ideas, and political cooperation flow between countries. Through globalization, the world is becoming a more interdependent system.

❏ **Remember and understand why and how organizations do business internationally**

Organizations expand internationally through a variety of methods with varying amounts of risk and investment. Many organizations start with global sourcing, that is, shopping for materials and labor worldwide. Importing and exporting involve buying and selling international goods. Through joint ventures, two companies create a separate entity to serve an international market. Finally, direct investment through partially or wholly owned subsidiaries in foreign counties requires the greatest investment and holds the highest risk.

❏ **Recognize barriers to trade and global trade agreements**

Barriers to trade are measures that governments take to make imported goods or services less competitive than those produced domestically. These barriers include tariff barriers, non-tariff barriers, quotas, subsidies, and embargos.

Globalization has been accelerated, at least in part though global trade agreements. These agreements, such as the North American Free Trade Agreement, The European Union, APEC, and the TPP are intended to eliminate trade barriers and encourage free trade between member nations.

❏ **Appreciate manager views on culture and differences in national culture**

Dutch psychologist Geert Hofstede identified five dimensions of national culture, which include power distance, uncertainty avoidance, masculinity, individuality, and long-term orientation. Robert House and his team expanded on Hofstede's research through the GLOBE project. In their studies, they identified 12 dimensions of national culture. The GLOBE dimensions are performance orientation, uncertainty avoidance, humane orientation, institutional collectivism, in-group collectivism, assertiveness, gender egalitarianism, future orientation, and power distance.

Other cultural differences include how cultures handle the issues of time and space and context. In low-context cultures, meanings are derived primarily from written and spoken words. In high-context cultures other nonverbal components of the message convey important meaning.

Questions for Review

1. Describe the concept of globalization and the global village. How does this trend affect organizations and managers?

2. Describe the various strategies organizations use to go global? What are the costs and benefits of each approach?

3. What are the implications of Hofstede's research? How does this research impact managers in organizations?

4. What are the challenges that might confront a Mexican manager transferred to the United States to manage a factory in Tucson, Arizona? Will those be the same as a U.S. manager who is transferred to Mexico? Explain.

5. How might the cultural differences outlined in the GLOBE project affect how managers (1) use work groups, (2) develop goals and plans, (3) reward outstanding employee performance, and (4) deal with conflict between employees?

Closing Case

It's Cool in Cuba

The fact that it has been off-limits for U.S. citizens for 50 years gives Cuba a high coolness factor. U.S. relations with Cuba have been quite cold since 1960. That's when President Eisenhower placed a temporary economic embargo on Cuba. Diplomatic relations were severed the next year. From there things got worse, with the disastrous U.S. backed "Bay of Pigs" invasion and the Cuban missile crisis, a U.S. Soviet stare down over nuclear missiles. President Kennedy made the embargo permanent in 1962 and it's stood ever since, through ten U.S. Presidents.

While the embargo is still in place (only Congress can lift it), U.S. relations with Cuba have been thawing quickly and for some time. In December 2014, President Obama and Cuban President Castro announced a new course in relations between the United States and Cuba. The following July, the U.S. Embassy in Havana, closed since 1961, reopened. The following March, President Obama became the first sitting president to visit Cuba in 88 years. Five months later, JetBlue began regularly scheduled flights to Cuba, the first commercial flights in 50 years.

While travel restrictions have eased, going to Cuba isn't as simple as visiting other Caribbean countries. All Americans need visas to enter Cuba, and traveling for pure tourism purposes is technically not allowed. Instead, Americans applying for visas need to cite one of 12 possible reasons, such as visiting family, humanitarian projects, journalism, educational activities, or professional research.

Current restrictions notwithstanding, visiting Cuba may become the cool tourist destination. Carnival Cruises began stopping there in May 2016. The next month, Starwood became the first American hospitality chain to manage a hotel in Cuba since the revolution, rebranding a 180-room Havana suburb hotel as a Four Points by Sheraton. Marriot, which is buying Starwood, is also in talks about taking over other Havana hotels.

Coolness is not all that Cuba has to offer, and that's a good thing because coolness will fade. Cuba is very interesting from a cultural perspective. It's not a typical beach island. There's art, dance, and culture. That's what Cuba has to sell to the United States.

Cubans are buyers as well. They have a highly literate population and close proximity to U.S. markets. Cuban consumers have been cut off from U.S. products for decades and Cuba needs everything: food, building products, and technology to name a few, assuming it can figure out a way to pay. The problem will be how to pay. The average Cuban makes about $25 per month.

There's still a lot to be worked out. U.S. corporate and citizen claims of lost property against Cuba total nearly $2 billion. Cuba is accused of continuing human rights violations and Cuban law limits freedom of expression, association, assembly, movement, and the press. But the goal of the White House in easing trade restrictions is to promote the independence of Cuban people so that they don't have to rely on the Cuban state. Time will tell, but normalization of relations with Cuba seems to have broad support in Washington.

Questions for Discussion

1. The travel and tourism seems well on its way in Cuba. What other U.S. companies and industries might benefit from normalized trade relations with Cuba? Explain.
2. What approach or approaches might U.S. companies take when expanding to Cuba? Explain.

End Notes

1. Kinicki, A. & Williams, B. (2013). *Management, A Practical Introduction* (6th ed.). McGraw-Hill, New York, p. 98.

2. Ibid, p. 99.

3. Daft, R. & Marcic, D. (2015). *Understanding Management* (9th ed.). Cengage, Stamford, CT, p. 102.

4. Robbins & Coulter, *Management*, 13e, p. 121.

5. http://www.huffingtonpost.com/aj-agrawal/ten-reasons-why-businesse_b_11512636.html (retrieved 9/26/16)

6. Schermerhorn, J. & Bachrach, D. (2015). *Management* (13th ed.). John Wiley & Sons, New York, p. 101.

7. Robbins, S., Coulter, M., & DeCenzo, D. (2017). *Fundamentals of Management* (10th ed.). Pearson, Upper Saddle River, p. 62.

8. Harley-Davidson, a U.S. icon, highlights offshoring's peril, James B. Kelleher, Reuters, July, 22, 2014, http://www.reuters.com/article/harleydavidson-results-offshoring-idUSL2N0PX1MT20140722

9. Lussier, R. (2017). *Management Fundamentals*, (7th ed.). Sage, Los Angeles, p. 73.

10. Kinicki, A., p. 108.

11. Ibid., p. 109.

12. Griffin, R. (2016). *Fundamentals of Management* (8th ed.). Cengage Learning, Boston, p. 52.

13. Robbins, Coulter, & DeCenzo, p. 64.

14. Schermerhorn, p. 103.

15. Robbins, S. & Coulter, M. (2016). *Management* (13th ed.). Pearson, Upper Saddle River, p. 106.

16. Daft, R. (2016). *Management* (12th ed.). Cengage, Boston, p. 125.

17. Robbins & Coulter, p. 107.

18. Lussier, R., p. 73.

19. Kinicki, p. 110.

20. Schermerhorn, J, p. 103.

21. http://ohio.honda.com/our-story (retrieved 8/29/16)

22. Robbins, S. & Coulter, p. 105.

23. Schermerhorn, J., p. 107.

24. http://www.forbes.com/global2000 retrieved 9/3/2016

25. http://www.investopedia.com/terms/m/multinationalcorporation.asp#ixzz4LOURSq4n http://www.investopedia.com/terms/m/multinationalcorporation.asp#ixzz4LOURSq4n (retrieved 9/26/16)

26. Daft, R., p. 118.

27. http://um.dk/en/tradecouncil/barriers/what-is (retrieved 9/26/16)

28. http://www.economicshelp.org/blog/glossary/trade-barriers/ (retrieved 9/26/16)

29. Griffin, R, p. 56.

30. Daft, R., p. 138.

31. Kinicki, A., p. 118.

32. Daft, R., p. 139–140.

33. Schermerhorn, J., p. 106.

34. Daft, R, p. 138.

35. Kinicki, A, p. 114.

36. http://www.bbc.com/news/uk-politics-32810887 (retrieved 8/26/16).

37. http://www.economist.com/blogs/economist-explains/2016/06/economist-explains-23 (retrieved 8/26/16)

38. Schermerhorn, J., p. 106.

39. http://www.apec.org/About-Us/About-APEC.aspx (retrieved 9/26/16)

40. http://www.bbc.com/news/business-32498715 (retrieved 8/29/16)

41. Kinicki, A., p. 118.

42. Schermerhorn, J., p. 109.

43. https://www.justice.gov/criminal-fraud/foreign-corrupt-practices-act (retrieved 9/26/16)

44. Daft, R., p. 132.

45. Gomez-Mejia, L. & Balkin, D. (2012). *Management*, Pearson, Upper Saddle River, p. 56.

46. Kinicki, A., New York, p. 109.

47. Robbins, S. & Coulter, M., p. 105.

48. Robbins, S. & Coulter, M., p. 111.

49. Schermerhorn, J., p. 115.

50. Jones, G. & George, J. (2015). *Essentials of Contemporary Management* (6th ed.). McGraw-Hill, New York, p. 143.

51. Ibid., p. 144.

52. Schermerhorn, J., p. 115.

53. Lussier, R., p. 86.

54. Robbins, S. & Coulter, M., p.111.

55. Aswathappa, A. (2006). *International Business* (2nd ed.). McGraw-Hill p. 225.

56. https://geert-hofstede.com/national-culture.html, retrieved 9/3/16

57. Gomez-Mejia, L., p. 46.

58. Ball, D., Geringer, J., McNatt, J. & Minor, M. (2013). *International business* (13th ed.). McGraw-Hill, New York, p. 438.

59. Schermerhorn, J., p. 113.

60. http://www.nytimes.com/2009/08/05/science/05hall.html?_r=0 retrieved 9/4/16

61. Schermerhorn, J., p. 112.

62. Kinicki, A., p. 121.

63. Daft, R., p. 114–115.

64. Ball, D., p. 280

Additional Notes and Acknowledgments

All boxed quotes adapted from https://www.thebalance.com/inspiring-quotes-on-globalization-importing-and-exporting-1953442 (retrieved 10/15/16)

Closing case adapted from http://time.com/money/4430542/cuba-flights-jetblue-cheap/, http://www.npr.org/sections/parallels/2014/12/17/371405620/the-u-s-and-cuba-a-brief-history-of-a-tortured-relationship, https://www.whitehouse.gov/issues/foreign-policy/cuba, and http://www.nytimes.com/2016/08/31/travel/how-to-go-to-cuba-now-jetblue.html , all retrieved 9/7/16

CHAPTER 4 PLANNING AND STRATEGY

Key Terms

Bankruptcy	Dogs	SMART objective
BCG matrix	Focus strategy	Stability strategy
Blue ocean strategy	Growth strategy	Stars
Cash cow	Liquidation	SWOT analysis
Competitive advantage	Mission statement	Turnaround strategy
Cost leadership	Porter's five forces	Unrelated diversification
Defensive strategy	Product life cycle	Vision statement
Differentiation	Question marks	
Divestiture	Related diversification	

Introduction

Planning is the first step in the management process. Strategic plans are long term in nature and determine the overall direction for the organization. In this chapter, we will explore the planning process from the perspective of strategic management, starting with the organization's mission and outlining tools for strategic management. We will discuss grand strategies and outline steps for analyzing an industry and reducing environmental uncertainty.

Learning Outcomes

After reading this chapter, you should be able to:

☐ Recall and understand the purpose of mission and vision statements

☐ Differentiate between strategic, tactical, and operational planning

☐ Remember and understand how different factors such as resources, capabilities, and other industry factors influence profitability

☐ Describe strategic concepts including grand strategies, generic strategies, and the BCG matrix

Planning and Strategy

Planning consists of translating an organization's mission and vision into goals and objectives. The organization's purpose is expressed through its mission statement, and the vision statement expresses where it wants to be in the future. From the organization's

FIGURE 1 THE PLANNING PROCESS. COURTESY OF JEFFREY ANDERSON.

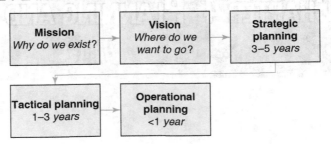

mission and vision, strategic, tactical, and operational planning follow. Figure 1 outlines the planning process.

Mission

The strategic planning process begins with establishing a mission, vision, and goals for the organization. An organization's mission expresses the purpose clearly and concisely. A **mission statement** describes what an organization does, its basic product or service, and its customers and values.[1]

Consider as an example, the mission statement of The Walt Disney Company:

> The Walt Disney Company operates a global entertainment portfolio of Media Networks, Parks and Resorts, Studio Entertainment, and Consumer Products. This wide array reaches out to the world through its television broadcasts, Internet businesses, theme parks, and the many ventures of The Walt Disney Company's subsidiaries.[2]

Mission statement describes what an organization does, its basic product or service, and its customers and values

A well-written mission statement includes some of the following elements[3]:

1. A purpose statement explains why the organization exists, it's purpose, and reason for being

2. A business statement identifies the organization's business activities and functions

3. A values statement explains the values held in common by the members of the organization

A clear sense of mission can inspire support from an organization's various stakeholders. Stakeholders are individuals or groups that are directly affected by an organization and its actions. Stakeholder groups include owners, employees, customers, shareholders, suppliers, distributors, creditors, and local communities.[4]

Vision statement statement provides an image of where the organization is headed and what it hopes to become

Vision

The mission describes how the organization currently operates. A **vision statement** looks to the future. A vision statement provides an image of where the organization is headed and what it hopes to become.[5]

A vision statement describes the organization as it would appear in the future if successful. An effective vision statement answers the question: If the organization were

TABLE 1 IMPORTANT CONSIDERATIONS FOR MISSION AND VISION STATEMENTS

Mission Statements

- ❏ Who are our customers?
- ❏ What are our major products or services?
- ❏ What geographic areas do we serve?
- ❏ What is our basic technology?
- ❏ What are our economic objectives?
- ❏ What are our beliefs and values?
- ❏ What is our competitive advantage?
- ❏ What are our responsibilities to the public?
- ❏ How do we treat employees?

Vision Statements

- ❏ Is our vision appropriate for the organization and for the times?
- ❏ Does our vision set high ideals?
- ❏ Does it clarify our direction and purpose?
- ❏ Is it enthusiastic and inspiring?
- ❏ Does it reflect the uniqueness of our organization?
- ❏ Is it ambitious?

to achieve all of its strategic goals, what would it look like 10 years from now? A well-written vision statement can be inspirational and aspirational, creating a mental image of the future state that the organization aspires to achieve. A vision statement should both challenge and inspire employees.[6]

Table 1 presents some important considerations for both mission and vision statements.

Levels of Managerial Planning

Clearly stated and inspiring mission and vision statements are the foundation for three types of planning.

Strategic planning is performed by top managers. With the mission and vision as a guide, strategic planning involves determining the organization's long-term goals. Strategic planning is organization wide and broad in nature. Strategic plans articulate how the organization will serve its customers and position itself against competition in the next 3–5 years or longer.

Tactical planning is performed by middle managers. With tactical planning, middle managers take the strategies developed by top managers and develop plans to implement these strategies in their respective divisions or units.

Operational planning is performed by first-line managers. Operational plans are the day-to-day plans that implement the organization's strategies. They have lots of details and typically cover a time-frame of 1 year or less.

Figure 2 illustrates the three levels of managerial planning.

FIGURE 2 THREE LEVELS OF ORGANIZATIONAL PLANNING. COURTESY OF JEFFREY ANDERSON.

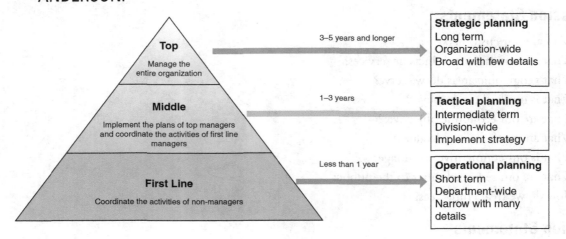

Objectives

After developing a mission and vision, objectives must be set at each level of the organization. Let's draw a distinction between goals and objectives. Goals state broad, general targets. **Objectives** state what is to be accomplished in specific, measurable terms and provide a target date.[7]

Specific

Measurable

Attainable

Results oriented

Target dates

The five characteristics of effective objective are represented by the acronym SMART.[8]

Specific—objectives should be stated in specific, rather than vague terms. They should state the exact level of desired performance.

Measurable—in order to achieve objectives, you must be able to observe and measure the progress toward that objective.

Attainable—objectives must be challenging, but they also must be realistic and attainable. Challenging objectives can motivate people more than easy ones.

Results oriented—objectives should support the organization's mission and vision and be results oriented and stated using action verbs.

Target dates—effective objectives have deadlines or target dates, dates by which the objectives should be accomplished.

Table 2 distinguishes between broad goals and specific SMART objectives.

Strategy and Competitive Advantage

Competitive advantage a superior position when an organization can provide greater value than its competitors

Developing an effective strategy is about creating and exploiting a competitive advantage. A competitive advantage is what sets an organization apart from its competitors. It is what gives an organization a distinctive edge over others in the market. This edge comes from an organization's core competencies by doing something that others cannot do or doing it better than others.[9]

TABLE 2 SMART AND NON-SMART OBJECTIVES

Goals	SMART Objectives
Reduce inventory	Reduce raw material inventory at the Cleveland plant by 10 percent by end of year
Improve customer satisfaction	Improve customer satisfaction by reducing caller wait time from 3.5 to 2.5 minutes by end of Q3
Decrease product costs	Decrease production set-up cost of the Acme product line by 20 percent by end of June

Some common sources of competitive advantage include:

Technology—organizations can use technology to achieve operational efficiencies, market exposure, and customer loyalty.

Cost and quality—providing greater product or service quality and greater efficiency.

Barriers to entry—creating strong markets that are protected from competitors.

Financial resources—having the potential to absorb short-term losses.

> Plans are only good intentions unless they immediately degenerate into hard work.
> —*Peter Drucker*

SMART objective an objective that is specific, measurable, achievable, and realistic with target dates

Resources and Capabilities

In the resource-based view, competitive advantage comes from resources and capabilities that are superior to those of competitors. Without this superiority, competitors could simply copy what an organization is doing and any competitive advantage would soon disappear.

Resources are organization-specific assets that can be used to create a cost or differentiation advantage and that few competitors can easily replicate. Some examples of such resources include:

❏ Trademarks and patents
❏ Proprietary knowledge
❏ Customer base
❏ Organizational reputation
❏ Brand value

The resource-based view suggests that sustainable competitive advantage results from the ownership and control of resources that are rare, valued by the market, non-tradable, non-substitutable, and difficult or impossible to imitate.

Capabilities refer to an organization's ability to use its resources effectively. One example is an organization's ability to bring a product to market more quickly than competitors. Often these capabilities are embedded in the culture of the organization and are not easily identified as procedures and are therefore difficult for competitors to copy.

An organization's resources and capabilities together form its distinctive competencies. Distinctive competencies drive innovation, quality, efficiency, and customer service, all of which can be used to create a cost or differentiation advantage.[10]

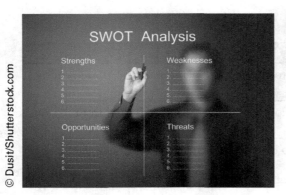
© Dusit/Shutterstock.com

SWOT Analysis

Formulating strategy begins with understanding the internal and external issues that shape an organization's competitive situation. This requires managers to conduct a SWOT analysis, which assesses the strengths and weaknesses of the organization along with opportunities and threats in the external environment.

Strengths are positive internal characteristics that the organization can exploit to achieve its performance goals. They can include any activities that an organization does well or any unique resources that it possesses. **Weaknesses** are internal characteristics that restrict or inhibit an organization's performance. They include activities that the organization does not do well or resources that it needs but does not possess. Managers perform an internal analysis of specific organizational functions to assess the organization's strengths and weaknesses. Often this analysis is done as a comparison with other companies.[11]

SWOT analysis assesses the strengths and weaknesses of the organization along with opportunities and threats in the external environment

We described the external environment in Chapter 2. Managers perform an external analysis to determine opportunities and threats presented by trends or changes in the political/legal, economic, sociocultural, and technological environments. **Opportunities** are presented by positive trends in the external environment whereas **threats** are implied from negative trends.

These combined internal and external analyses are called a SWOT analysis. SWOT is an acronym for strengths, weaknesses, opportunities, and threats. After completing a SWOT analysis, managers should be ready to formulate strategies that exploit an organization's strengths and external opportunities, minimize the organization's risk from external threats, and correct key weaknesses.[12]

Table 3 provides some general factors that may represent strengths, weaknesses, opportunities, and threats.

We will use Starbucks as an example to illustrate several concepts in this chapter. Starbucks operates limited service restaurants that serve specialty snack items or nonalcoholic beverages for consumption on-premises. This industry includes retailers such as bagel shops, coffee shops, doughnut shops, ice cream parlors, juice bars, and smoothie shops. Major companies in the industry include Dunkin' Brands, Einstein Noah Restaurants, Krispy Kreme Doughnuts, and Starbucks (all US-based), along with Costa Coffee (UK) and Tim Hortons (Canada).

Table 4 presents a SWOT analysis for Starbucks.

Porter's Five Forces

Porter's five forces a model of industry analysis that proposes five competitive forces in an organization's environment

Industries vary greatly in terms of their make-up, competitive situation, and potential for growth. In Porter's model for industry analysis, Michael Porter proposed five primary competitive forces in an organization's environment: (1) threat of new entrants, (2) bargaining power of suppliers, (3) bargaining power of buyers, (4) threat of substitute products or services, and (5) rivalry among competitors.[14]

1. **Threat of new entrants**—the threat of new competitors entering the market. The threat of new entrants is based on the presence or absence of barriers to entry.

2. **Bargaining power of suppliers**—the ability of suppliers to influence the price that an organization pays for supplies and services.

TABLE 3 SWOT ANALYSIS WITH POTENTIAL STRENGTHS, WEAKNESSES, OPPORTUNITIES, AND THREATS

Internal Factors	
Strengths Possible strengths include: ❏ Manufacturing efficiencies ❏ Talented workforce ❏ Strong market share ❏ Strong financial resources ❏ Superior reputation	**Weaknesses** Possible weaknesses include: ❏ Outdated facilities or equipment ❏ Inadequate research and development ❏ Obsolete technology ❏ Weak management ❏ Weak organizational culture
Opportunities Some possible opportunities include: ❏ Potential new markets ❏ Weak competitors ❏ Strong economic conditions ❏ Emerging technologies ❏ Growth in existing markets	**Threats** Possible threats include: ❏ New competitors entering the market ❏ Shortage of raw materials ❏ Changing consumer tastes ❏ New government regulations ❏ Substitute products
External Factors	

TABLE 4 SWOT ANALYSIS FOR STARBUCKS

SWOT Analysis for Starbucks[13]	
Strengths ❏ Strong brand name recognition ❏ Large distribution network (16,635 stores worldwide) ❏ Customers are satisfied with the quality of the product ❏ Strong human resources ❏ Good supplier relations ❏ Excellent customer service	**Weaknesses** ❏ High prices compared to the competitors ❏ High operating costs ❏ Highly dependent on coffee for sales ❏ Starbucks has less control on stores located outside the United States ❏ Protests against the company
Opportunities ❏ Growth opportunities in Asian markets ❏ Product diversification ❏ Market penetration in international locations ❏ Co-branding with other food companies ❏ Whole bean sales in grocery stores	**Threats** ❏ Economic conditions can impact sales ❏ Increasing number of competitors ❏ Health conscious trends ❏ Competitors can imitate Starbucks, weakening its differentiation

3. **Bargaining power of buyers**—the ability of customers to influence the price that they will pay for the organization's goods and services.
4. **Threat of substitute products or services**—the ability of customers to use alternative products or services
5. **Rivalry among competitors**—the intensity of rivalry between existing firms in the industry and how they compete with one another.

Figure 3 presents the five forces as well as some factors that impact the severity of each force.

The combination of these five forces influences the attractiveness, or potential to be profitable over the long term. Table 5 presents a Porter's five forces analysis of the specialty eatery industry where Starbuck's competes. Upward point arrows in the table signify forces that increase industry profitability, and downward point arrows identify forces that decrease industry profitability.

Growth strategy a grand strategy with the goal of making the organization bigger by increasing sales, market share, the number of locations, or the number of employees

Apple is pursuing a growth strategy. Company-owned Apple stores are an example of forward vertical integration.

Grand Strategies

From a macro perspective, an organization has a choice of three common grand strategies; growth, stability, and defensive.

A growth strategy involves expansion, such as increasing sales, market share, locations, and the number of employees. With a growth strategy, a company may expand into new markets or add new products.

There are several ways that an organization can grow. A concentration strategy focuses on realizing the growth of a single product or a few closely related products or services. This is also known

FIGURE 3 PORTER'S FIVE FORCES. COURTESY OF JEFFREY ANDERSON.

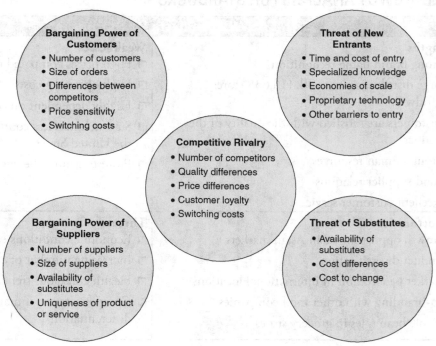

TABLE 5 A PORTER'S FIVE FORCES ANALYSIS FOR THE SPECIALTY RESTAURANT INDUSTRY. STARBUCK'S LOGO © SHUTTERSTOCK.COM

Threat of new entrants
The threat of new entrants is high because little capital investment is needed in this industry.

Bargaining power of suppliers	**Rivalry among competitors**	**Bargaining power of customers**
The bargaining power of suppliers is limited because a there is a diversity of suppliers across many different countries.	There are many different competitors. Coffee is a commodity that is widely traded. Switching costs and customer loyalty are low.  © Sergey Kohl/ Shutterstock.com	Customers have little individual bargaining power as individual purchases are very small. There are a variety of customers thus no single customer or type of customer carries enough weight to significantly influence Starbucks' pricing. Since there are no switching costs companies must be sensitive to such issues as how much of a premium its customers are generally willing to pay.

Threat of substitute products
This is significant market force. There are many alternate food and beverage products that consumers can choose in place of Starbucks' products.

There are no switching cost when choosing alternate products. Bars or restaurants are readily available substitute choices for a coffee shop.

as "market penetration strategy." The aim is to gain a larger share of the current market by expanding into new markets with the same product or with developing closely related new products.

A company might choose to grow by vertical integration. In backward vertical integration, the organization becomes its own supplier controlling access to raw materials, suppliers, or services. For example, eBay owns PayPal in order to control secure payments for their online auctions.

In forward vertical integration, a company becomes its own distributor. For example, Apple distributes its own products through more than 400 worldwide company-owned Apple stores.[14]

Horizontal integration involves growth through acquisition. With horizontal integration, an organization acquires a competitor, eliminating that competitor as a threat and broadening the reach of its product line by acquiring a competitor's customers.

A stability strategy involves maintaining existing operations with little or no change. With a stability strategy, a company would serve the same customers by offering the same products and services. The goal is to maintain market share and sustain current operations.

A no change strategy, as the name itself suggests, is a stability strategy that is followed when an organization aims at maintaining its present business definition. Simply, the decision of not doing anything new and continuing with the existing business operations and the practices is referred to as a no-change strategy.

There are several reasons why a company might adopt a stability strategy:[16]

- ❑ When there is a slowdown or recession in the economy
- ❑ When the company wants to reduce debt on its balance sheet
- ❑ When the industry has reached the maturity phase
- ❑ When gains from expansion are less than the costs involved

Stability strategy a grand strategy with the goal of maintaining existing operations with little or no change

Defensive strategy a grand strategy with the goal of reducing the organization's size or the number of offerings

A defensive strategy involves reducing the organization's size or offerings. Defensive strategies become necessary during times of market decline. In 2014, Redbox began to reduce their kiosks in the US market as a result of declining rentals.[17]

Defensive strategies include harvest, turnaround, divestiture, bankruptcy, and liquidation. With a harvest strategy, an organization minimizes its investments and attempts to maximize short-run cash flow and profits with the intention of eventually liquidating the company.

In a turnaround strategy, an organization attempts to move from a negative direction to a positive one.

In 2003, the Danish firm Lego was on the verge of bankruptcy. The company was struggling to meet the changing demands of customers and effectively manage costs. In 2004, the company hired Jorgen Vig Knudstorp as CEO. Knudstorp implemented a defensive strategy of cutting costs by trimming Lego's product line, restructuring its supply chain and refocusing the company's image around plastic blocks. The strategy worked and in less than 10 years, the company quadrupled its revenues and brought Lego back to households around the world. Today, Lego occupies the top spot in toy manufacturing.[18]

Divestiture is the process of selling off divisions or subsidiaries to restructure a company into a smaller but stronger portfolio of businesses. This strategy is especially useful with poorly performing divisions that might be sold to a competitor. Cash from that sale can be used to finance other business lines.

Danish toy producer Lego adopted a defensive strategy to avoid bankruptcy.

Turnaround strategy a defensive strategy that attempts to return an organization to profitability

Divestiture the process of selling off divisions or subsidiaries to create a smaller portfolio of businesses

> The essence of strategy is choosing what not to do.—*Michael Porter*

Bankruptcy a form of court protection from creditors when an organization is unable to meet its obligations

Bankruptcy is the ultimate defensive strategy. Also known as chapter 11, bankruptcy is a form of court protection from creditors when an organization has been in decline for a long period of time and is unable to meet its obligations and needs time and opportunity to reorganize itself for a turnaround.

During the economic crisis, General Motors was losing billions of dollars as consumers stopped buying cars. The company filed for bankruptcy in 2009. Five years after their filing, General Motors became one of the most profitable companies in the world.

Through the bankruptcy, the company reached new labor agreements, and shed debt, nonproductive factories, and weak brands and dealerships.[19]

Liquidation simply means ending or terminating the business. The company exits the business either by liquidating its assets or by selling the whole business, thus ending its existence in the current form.

Table 6 presents the variations of the three grand strategies.

Liquidation the process of ending or terminating the business

Porter's Generic Strategies

Harvard professor Michael Porter argued that a company's competitive advantage lies in one of two areas: cost advantage and differentiation. By applying this advantage in either a broad or narrow market scope, three generic strategies emerge: (1) cost leadership, (2) differentiation, and (3) focus. Figure 4 outlines each of these strategies.

An organization creates a competitive advantage by using its resources and capabilities to achieve either a lower cost structure or a differentiated product. An organization's positions itself is in its industry by choosing between low cost or differentiation strategies. This decision is a central component of the firm's competitive strategy.

With a cost-leadership strategy, an organization's goal is to become the low-cost producer in an industry for a given level of quality. The company then sells its products and services at industry average prices and earns a higher profit than competitors, or sells below industry average prices to gain market share. The cost-leadership strategy is applied in a broad market, that is, one with many customers.[20] Retailing giant Walmart

Cost leadership a generic strategy where an organization becomes the low-cost producer serving a wide market

TABLE 6 WAYS TO IMPLEMENT GRAND STRATEGIES.

Growth Strategy

❏ Improve existing products or services to attract more customers
❏ Increase advertising and promotion to try to increase market share
❏ Expand operations through vertical integration
❏ Expand into new products and services
❏ Acquire a similar or complementary business
❏ Merge with another company to form a bigger company

Stability Strategy

❏ Implement a "no-change" strategy
❏ Implement a "little-change" strategy

Defensive Strategy

❏ Reduce costs through a hiring freeze or spending cuts
❏ Liquidate assets such as land, buildings, and inventory
❏ Discontinue selected products or services
❏ Divest or "spin-off" part of its business
❏ Declare bankruptcy
❏ Attempt a turnaround and move toward reestablishing profitability

FIGURE 4 PORTER'S GENERIC STRATEGIES. COURTESY OF JEFFREY ANDERSON.

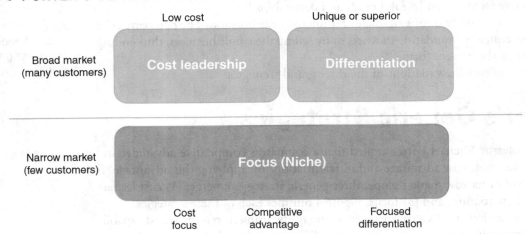

Low cost   Unique or superior

Broad market (many customers) — **Cost leadership** | **Differentiation**

Narrow market (few customers) — **Focus (Niche)**

Cost focus   Competitive advantage   Focused differentiation

Retailing giant Walmart competes with a cost-leadership strategy.

© fotomak/Shutterstock.com

is an obvious example. Walmart focuses on lowering its costs through efficient operations. The cost to operate Walmart's stores is much less than those of their competitors, allowing them to offer lower prices to their customers.

Other examples of companies with a cost-leadership strategy include Timex, hardware retailer Home Depot, and Bic pens.

> However beautiful the strategy, you should occasionally look at the results.—*Winston Churchill*

A differentiation strategy requires a firm to offer unique or superior products to a broad market. This strategy is used by companies trying to create brands that set themselves apart from competitors. Coca-Cola spends millions every year in advertising to reinforce their brand image.[21] Examples of companies with differentiation strategies include Mercedes-Benz, Lexus, and Ritz-Carlton hotels.

With a focus or niche strategy, an organization focuses on a more narrow market segment, one with fewer potential customers. The objective is to serve the needs of a particular market segment better than competitors. Competitive advantage is achieved through a cost-leadership differentiation approach in a narrow market segment.

A focused differentiation strategy involves selling unique or superior products to a narrow market.

Ferrari is an Italian sports car manufacturer that specializes in high-performance luxury vehicles. Ferrari models are known for their sleek design, speed, and high sticker prices. Since Ferrari car prices start at around $190,000 and go up, there are very few customers in this market segment. This is an example of a focused differentiation strategy. Other companies that operate in this segment include Bentley, Rolls Royce, and Lamborghini.

With a cost-focus strategy, a company competes by being a cost leader in a narrow market. Claire's appeals to young women, a narrow-market segment, with inexpensive jewelry, accessories, and ear piercing. Claire's has more than 3,000 stores across the United States and is located in 95percent of the malls of the country.[22]

© ruangrit jukong/Shutterstock.com

Coca-Cola is a highly differentiated product.

© yousang/Shutterstock.com

© Jason Batterham /Shutterstock.com

Differentiation a generic strategy where an organization offers a unique or superior product or service to a wide market

Focus strategy a generic strategy where a company focuses on a narrow market, competing on low cost or differentiation

Consider the companies listed in Table 7. Southwest Airlines pursues a cost-leadership strategy. Their operations are designed to increase efficiencies and decrease costs, allowing Southwest to compete in a wide market. Companies such as Delta, United, and American Airlines compete by offering unique or superior services. These companies target a wide, international market with a differentiation strategy. European ultra-discount airline Ryan Air, along with US companies such as Allegiant and Spirit, competes in a more narrow market segment. There are fewer customers in this ultra-discount, bare-bones market segment. These companies are competing with a cost-focus strategy. Finally, NetJets offers private, secure, and luxury flights to a very narrow segment of customers who are able to pay very high prices.

TABLE 7 EXAMPLES OF GENERIC STRATEGIES IN THE AIRLINE INDUSTRY. PHOTOS © SHUTTERSTOCK.COM

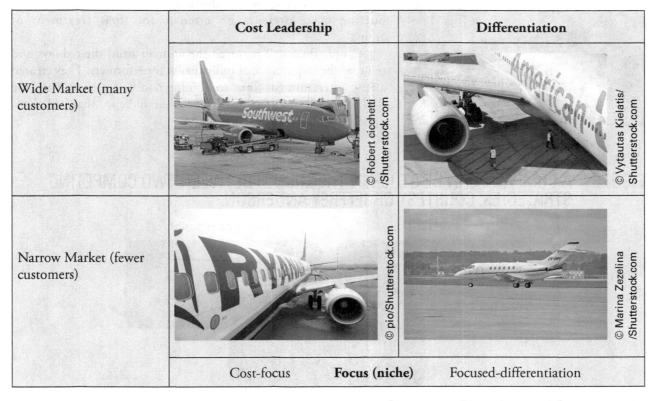

	Cost Leadership	**Differentiation**
Wide Market (many customers)	© Robert cicchetti /Shutterstock.com	© Vytautas Kielatis/ Shutterstock.com
Narrow Market (fewer customers)	© pio/Shutterstock.com	© Marina Zezelina /Shutterstock.com
	Cost-focus **Focus (niche)**	Focused-differentiation

Blue Ocean vs. Stuck in the Middle

Blue ocean strategy a strategy that combines cost leadership and differentiation to create value innovation

Porter's generic strategies call for companies to compete on the basis of either cost or differentiation. Can companies compete with both strategies? Generally, the answer is no as each strategy has inherent trade-offs and conflicts in the two different strategic positions. For example, if a company offers differentiated, high-quality products, it risks undermining the perception of that quality if it offers lower prices. Figure 5 illustrates the strategic position Porter called "stuck-in-the-middle." He argued that to compete with both strategies, the company should separate into separate business units to serve the different markets associated with each strategy.[23]

Strategy scholars Kim and Mauborgne offer the idea of a blue ocean strategy where a successful business unit can combine cost leadership and differentiation. Companies with a blue ocean strategy reconcile the differences between the two strategic positions by offering innovative value. They call this approach blue ocean because the companies compete in wide-open markets.[24]

The regional grocery chain Trader Joe's competes with a blue ocean strategy. Trader Joe's has a much lower cost structure than Whole Foods. Both companies compete for the same customers, those wanting high-quality health-conscious food. The perception among customers is clear; Whole Foods is notoriously expensive, whereas Trader Joe's is relatively cheap.[25]

Another example is Cirque du Soleil, the Canadian company that reshaped the dynamics of the declining circus industry in the 1980s. With a Porter's five forces

analysis, the circus industry was a loser. Performers had "supplier power" over the company. Stiff competition came from alternative forms of entertainment, such as sporting events and home entertainment systems. In addition, animal rights groups were putting more pressure on circuses for their treatment of animals.

Cirque du Soleil removed the animals from their shows and reduced the importance of individual star performers. They created a new entertainment form combining dance, music, and athletic skill to appeal to a more expensive adult audience that had abandoned traditional circus shows.

FIGURE 5 A COMPANY CAN BE STUCK IN THE MIDDLE BETWEEN TWO COMPETING STRATEGIES. COURTESY OF JEFFREY ANDERSON.

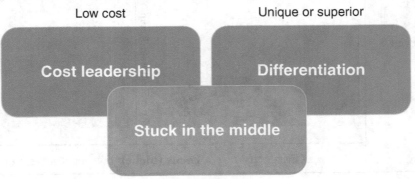

As a replacement for of "five forces," Kim and Mauborgne cite "four actions" that can help create a blue ocean strategy. These actions are found by answering the following questions[26]:

—*Which of the factors that the industry takes for granted should be eliminated?* For Cirque du Soleil that included animals, star performers, and the three separate rings.

—*Which factors should be reduced well below the industry's standard?* Cirque du Soleil reduced a considerable amount of the thrill and danger found in conventional circuses.

—*Which factors should be raised well above the industry's standard?* Cirque du Soleil improved the uniqueness of the setting by developing their own tents, as opposed to performing in existing venues.

—*Which factors should be created that the industry has never offered?* Cirque du Soleil presented dramatic themes, artistic music, and dance, presented in a more fashionable, refined environment.

> A satisfied customer is the best business strategy of all.—*Michael LeBoeuf*

The Product Life Cycle

Product life cycle a life cycle for products that includes the introduction, growth, maturity, and decline phases

Most successful products pass through a life cycle of recognizable stages; introduction, growth, maturity, and decline. This lifecycle is presented in Figure 6.[27]

Stage 1—Introduction. During the introduction stage, a product is brought to the market for the first time, often before there is a proven demand and before the product is fully developed. Sales are low because the product is new.

Stage 2—Growth. Demand accelerates during the growth stage and the total size of the market expands greatly.

FIGURE 6 THE PRODUCT LIFE CYCLE

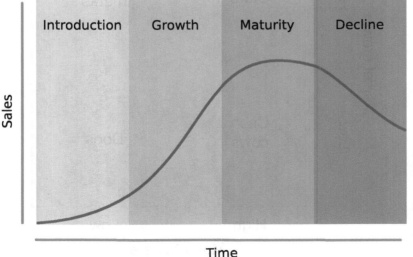

Product life cycle

Introduction — Growth — Maturity — Decline

Sales

Time

© Niki99/Shutterstock.com

Stage 3—Maturity. During the maturity phase, sales level off. Often sales during this period are for replacement products.

Stage 4—Decline. Finally, during the decline sage, products lose their appeal and sales drop.

Understanding the four stages of the product life cycle helps managers recognize the different strategies required as sales volume changes over time. Organizational strategies can change during the product life cycle. During the introduction and growth stages, an organization might use a growth strategy to capitalize on the increased product demand. During the maturity stage, the organization should shift to a stability strategy and finally a defensive strategy during the decline stage. An organization may also shift from a differentiation strategy to a cost-leadership or cost-focus strategy as demand begins to level-off and decline.

BCG Matrix

BCG matrix a portfolio strategy that evaluates products on the basis of their market share and market growth rates

Developed by the Boston Consulting Group, the BCG matrix is a method of evaluating strategic business units on the basis of the market growth rate of their industry and their share of the market. Market growth rate is an indication of how fast the entire industry is growing. Market share is concerned with an organizations portion of total industry sales. The BCG matrix suggests that companies will do well in a fast-growing market in which it has a large market share.[28]

Figure 7 illustrates the matrix. In the figure, market share is on one axis, high and low, and market growth is on the other axis, high and low. The resulting matrix presents four different quadrants.

FIGURE 7 THE BCG MATRIX. COURTESY OF JEFFREY ANDERSON.

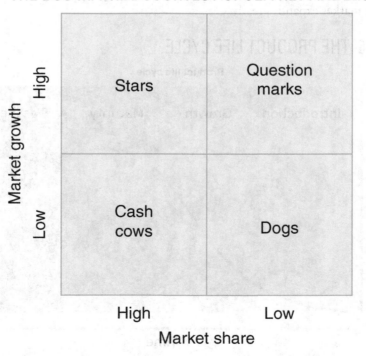

- **Stars** are products or services with a high market share in a high-growth market.
- **Cash cows** are products or services with a high market share in a low-growth market.
- **Question marks** are products or services with a low share of a high-growth market.
- **Dogs** are products or services with a low share in low-growth market.

A strategic business unit's location on the matrix determines its strategy. Dogs call for a defensive strategy, scaling back offerings or selling off product lines. A stability strategy is appropriate for cash cows. Profits from these units are used to fund other units. A growth strategy is appropriate for stars. Companies with star products should take maximum advantage of their high market share and the potential for growth in the market. Question marks are risky propositions as these units may become stars, or dogs.

Figure 8 provides an example of a BCG matrix for Starbucks products[29]:

Coffee and packed food are stars. These products operate in high-growth markets and have high market share. These are proven products that tend to generate great amounts of cash for Starbucks.

Tea is a question mark for Starbucks. Tea is a product with a high market growth rate. However, Starbucks is more famous for coffee and they have a very low share of the fast-growing tea market.

Stars a BCG matrix classification for a product with a high market share of a high-growth industry

Cash cow a BCG matrix classification for a product with a high market share of a low-growth industry

Question marks a BCG matrix classification for a product with a low market share of a high-growth industry

Dogs a BCG matrix classification for a product with a low market share in a low-growth industry

FIGURE 8 BCG ANALYSIS OF STARBUCKS. PHOTOS © SHUTTERSTOCK.COM

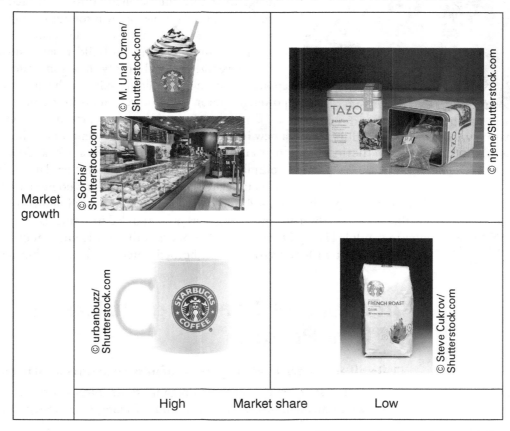

Mugs are a cash cow. These products have a high market share operating in a low-growth market. This is a mature market and the products are very well established, therefore generating exceptional cash flow. Mugs provide Starbucks with profits according to seasonal trends.

Finally, packaged coffee beans are dogs. These products have a low market share and operate in a low-growth market. Starbucks' packaged coffee beans do not generate significant cash for the company as customers tend to go to Starbucks for quick service for coffee and food.

Diversification

Related diversification when a company moves into a new industry that has important similarities to their existing industry

Organizations use diversification strategies to enter new industries. Through vertical integration, a company moves forward or backward to a new part of the value chain. Diversification involves moving into new value chains. Often this is done through acquisitions or mergers.

© Chere/Shutterstock.com

Honda pursues a strategy of related diversification with a wide range of products including cars, motorcycles and marine engines.

Unrelated diversification when a company moves into a new industry that lacks any important similarities to its existing industry

Related diversification happens when a company moves into a new industry that has important similarities with their existing industry or industries. Disney's purchase of ABC is an example of related diversification as films and television are an important part of entertainment. Some organizations engage in related diversification to exploit a core competency. Honda Motor Company provides a good example of leveraging as they leverage their core competencies through related diversification. While Honda is best known for automobiles, the company actually started in motorcycle business where they developed a unique ability to build reliable small engines. Honda leveraged this ability with automobiles. They also applied their engine-building skills in the all-terrain vehicle, power generator, lawn mower, and boat motor industries.

Unrelated diversification occurs when a company enters a new industry, one that lacks any important similarities with their existing industry or industries. Coca-Cola invested in Columbia Motion Pictures, which they later sold to Sony. Many unrelated diversification efforts do not have happy endings. For example, Harley-Davidson once tried to sell Harley-branded bottled water. Starbucks tried to diversify by offering Starbucks-branded furniture. Both attempts were disasters. While Harley-Davidson and Starbucks both enjoy iconic brands, this resource simply did not transfer effectively to the bottled water and furniture businesses.[30]

Summary of Learning Outcomes and Key Points

❏ **Recall and understand the purpose of mission and vision statements**

A mission statement describes an organization's purpose or reason for being. A vision statement describes the organizations long-term strategic intent.

❑ **Differentiate between strategic, tactical, and operational planning**

Strategic planning is performed by top managers. Strategic plans are organization wide and long term, typically 3 years or more. Tactical plans are made at the middle levels of management. Tactical plans are division wide and intermediate in time frame, typically 1–3 years. Operational plans are made by first-line managers. Operational plans are department wide and short term in time frame, typically 1 year or less.

❑ **Remember and understand how different factors such as resources, capabilities, and other industry factors influence profitability**

In the resource-based view, competitive advantage comes from having resources and capabilities that are superior to competitors. Resources include assets such as patents and trademarks, proprietary knowledge, and brand value. Capabilities refer to an organization's ability to use its resources more effectively than competitors.

Harvard Professor Michael Porter identified five factors that influence industry profitability. These include the competitive rivalry in the industry, the power of suppliers and customers to influence prices, the threat of substitute products, and the threat of new entrants.

❑ **Describe strategic concepts including grand strategies, generic strategies, and the BCG matrix**

Organizations may pursue one of three grand strategies; growth, stability, and defensive. Growth strategies involve increasing the size of the organization, stability strategies maintain the status quo, and defensive strategies typically seek to make an organization smaller.

Michael Porter proposed that organizations may pursue one of two generic or competitive strategies. A differentiation strategy involves selling a product or service that is unique or superior to competitor offerings. With a cost-leadership strategy, organizations minimize costs so as to offer lower prices than competitors or to make higher margins. Both of these strategies can be applied to narrow markets, ones with relatively few customers. This is known as a focus or niche strategy.

In the BCG matrix, products are categorized along two factors; market growth and market share. Products with a high market share and in a high growth market are stars. Products with a high market share of a low-growth market are cash cows. Products with a low-market share in a low-growth market are dogs, whereas products with a low share in a high-growth market are questions marks.

Closing Case

One company is using technology to push new methods into the age-old whiskey industry. Cleveland Whiskey, based in Cleveland, Ohio, is using carefully guarded proprietary technology to age whiskey in a fraction of traditional time of 6–12 years. The company uses pressure aging, , which shortens the aging process by using intense pressure in stainless steel tanks to push young spirits in and out of wood, which gives the whiskey its flavor.

Company founder and CEO Tom Lix was inspired by the 1970 film MASH and first learned distilling while stationed on a US Navy Destroyer. In the Navy, he made bootleg spirits from fermented fruit juice, discarded steel piping and patched up seawater condensers.

The American craft distillery market has grown with more than 750 craft distilleries in production as of 2015. The industry produces about one million cases of spirits a year. While this is a fraction of the overall distilled spirits industry, craft brands are influencing larger distillers to introduce their own so-called craft brands. Jim Beam's Signature Craft series of "small batch bourbons" that include a premium packaged and premium priced 12-year old bourbon, as well as new bourbon finished with Spanish brandy are two examples.

Lix created Cleveland Whiskey in 2012 in response to the whiskey shortage. While bourbon production topped the one million barrel mark in 2014, people are drinking bourbon faster than distillers can make it. There's lots of evidence of this shortage in the industry. Four Roses has stopped exports because they can't meet demand. Maker's Mark tried to water down their bourbon. Knob Creek actually ran out of whiskey at one point and other brands have put products on allocation.

The opportunity for growth in the whiskey market comes from upscale brands. While whiskey market volume has grown, sales of value whiskey brands (the lowest-end price segment) has been flat. The volume for premium categories has seen double-digit growth. This phenomenon, known as "premiumization," is part of the current buyer's desire to trade up to "affordable luxuries." As producers struggle to meet demand, the market continues to encourage consumers to move to small-batch, upscale brands.

Flavor is also appearing as an opportunity growth for American whiskey. While the overall whiskey segment grew 7.8 percent in the United States in 2015, it's estimated that 44 percent of that growth came from flavored brand extensions such as Sazerac Co.'s Fireball Cinnamon, Jack Daniel's Tennessee Honey, Jim Beam Red Stag, and Wild Turkey American Honey.

Cleveland Whiskey's production process allows them to quickly adapt to market demands. While other whiskey takes years to produce, Cleveland Whiskey is made in as little as one day. This gives them lots of flexibility to adjust their production. The company's "just-in-time" process also gives them the ability to produce new flavors that can reach markets in a fraction of the time previously necessary.

Cleveland Whiskey's production process is also much more efficient than that of other distillers. Traditionally aged whiskies lose about 3 to 6 percent of their volume each year through evaporation. This evaporation is known as the "angel's share" and a whiskey stored in a barrel for 10 years can lose up to 50 percent of its original volume. Cleveland Whiskey's rapid aging process eliminates the angel's share.

Lix chose Cleveland because it offered important assets including abundant freshwater, affordable real estate, and a strong entrepreneurial support network. Cleveland also tested well as a brand name in markets such as Boston, Seattle, Los Angeles, Dallas, and Chicago. People said that Cleveland to them stood for something that was authentic, genuine, hardworking, entrepreneurial, and edgy.

The company's annual sales topped $1 million in 2015 and currently Cleveland Whiskey is available in 13 states. They've also exported small batches to Germany, France, Belgium, Switzerland, and Japan.

Questions for Discussion

1. Perform a SWOT analysis for Cleveland Whiskey. What are the company's strengths and weaknesses? What are opportunities and threats in the distilled spirits industry?

2. Describe Cleveland Whiskey's generic strategy. Is the company well positioned to take advantage of market opportunities?

3. Evaluate the distilled spirits industry in terms of Michael Porter's five factors of competition. How profitable is this industry on a scale of 1–5 (5 being the most profitable)?

End Notes

1. Bateman, T. & Snell, S. (2013). *Management* (3rd ed.). McGraw-Hill, New York, NY, p. 99.

2. Retrieved February 3, 2017, from https://www.missionstatements.com/fortune_500_mission_statements.html.

3. Cherrington, D. & Dyer, W. (2009). *Creating Effective Organizations* (5th ed.). Kendall Hunt, Dubuque, Iowa, p. 41.

4. Schermerhorn, J. & Bachrach, D. (2015). *Management* (13th ed.). John Wiley & Sons, New York, NY, p. 221.

5. Bateman, T. & Snell, S. (2013). *Management* (3rd ed.).McGraw-Hill, New York, NY, p. 99.

6. Retrieved February 16, 2017, from https://www.shrm.org/resourcesandtools/tools-and-samples/hr-qa/pages/isthereadifferencebetweenacompany%E2%80%99smission,visionandvaluestatements.aspx.

7. Lussier, R. (2017). *Management Fundamentals* (7th ed.). Sage Thousand Oaks, CA, p. 138.

8. Kinicki, A. & Williams, B. (2016). *Management: A Practical Introduction* (7th ed.). McGraw-Hill, New York, NY p. 158.

9. Robbins, S. & Coulter, M. (2016). *Management* (13th ed.). Pearson, Upper Saddle River, p. 244.

10. Retrieved February 16, 2017, from http://www.quickmba.com/strategy/competitive-advantage/.

11. Daft, R. & Marcic, D. (2015). *Understanding Management* (9th ed.). Cengage, Stamford, CT, p. 203.

12. Robbins, S. & Coulter, M. (2016). *Management* (13th ed.). Pearson, Upper Saddle River, p. 238.

13. Adapted from http://www.mba-tutorials.com/marketing/swot-analysis-marketing/310-starbucks-swot-analysis.html, Retrieved February 10, 2017 and Lussier, R. (2016). *Management* (6th ed.). Sage, San Francisco, CA, p. 135.

14. Kinicki, A. & Williams, B. (2016). *Management*: A Practical Introduction (7th ed.). McGraw-Hill, New York, NY p. 173.

15. Robbins, S. & Coulter, M. (2016). *Management* (13th ed.). Pearson, Upper Saddle River, p. 242.

16. Retrieved February 16, 2017, from http://www.letslearnfinance.com/what-is-stability-strategy.html.

17. Kinicki, A. & Williams, B. (2016). *Management: A Practical Introduction* (7th ed.). McGraw-Hill, New York, NY p. 175.

18. Retrieved February 9, 2017, from http://www.businessinsider.com/how-lego-made-a-huge-turnaround-2014-2.

19. Retrieved February 16, 2017, from http://money.cnn.com/2014/05/29/news/companies/gm-profit-bailout/.

20. Retrieved February 3, 2017, from http://www.quickmba.com/strategy/generic.shtml.

21. Kinicki, A. & Williams, B.(2016). *Management: A Practical Introduction* (7th ed.). McGraw-Hill, New York, NY p. 177.

22. Retrieved February 9, 2017, from http://2012books.lardbucket.org/books /strategic-management-evaluation-and-execution/s09-04-focused-cost-leadership-and-fo.html.

23. Retrieved February 9, 2017, from http://www.quickmba.com/strategy/generic. shtml.

24. Rothaermel, F. (2017). *Strategic Management* (3rd ed.). McGraw-Hill, New York, NY, p. 194.

25. Retrieved February 9, 2017, from http://www.businessinsider. com/i-compared-the-price-of-whole-foods-365-items-to-trader-joes-heres-what -i-found-2016-2/#cheddar-cheese-6.

26. Retrieved February 16, 2017, from http://guides.wsj.com/management/strategy /what-is-blue-ocean-strategy/.

27. Retrieved February 9, 2017, from https://hbr.org/1965/11/exploit-the-product-life-cycle.

28. Kinicki, A. & Williams, B. (2016). *Management: A Practical Introduction* (7th ed.). McGraw-Hill, New York, NY p. 179.

29. Retrieved February 9, 2017, from http://starbuckscompanynews.blogspot. com/2014/02/boston-matrix.html.

30. Retrieved February 12, 2017, from http://catalog.flatworldknowledge.com/ bookhub/reader/3085?e=ketchen_1.0-ch08_s03.

CHAPTER 5 MAKING DECISIONS

Key Terms

Bounded rationality
Brainstorming
Certainty
Creativity
Decision tree
Decision tree

Delphi technique
Expected value
Groupthink
Heuristics
Innovation
Mind map

Nominal Group Technique (NGT)
Nonprogrammed decision
Programmed decisions
Risk
Satisficing model
Uncertainty

Introduction

As discussed in Chapter 1, managers perform in four different decisional roles; resource allocator, disturbance-handler, entrepreneur, and negotiator. In this chapter, we will explore the decision-making process. We will discuss the cognitive and individual limits on rational decision-making. We will explore the differences, advantages, and disadvantages that groups offer to the decision-making process and we will examine the phenomena of groupthink.

Ordering more products to maintain inventory levels is an example of a programmed decision.

© Dave Nelson/Shutterstock.com

Learning Outcomes

After reading this chapter, you should be able to:

❏ Understand and remember types of problems, decisions, and decision-making styles
❏ Explain the rational decision-making process
❏ Identify the limits on rational decision-making
❏ Recognize heuristics and cognitive biases
❏ Describe techniques for innovative decision-making
❏ Explain the advantages and disadvantages of group decision-making

Problems and Decisions

Problem solving is the process of identifying differences between actual and desired situations. To solve problems, managers make decisions. A **decision** is a choice among alternative courses of action.[1]

We can distinguish between two types of decisions; programmed decisions and nonprogrammed decisions.

Programmed decisions involve situations that have occurred before often enough so that procedures, policies, or rules have been established to guide these decisions. Programmed decisions involve structured problems, ones that are well defined and where the issues, alternatives, and potential outcomes are known to a large degree.

Programmed decisions A routine or repetitive decision that can be handled by established business rules or procedures

Nonprogrammed decision A decision regarding an unique and unstructured problem

Programmed decisions include routine issues like inventory management. A manager of a carryout would develop rules to help make decisions on when and how much beer to order from distributors. For example, when the supply of Natural Light falls below fifteen cases, order fifteen from the distributor. The decision rules for programmed decisions follow the logic as the "if, then" statements in computer programming. For example, if a customer has a valid receipt, less than 30 days old and the merchandise is in new condition, then we will issue cash refund. Most programmed decisions are related to daily activities.

By contrast, nonprogrammed decisions are made in response to situations that are unique. These problems are poorly defined and largely unstructured. Since these nonprogrammed decisions are not routine, no decision rules have been developed. Nonprogrammed decisions involve problems that are unstructured, where the issues are complex and all alternatives and potential outcomes of the alternatives are relatively unknown.

A company's decision as to where to build a new factory is an example of a nonprogrammed decision.

© EML/Shutterstock.com

Selecting the location for a new warehouse is an example of a nonprogrammed decision.

There are many factors to consider in this decision, the local economy, infrastructure, the availability of skilled workers, tax consequences, and others.

Nonprogrammed decisions are inherently challenging as they have more chance for errors and are more difficult for managers to handle. Managers must rely on their intuition to quickly respond to the urgent nature of nonprogrammed decisions.[2]

Cognitive Styles in Decision-Making

Just as there are different types of decisions, there are different types of decision makers. Researchers Row and Boulgarides developed a matrix of decision-making styles based on an individual's cognitive complexity (ambiguity tolerance vs. need for structure) and value orientation (social/human vs. instrumental/task-centered). These dimensions yield four decision-making styles: (1) directive (2) analytical, (3) conceptual, and (4) behavioral.[3] This matrix is presented in Figure 1.

FIGURE 1 THE FOUR COGNITIVE DECISION-MAKING STYLES.

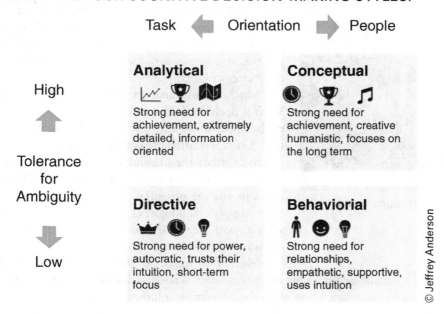

Directive (Low-ambiguity tolerance, Task focus): Directive individuals need and value structure. They prefer to make decisions based on clear, undisputed facts and impersonal rules and procedures.

Analytical (High-ambiguity tolerance, Task focus): Analytically decision makers can process ambiguous problems with time and information. They rely heavily on abstractions and instrumental logic, and tend to review all aspects of a problem carefully by acquiring and organizing large amounts of data. They consider every aspect of a given problem, acquiring information by careful analysis. Their solutions are comprehensive, detailed, and thorough.

Conceptual (High-ambiguity tolerance, Social focus): Conceptual decision makers are creative, probing, interested in novelty, and comfortable taking risks. The creative thinkers like to consider many different options and possibilities. They gather and evaluate information from many different perspectives, integrating diverse cues, and passing intuitive judgments as they work to identify emerging patterns.

Behavioral (Low-ambiguity tolerance, Social focus): Behavioral decision makers focus on the feelings and welfare of group members and other social aspects of work. They look to others for information, both explicit information in what others say and implicit information sensed during interactions with them. They evaluate information emotionally and intuitively.

Facing Certainty, Risk, and Uncertainty

It's not only that personal styles differ in problem-solving, the environment matters as well. There are three different situations or problem environments in which managers make decisions; certainty, risk, and uncertainty.

Managers typically encounter decisions under risk and uncertainty.

Certainty A decision situation where decision maker has complete information on possible alternatives and outcomes

Risk A decision situation where the decision maker has incomplete information about available alternatives but has a good idea of the probability of outcomes for each alternative

Uncertainty A decision situation where the decision maker cannot list all possible outcomes and/ or cannot assign probabilities to the various outcomes

With decisions under certainty, the decision maker has complete information on possible alternatives and outcomes. In this situation, all the information that the decision maker needs is fully available. As you might imagine, very few decisions are made under these circumstances.

Most often, managers face decisions under risk. With a decision under risk, managers can assess the probabilities of the outcomes for each alternative solution. Managers often use computerized statistical analysis to calculate the likelihood of the success or failure of each option. For example, restaurants like McDonalds can analyze potential customer data, traffic patterns, supply chain logistics, and competition come up with a good idea of the success of a restaurant when considering new store locations.

Most of the major decisions in contemporary organizations are made under a state of uncertainty. With decisions under uncertainty, the decision maker does not know all of the alternative solutions, the risks associated with each, or the likely outcomes of each alternative. This uncertainty stems from the complexity and dynamic nature of modern organizations and their environment.[4]

Making Rational Decisions

The **rational model** of decision-making, also called the classical model, explains how managers should make decisions. The rational model assumes that mangers will make logical decisions that will seek the optimum solution to further the organization's best interests. Figure 2 presents the rational decision-making model in four stages.[5]

The first stage of the decision-making process involves identifying a problem. A problem could represent the difference between goals and actual performance. For example, Bill, a department manager has a goal of $1,000,000 in sales for his department but is on track to earn only $750,000. This is a problem.

After the problem has been identified, the decision maker needs to generate alternative solutions to solve the problems. There are several alternatives that might solve Bill's problem of slacking sales. Here are some possible alternative; (1) hire additional sales staff, (2) pay current sales staff overtime, and (3) transfer employees from another division.

FIGURE 2 THE RATIONAL DECISION-MAKING PROCESS.

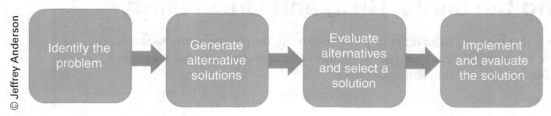

In the third step, the decision maker would evaluate each of the alternatives in terms of the costs and potential benefits of each. Then the decision maker would select the alternative solution with the best cost to benefit ratio.

Finally, the manager would implement the selected alternative and evaluate the success of this action.

Decision Trees

Decision tree A choice among alternative courses of action

Decision tree A decision support tool that uses a tree-like graph to model alternatives and their possible consequences.

Decision trees are tools to aid in choosing between multiple courses of action. They provide an effective structure allowing the decision maker to lay out options and examine the possible outcomes of those options. Decision trees also help the decision maker to form a balanced picture of the risks and rewards associated with each possible course of action.[6]

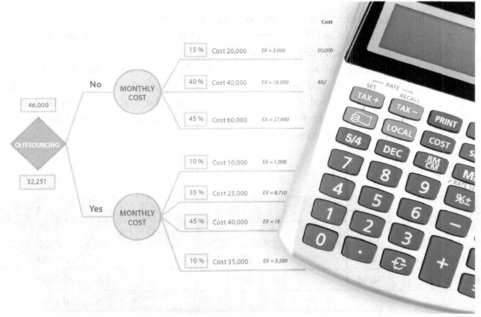

A decision tree is a decision support tool that uses a tree-like graph to model of decisions and their possible consequences.

With decision trees, all options and possible values of outcomes are mapped out. Then the probability of each outcome is assessed. The resulting analysis reveals an expected or most likely outcome.

Figure 3 shows a simplified decision facing a manager. Should the company build a large factory or a small one? In either case, the manager assesses a 70 percent likelihood that there will be a high demand for the company's product in the future, while there is a 30 percent chance that demand will be low. If the manager builds a large factory and demand is high, a payoff of $10 million per year is expected. If demand is low, then only a $1 million per year payoff is predicted.

FIGURE 3 A DECISION TREE SHOWS THE POSSIBLE ALTERNATIVES AND OUTCOMES OF A DECISION.

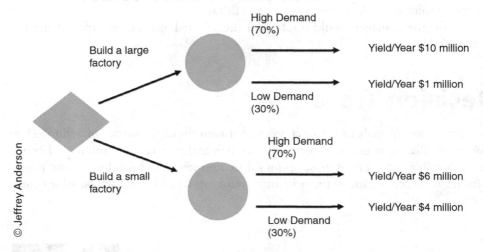

© Jeffrey Anderson

On the other hand, if the manager builds a small factory and demand is high, the payoff will be $6 million and if demand is low, the payoff will be $4 million.

Table 1 shows the expected values for each option. The expected value is a probability weighted average of all possible outcomes. The expected value is calculated by multiplying the probability of each outcome by the payoff, then adding the outcomes for each option. The optimal decision is the one with the highest payoff or expected value. In this case, the manager would choose to build a large factory as this alternative offers the highest expected (most likely) value.

Expected value A probability weighted average of all possible outcomes for each decision alternative.

TABLE 1 EXPECTED VALUE PAYOFF TABLE.

Payoff Table				
Option	**Outcome**	**Probability**	**Payoff**	**Expected Value**
Large factory	High Demand	70%	$10,000,000	$7,000,000
	Low Demand	30%	$ 1,000,000	$ 300,000
			Total Expected Value	$7,300,000
Small factory	High Demand	70%	$ 6,000,000	$4,200,000
	Low Demand	30%	$ 4,000,000	$1,200,000
			Total Expected Value	$5,400,000

Bounded rationality The idea that rationality in decision-making in individuals is limited by the information they have, the cognitive limitations of their minds, and the finite amount of time they have to make a decision

Bounded Rationality

The rational model makes assumptions about how a decision should be made rather than describing how a decision is actually made. Bounded rationality suggests that individual judgment is bounded by multiple constraints and that we can better understand decision-making by explaining actual rather than theoretic decision processes.

Bounded rationality acknowledges that decision makers often lack important information on the definition of the problem and the relevant criteria. Time and cost constraints also limit the amount and quality of available information. Further, decision makers retain only a relatively small amount of information in their usable memory. Finally, limitations on intelligence and perceptions constrain the ability of decision makers to calculate the optimum alternative from available information.

Together, these limitations keep decision makers from making the optimum choice as outlined in the rational model. Figure 4 illustrates the constraints placed on rational decision-making.

Because of the constraints placed on decision-making, managers often don't make exhaustive search for the best alternative solution. Instead, they follow the satisficing model. With the satisficing model, decision makers seek alternative solutions until they find one that solves the problem. The resulting solution is satisfactory but not necessarily optimum.[7] Figure 5 outlines the satisficing decision model.

In his 1975 study of managerial behavior, Mintzberg found that the average manager engages in a different activity every nine minutes. Further, he found that when making decisions, managers tend to avoid hard data and rely more on their intuitive judgment.[8]

FIGURE 4 BOUNDED RATIONALITY.

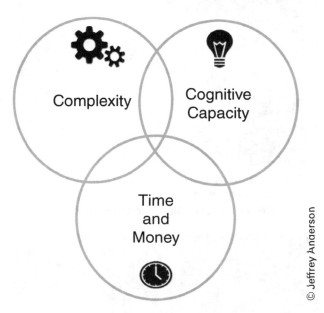

Satisficing model A decision-making strategy or cognitive heuristic that entails searching through the available alternatives until an acceptability threshold is met

FIGURE 5 THE SATISFICING MODEL.

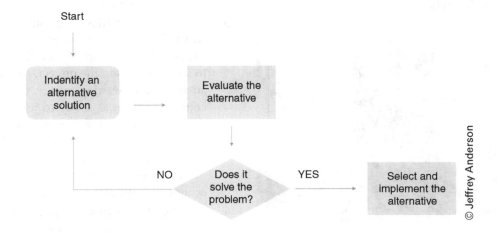

The availability bias, fueled by reports in the media, cause many to believe that travel by air is more dangerous than traveling by car.

The sunk cost bias explains why the French and British governments continued to invest in the Concorde supersonic airline despite decades of financial losses.

The VietnNam war provides an example of the escalation of commitment bias. The UnitedStates sent increasing numbers of troops to fight in the war even though it was clear to many that the war could not be won.

Heuristics and Cognitive Biases

Research suggests that people rely on a number of strategies, or rules of thumb, when making decisions. These simplifying strategies are known as heuristics. They are the rules that direct our judgment implicitly. They serve as a useful means of dealing with the complex environment that surrounds many of our decisions. In general, heuristics are helpful but in some cases they can lead systematically biased outcomes with the potential for significant errors. Cognitive bias happens in situations where a heuristic is inappropriately applied in making a decision.[9] Here are nine cognitive biases that commonly affect decision-making[10]:

1. **Availability Bias**—With the availability bias, managers use information readily available from memory to make judgments. However, what's readily available in memory may not present a complete picture of the situation. The availability bias may be fueled by what we see in the news media.

2. **Representative Bias**—The representative bias is the tendency to generalize from a small sample or single event. The bias here is that just because something has happened once doesn't mean that it's representative of what will happen again. Also, people tend to judge the probability of an event by finding a "comparable known" event and assuming that the probabilities will be similar.

3. **The Sunk-Cost Bias**—The sunk-cost bias or sunk-cost fallacy is when managers, after adding up all of the money already spent, and decide it is too costly to simply abandon the project. As many people have an aversion to wasting money, they may continue a course of action as a way to justify money already spent. The sunk-cost bias is sometimes called the "Concorde" effect as the British and French governments both continued to invest money in the supersonic jet even when it was clear that there was no economic justification for the plane.

4. **The Escalation of Commitment Bias**—With the escalation of commitment bias, decision makers increase their commitment to a project even when faced with negative outcomes rather than altering their course of action. Consider the Vietnam War; when Lyndon Johnson took office, the United States

had committed 16,000 troops to support South Vietnam. Near the end of his presidency, the initial commitment had spiraled to 537,000 troops.[11]

5. **The Anchoring and Adjustment Bias**—The anchoring and adjustment bias is the tendency to make decisions based on some suggested reference point (the "anchor") and make adjustments to it to reach their estimate. The problem is that the initial starting point may not reflect market realities.

6. **The Confirmation Bias**—The confirmation bias occurs when people seek out information that confirms to their point of view and discount data which does not. This bias is practiced when people listen for information that they want to hear and ignore the rest.

7. **The Framing Bias**—The framing bias is the tendency for a decision maker to be swayed by the way a situation or problem is presented. For example, customers have been found to prefer meat that is 85 percent lean instead of 15 percent fat, even though they are the same thing. In general, people prefer alternatives when they are framed in terms of gains rather than losses. Advertisers capitalize on the framing bias by presenting information in a manner that influences how viewers interpret that information.

8. **The Overconfidence Bias**—The overconfidence bias occurs when individuals overestimate their ability to predict future events. With this bias, people's subjective confidence in their decision-making ability is greater than their objective accuracy.

9. **The Hindsight Bias**—With the hindsight bias, people tend to view events as being more predictable than they really are. Sometimes known as the "I-knew-it-all-along" effect, this bias occurs when we look back at a decision and try to reconstruct why we decided to do something.

Heuristics A strategy to simplify the process of making decisions

Framing is a cognitive bias where people react in different ways to the same choice depending on the way it is presented to them.

The hindsight bias is the inclination, after an event has occurred, to see the event as having been predictable, despite there having been little or no objective basis for predicting it.

Biases in Action

Cognitive biases help explain the tragedy on Mount Everest memorialized in Jon Krakauer's book *Into Thin Air* and depicted in the 2015 film *Everest*. On May 10, 1996, twenty-three people reached the summit of the world's highest mountain, including Rob Hall and Scott Fischer, two of the world's most skilled and experienced high-altitude climbers. Unfortunately, Hall, Fischer, and three members of their expedition died as a storm enveloped the mountain during their descent.[12]

Cognitive biases including the sunk-cost, overconfidence, and availability biases help explain the Everest tragedy of 1996.

The sunk-cost bias causes normally rational people to discard common sense, allowing past investment decisions to influence their future choices. The expedition cost more than $70,000. Each climber had spent years training and preparing, and the final push to the summit was over eighteen hours long, following weeks of difficulty acclimating, and hiking to base camp. The final thrust to the summit was incredibly dangerous and required perfect timing so that auxiliary oxygen supplies would last and climbers would not get caught in darkness on their return to camp.

Hall and Fischer knew that climbers would find it difficult to turn around after coming so far and expending such an effort. Past Everest guides even reported climbers laughing in their face when told that they would not be able to summit. Despite mentioning numerous times that climbers would be turned around if they could not make the summit by 1:00 p.m. or 2:00 p.m. at the very latest, Hall and Fischer did not turn the climbers around. None of the twenty-three climbers made it to the summit by 1:00 p.m., and only six climbers made it by 2:00 p.m. One climber expressed this sentiment during his final descent: 'I've put too much of myself into this mountain to quit now without giving it everything I've got.' He had climbed the mountain with Hall's expedition the year before, and Hall had turned him around just 330 vertical feet from the summit. He did not reach the summit until after 4:00 p.m., and he died on his way down the mountain. His thinking was clouded by the sunk-cost bias, and he paid with his life. Other climbers experienced severe blindness and sickness, and yet still pressed on.

The overconfidence bias also may have impaired the judgment of the climbers. Hall had reached the summit of Everest four times before and had led thirty-nine people to the top. This caused him to believe that he couldn't fail. Both Hall and Fischer made bold statements that demonstrated the overconfidence bias. Fischer once told his team "We've got the Big E figured out, we've got it totally wired." This overconfidence also extended to the climbers, causing them to develop overly positive assessments of the risks and obstacles associated with climbing Everest.

Finally, the availability caused Hall and Fischer's incorrect assumption that the weather would be calm and fair. They had both led previous expeditions on Everest for several seasons and experienced only calm weather; however, this was the outlier, not the norm. For many seasons prior to Hall and Fischer's expeditions, storms were normal. In fact, there were three consecutive years in the mid-1980s where no one made the summit due to terrible winds. Both guides failed to look at past recent weather patterns and didn't realize that they had experienced abnormally calm weather.

The sunk-cost, overconfidence, and availability biases, magnified by the high altitude of the mountain, resulted in irrational decision-making with tragic results.[13] Fortunately, managers don't typically make life or death decisions, but the Everest disaster illustrates how multiple cognitive biases can impair our ability to make rational decisions.

Creativity and Innovation

Creativity A way of thinking that produces new ideas to solve problems or exploit opportunities

Innovation The implementation of a new idea

Creativity is a way of thinking that produces new ideas. Creativity is the driver of innovation. It's about seeing things from a different view, often called thinking "outside the box". It's about coming up with new ways to solve problems or exploit opportunities. Innovation, is the implementation of a new idea. Two important types of innovation are product innovation (new goods or services) and process innovation (new ways of doing things). Creativity is needed, but useless unless implemented. After years of discarding cranberry seeds used to make juice, an employee of Ocean Spray thought of the idea of turning them into a snack like Craisins.[14]

There are a number of techniques to foster creativity and innovation in decision-making including brainstorming, nominal group technique, the Delphi technique, and mind mapping.

Brainstorming

Brainstorming is a process for creating a broad list of alternative ideas in response to an initial question or idea. Brainstorming emphasizes broad and creative thinking by inviting points of view inviting from all participants. The idea is to ensure that all relevant aspects of an issue or question are considered.[15]

Here are four key ground rules that are useful when conducting a brainstorming session[16]:

1. **No ideas are criticized.** This is not a debate, discussion, or forum where one person displays superiority over another.

2. **Freewheeling is encouraged.** The free association of ideas is promoted. The more farfetched an idea, the better.

3. **Reverse the thought of "quality over quantity."** Here we want quantity; the more creative ideas the better. Facilitators can make it a challenge to come up with as many ideas as possible.

4. **Hitchhiking is encouraged.** Often an idea suggested by one person can trigger a bigger, better idea by another person. Building on others ideas leads to out of the box thinking and innovative ideas.

A brainstorming session is not a serious matter that requires only serious solutions. Remember, this is one of the more fun tools of decision-making, so keep the entire team involved! But also be realistic, empirical research suggests that brainstorming may not produce more creative ideas than individuals working alone.[17]

Brainstorming A group creativity technique by which efforts are made to find a conclusion for a specific problem by gathering a list of ideas spontaneously contributed by its members.

Brainstorming is a group creative technique which creates a list of ideas spontaneously contributed by its members.

© stockfour/Shutterstock.com

Nominal Group Technique

The Nominal (meaning in name only) Group Technique (NGT), is a structured variation of a small-group discussion designed to reach consensus. With the Nominal Group Technique, information is gathered by asking individuals to respond to questions posed by a moderator. Then participants are asked to prioritize the ideas or suggestions of all group members. The process is designed to prevent the domination of the discussion by a single person, encourages all group members to participate, and can result in a set of prioritized solutions or recommendations that represent the group's overall preferences. The procedure for conducting a NGT follows these steps[18]:

1. The facilitator outlines the problem, and participants work individually to develop their ideas.

Nominal Group Technique (NGT) A group process involving problem identification, solution generation, and decision-making

2. In a round-robin fashion, group members present their ideas. There is no criticism or evaluation of ideas at this stage.

3. The group discusses the ideas, asking questions for clarification and critiquing each alternative.

4. When all alternatives have been discussed, each group member ranks each of the options from most to least preferred. The alternative receiving the highest ranking is chosen.

Table 2 outlines the advantages and disadvantages of NGT.[19]

TABLE 2 ADVANTAGES AND DISADVANTAGES OF THE NOMINAL GROUP TECHNIQUE.

Advantages of NGT	Disadvantages of NGT
❑ Generates more ideas than traditional group discussions. ❑ Balances the influence of individuals by limiting the power of opinion makers (this is particularly advantageous for use where peer leaders may have an exaggerated effect over group decisions or in meetings where established leader tend to dominate the discussion). ❑ Reduces competition and pressure to conform, based on status within the group. ❑ Encourages participants to address issues through constructive problem-solving. ❑ Allows the group to prioritize ideas in a democratic process. ❑ Generally provides a greater sense of closure than can be obtained through group discussion.	❑ Requires preparation. ❑ Is rigid and lends itself only to a single-purpose, single-topic meeting. ❑ Minimizes discussion, and thus does not allow for the full development of ideas, which can be a less stimulating group process than some other techniques.

Delphi technique
A method of group decision-making and forecasting that involves successively collating the judgments of experts

Named after the ancient Greek oracle who could predict the future, the Delphi technique is a group decision-making technique that aggregates the results of multiple questionnaires.

The Delphi Technique

The RAND Corporation developed the Delphi technique in the 1950s. The name refers to the Oracle of Delphi, a priestess at a temple of Apollo in ancient Greece known for her prophecies. Originally, it was intended to forecast the impact of technology on warfare. The method involves a group of experts who anonymously reply to questionnaires and later receive feedback in the form of a statistical representation of the "group response," after which the process repeats itself. The goal is to reduce the range of responses and arrive at something closer to expert consensus. The Delphi Method has been widely adopted and is still in use today.[20]

The Delphi technique is a forecasting method based on the results of questionnaires sent to a panel of experts.

Several rounds of questionnaires are sent out, and the anonymous responses are aggregated and shared with the group after each round. The experts are permitted to amend their answers in subsequent rounds. Since multiple rounds of questions are asked and the panel is informed as to what the group thinks as a whole, the Delphi technique seeks to reach the optimum solution through consensus.

The Delphi technique provides the benefits of aggregating opinions from a diverse set of experts, and it can be done without the need to have a physical meeting. Since the responses of the participants are anonymous, individual panelists don't have to worry about potential repercussions for their opinions. Consensus can be reached over time as opinions are swayed.

Although the Delphi method allows for commentary from a diverse group of participants, it does not result in the same type of interactions as a live discussion. Response times can be long, which slows the discussion. It is also possible that the information received back from the experts won't provide value.[21]

Mind Mapping

A mind map is an easy way to brainstorm organically without concern for order and structure. It allows participants to visually structure ideas and helps with analysis and recall.

A mind map is a diagram which links tasks, words, concepts, or items arranged around a central concept or subject using a nonlinear graphical layout allowing the users to build an intuitive framework around a central concept. A mind map can turn a long list of monotonous information into a colorful, memorable, and highly organized diagram that works in line with the brain's natural way of doing things.

Mind maps have a natural organizational structure that radiates from the center and use lines, symbols, words, color, and images according to simple, brain-friendly concepts.

One simple way to understand a mind map is to compare it to a map of a city. The city center represents the main idea; the main roads leading from the center represent the key thoughts; the secondary roads or branches represent secondary thoughts; and so on. Special images or shapes can represent landmarks of interest or particularly relevant ideas.[22]

Mind mapping allows decision makers to link ideas in a non-linear graphical format

© stockfour/Shutterstock.com

Mind map A diagram used to visually organize information into a hierarchy showing relationships among pieces of the whole

Group Decisions

Group decision-making offers the advantages of drawing from the experiences and perspectives of a larger number of people. Therefore, groups have the potential to be more creative which could lead to a more effective decision. In fact, often groups achieve results beyond what they could have done as individuals. Groups also offer the opportunity for social interaction making tasks more enjoyable for members. Finally, when the decision is made by a group rather than an individual, implementing the decision will be easier because group members will be invested in the decision.

© g-stockstudio/Shutterstock.com

Groups allow for multiple perspectives and skill sets and can enhance the quality of decisions.

If the group is diverse, better decisions may be made because different group members may have diverse ideas based on their background and experiences. Research indicates that for top management teams, groups that debate issues and that are diverse make decisions that are more comprehensive and better for the bottom line in terms of profitability and sales.

Notwithstanding its popularity within organizations, group decision-making suffers from a number of disadvantages. Group decisions take time. Time is needed to coordinate schedules and hear input from each group member. Groups can be subjected to domination by one or a few individuals which can derail the group process. Furthermore, groups can suffer from social loafing which is the tendency of some members to put forth less effort while working within a group. Finally, groups may also suffer from groupthink, the tendency to avoid critical evaluation of ideas the group favors.

Thus, whether an individual or a group decision is better will depend on the specifics of the situation. For example, if there is an emergency and a decision needs to be made quickly, individual decision-making might be ideal. Individual decision-making may also be appropriate if the individual in question has all the information needed to make the decision and the implementation of the decisions is expected to go smoothly. However, if one person does not have all the information and skills needed to make the decision, if implementing the decision will be problematic without the involvement of those who will be affected by the decision, and if the timeline is not urgent, then decision-making by a group may be more effective.[23]

Table 3 outlines the advantages and disadvantages of both individual and group decision-making.

TABLE 3 GROUP AND INDIVIDUAL DECISION MAKING, ADVANTAGES AND DISADVANTAGES.

Group Decision-Making		Individual Decision-Making	
Advantages	**Disadvantages**	**Advantages**	**Disadvantages**
More information and knowledge are available	The process takes longer and costs more	Typically faster than groups	Fewer ideas
More alternatives are likely to be generated	Compromise decisions resulting from indecisiveness may emerge	Accountability is easy to determine	Prone to procrastination
More acceptance of the final decision is likely	One person may dominate the group		
Enhanced communication about the decision may result	Groupthink may occur		
Better decisions generally emerge			

Groupthink

Groupthink is a psychological phenomenon that occurs within groups of people. It is the mode of thinking that happens when the desire for harmony in a decision-making group overrides a realistic appraisal of alternatives. Group members try to minimize conflict and reach a consensus decision without critical evaluation of alternative ideas or viewpoints.[24]

Cohesiveness is normally a good thing, but sometimes it can lead to problems. Groupthink occurs when group members fail to critically evaluate circumstances and proposed ideas. They don't actually lose the ability to criticize, they simply don't exercise it. Members go out of their way to conform, as cohesiveness actually works against the group."[25] The majority of the initial research on groupthink was performed by Irving Janis, a research psychologist from Yale University.

Examples of groupthink "fiascoes" studied by Janis include U.S. failure to anticipate the attack on Pearl Harbor, the Bay of Pigs invasion, the escalation of commitment in the Vietnam war, and the doomed hostage rescue in Iran.

According to Yale psychologist Irving Janus, groupthink caused the ill-fated decision to launch the space shuttle Challenger during freezing weather.

A contemporary example of groupthink can be found in the decision to pursue an invasion of Iraq based on a policy of "preemptive use of military force against terrorists and rogue nations". The decision to rush to war in Iraq before a coalition of allies could be built has placed the United States in an unenviable military conflict that has been costly in terms of military deaths and casualties, and our diplomatic standing in the world.[26]

Janis came up with the idea of groupthink during a Yale seminar on the psychology of small groups. His examination of the Bay of Pigs disaster had led him to wonder how intelligent people like John F. Kennedy and his advisers could have been "taken in by such a stupid, patchwork plan as the one presented to them by the CIA representatives." During the seminar, Janis found himself suggesting that what had happened in the White House might be similar to what happened among ordinary citizens in the groups he studied for his research: they often developed a "pattern of concurrence-seeking . . . when a 'we' feeling of solidarity is running high."

In each case that Janis studied, group members "adhered to group norms and pressures toward uniformity, even when their policy was working badly and had unintended consequences that disturbed the conscience of the members," he wrote. "Members consider loyalty to the group the highest form of morality."

Those that participated in those critical decisions, Janis found, had failed to consider the full range of alternatives or consult experts who could offer different perspectives. The group rejected outside information and opinion unless it supported their preferred strategy. Moreover, the harsher the preferred action, the more zealously members clung to their consensus: "Each member is likely to become more dependent than ever on the in-group for maintaining his self-image as a decent human being and will therefore be more strongly motivated to maintain group unity."

Janis devised the following eight symptoms indicative of groupthink.[27]

Groupthink A psychological phenomenon that occurs within a group of people in which the desire for harmony or conformity in the group results in an irrational or dysfunctional decision-making outcome.

1. **Illusions of invulnerability** creating excessive optimism and encouraging risk taking.

2. **Unquestioned belief in the morality of the group**, causing members to ignore the consequences of their actions.

3. **Rationalizing warnings** that might challenge the group's assumptions.

4. **Stereotyping those who are opposed** to the group as weak, evil, biased, spiteful, impotent, or stupid.

5. **Self-censorship of ideas** that deviate from the apparent group consensus.

6. **Illusions of unanimity** among group members, silence is viewed as agreement.

7. **Direct pressure to conform** placed on any member who questions the group, couched in terms of "disloyalty."

8. **Mind guards**—Self-appointed members who shield the group from dissenting information.

Janis suggested several steps for preventing groupthink, though he warned that they were hypothetical. His recommendations suggest careful impartiality on the part of the leader as to what decision the group should make; formation of competing teams to study the same problem; and giving "high priority to airing objectives and doubts."[28]

What Managers Need to Know About Group Decision-Making

If you're a manager and deciding whether to call a meeting for group input, here are four things to consider.[29]

1. **Groups are less efficient**—Groups take more time to make decisions. If a timely decision is needed, you may want to make the decision yourself.

2. **Group size affects quality**—Generally, the larger the group, the lower the quality of the decision. Some researchers suggest that seven people is the optimum group size, others suggest five. An odd number may be best when the group used majority rule.

3. **Groups may be too confident**—Groups are more confident about their judgments and choices than individuals. This can be a liability that leads to groupthink.

4. **Knowledge matters**—Group decision-making accuracy is higher when group members know a good deal about the relevant issues. Groups also tend to do better when members of the group know each other.

Table 4 presents some guidelines for using groups.

TABLE 4 WHEN A GROUP CAN HELP IN DECISION-MAKING;
A PRACTICAL GUIDELINE.

When to Use a Group
1. **When it can increase quality**—If additional information would increase the quality of a decision, managers should involve people who can provide that information. If a decision occurs frequently, such as promotions, a group may be better because groups tend to produce more consistent results over time.
2. **When it can increase acceptance**—Managers should use groups when it's important the decision is accepted by the organization. Involving individuals who are affected can increase acceptance.
3. **When it can increase development**—Groups provide the opportunity for people to develop by their participation. Managers may want to involve people whose development is important.

Summary of Learning Outcomes and Key Points

☐ **Understand and remember types of problems, decisions, and decision-making styles**

Managers make two types of decisions; programmed decisions and nonprogrammed decisions. Programmed decisions involve structured problems that are well defined and where the issues, alternatives, and potential outcomes are known to a large degree. Most programmed decisions are related to daily activities. Nonprogrammed decisions are made in response to situations that are unique. These problems are poorly defined and largely unstructured. As these nonprogrammed decisions are not routine, no decision rules have been developed. Nonprogrammed decisions involve problems that are unstructured, where the issues are complex and all alternatives and potential outcomes of the alternatives are relatively unknown.

Individuals have a preferred decision-making style that is a combination of how an individual perceives and responds to information. Value orientation reflects the extent to which a person focuses on people or task concerns when making a decision. A second dimension, tolerance for ambiguity, indicates whether or not a person has a high need for structure or control. These two variables form a matrix with four resulting styles of decision-making; (1) analytical, (2) conceptual, (3) directive, and (4) behavioral.

☐ **Explain the rational decision-making process**

The rational decision-making process outlines how decisions should be made. The rational model follows the following steps; (1) Define the problem,

(2) Identify alternative solutions to the problem, (3) Evaluate alternatives and select the optimal solution, and (4) Implement and evaluate the solution.

❏ **Identify the limits on rational decision-making**

The rational model describes how decisions should be made. However, there are real-world constraints that limit a decision maker's ability to be rational. Bounded rationality describes the fact that the rational model is limited by constraints including problem complexity, cognitive capacity, time, and money. Satisficing is a function of bounded rationality where the decision maker chooses the first available alternative that reasonably solves the problem instead of evaluating all available alternatives.

❏ **Recognize heuristics and cognitive biases**

Heuristics are simplifying strategies that individuals use to make decisions. They are individual rules that implicitly guide our judgment. Heuristics provide time-pressured managers a simple way of dealing with a complex world. They produce correct or partially correct judgments more often than not.

The misapplication of heuristics, however, can lead to systematically biased outcomes. These biases include; the availability, representative, sunk-cost, escalation of commitment, overconfidence, anchoring and adjustment, hind-sight, and framing biases.

❏ **Describe techniques for creative decision-making**

Creativity is a way of thinking that produces new ideas. It's about seeing things from a different view, often called thinking "outside the box." Innovation is the implementation of a new idea. Two important types of innovation are product innovation (new goods or services) and process innovation (new ways of doing things). Techniques for producing creative decisions include brainstorming, the Nominal Group Technique (NGT), the Delphi Technique, and Mind Mapping.

❏ **Explain the advantages and disadvantages of group decision-making**

Groups often produce higher-quality decisions because there is more knowledge and a wider variety of perspectives. Generally, decisions made by groups are more likely to be accepted and group decision-making can make communication easier. However, groups take more time than individuals to make a decision. A group can be dominated by one or two individuals and groups are subject to groupthink.

Closing Case—The Jindra Winery

In September 2016, Robert Jindra, owner of the Jindra Winery, had to make a decision: should he harvest the Riesling grapes immediately, or leave them on the vines despite the approaching storm? A storm just before the harvest is usually detrimental, often ruining the crop. A warm, light rain, however, will sometimes cause a beneficial mold, botrytis cinerea, to form on the grape skins. The result is a luscious, complex sweet wine, highly valued by connoisseurs.

Robert Jindra faces a decision; harvest grapes now or wait for a possible storm which could produce a more expensive wine.

The Winery

The Jindra winery is located in the Napa Valley of California. The winery produces only premium wines from the best grape varieties. Of the 25,000 cases of wine bottled each year (about the same as Chateau Lafite-Rothschild) most were Cabernet Sauvignon and Chardonnay. About 1,000 cases of Riesling and 500 cases of Petite Syrah were also bottled. (A case contains twelve bottles of wine.)

The Napa Valley extends for 30 miles, from Calistoga in the north to Napa in the south. The average temperature decreases as one moves south, closer to San Francisco Bay and the cold ocean waters. Jindra's grapes came from an ideal climate in the central and southern parts of the valley.

Winemaking

Wine is produced when the fruit sugar, which is naturally present in the juice of grapes, is converted by yeast, through fermentation, into approximately equal molecular quantities of alcohol and carbon dioxide. Sparkling wines excepted, the carbon dioxide is allowed to bubble up and dissipate. The wine then ages in barrels for one or more years until it is ready for bottling.

By various decisions during vinification—for example, the type of wooden barrel used for aging—the winemaker influences the style of wine produced. The style adopted by a particular winery depends mainly on the owners' preferences, though it is influenced by marketing considerations. Usually, as the grapes ripen, the sugar levels increase and the acidity levels decrease. The winemaker tries to harvest the grapes when they have achieved the proper balance of sugar and acidity for the style of wine sought. The ripening process is variable, however, and if the weather is not favorable, the proper balance might never occur.

Several different styles of Riesling (more accurately, Johannesburg Riesling) are on the market. If the grapes are harvested at 20 percent sugar, the wine is fermented "dry" (all the sugar is converted to alcohol and carbon dioxide) or "near dry." The resulting wine, at about 10 percent alcohol is light bodied. If the grapes are harvested at 25 percent sugar, the winemaker can produce a wine with the same 10 percent alcohol but with 5 percent residual sugar; this wine is sweet and relatively full bodied.

A third and rare style results when almost ripe Riesling grapes are attacked by the botrytis mold. The skins of the grapes become porous, allowing water to evaporate while the sugar remains. Thus, the sugar concentration increases greatly, sometimes to 35 percent or more. The resulting wine, with about 11 percent alcohol and 13 percent residual sugar, has extraordinary concentration, and the botrytis itself adds to the wine's complexity. Jindra had already produced a botrytized Riesling from its 2009 vintage.

Jindra's Decision Problem

From the weather reports, Jindra concluded that there was a fifty–fifty chance that the rainstorm would hit the Napa Valley. Since the storm had originated over the warm waters of Mexico, he thought there was a 40 percent chance that, if the storm did strike, it would lead to the development of the botrytis mold. If the botrytis did not form, however, the rainwater, which would be absorbed into the grapes through the roots of the vines, would merely swell the berries by 5–10 percent, decreasing their concentration. This would yield a thin wine that would sell wholesale for only about $6.00 per bottle, about $2.50 less than Jindra could obtain by harvesting the not quite ripe grapes immediately and eliminating the risk. Jindra Winery always had the option of not bottling a wine that was not up to standards. It could sell the wine in bulk, or it could sell the grapes directly. These options would bring only half as much revenue, but would at least avoid damaging the winery's reputation, which would be risked by bottling an inferior product.

If Jindra decided not to harvest the grapes immediately in anticipation of the storm and the storm did not strike, Jindra would probably leave the grapes to ripen more fully. With luck, the grapes would reach 25 percent sugar, resulting in a wine selling for around $12.00 wholesale. Even with less-favorable weather, the sugar levels would probably top 20 percent, yielding a lighter wine selling at around $9.00. Jindra thought these possibilities were equally likely. In the past, sugar levels occasionally failed to rise above 19 percent. Moreover, while waiting for sugar levels to rise, the acidity levels must also be monitored. When the acidity drops below about 0.7 percent, the grapes must be harvested whatever the sugar level. If this happened, the wine would be priced at only about $7.50. Jaeger felt that this event had only about .2 probability.

The wholesale price for a botrytized/Riesling would be about $32.00 per bottle. Unfortunately, the same process that resulted in increased sugar concentration also caused a 30 percent reduction in the total juice. The higher price was therefore partly offset by a reduction in quantity. Although fewer bottles would be produced, there would be essentially no savings in vinification costs. The costs to the winery were about the same for each of the possible styles of wine and were small relative to the wholesale price.

Questions for Discussion

1. Describe the decision situation facing Jindra. Is this a programmed or nonprogrammed decision? Is this a situation under certainty, risk, or uncertainty? Explain

2. What decision making approaches or methods might Jindra use to reach a decision?

3. What should Jindra do?

End Notes

1. Schermerhorn, J. & Bachrach, D.(2018). *Exploring Management* (6th ed.). John Wiley and Sons, New York, NY, p. 66.

2. http://www.mba-tutorials.com/management/535-types-of-decisions.html (retrieved 3/1/2018).

3. Rowe, A. J. & Boulgarides, J. D. (1992). *Managerial Decision Making.* Macmillan Publishing Company, New York.

4. Griffin, R. (2016). *Fundamentals of Management* (8th ed.). Cengage Learning, Boston, MA, p. 103.

5. Kinicki, A. & Williams, B. (2018). *Management: A Practical Introduction* (8th ed.). McGraw-Hill, New York, NY, p. 204.

6. https://www.mindtools.com/dectree.html (retrieved 3/8/18).

7. Kinicki & Williams, p. 208.

8. Bazerman, M. *Judgment in Managerial Decision Making* (4th ed.). John Wiley and Sons, New York, NY, p. 4–5.

9. Ibid., p. 5 and 11.

10. Kinicki & Williams, p. 225.

11. https://www0.gsb.columbia.edu/mygsb/faculty/research/pubfiles/11642/vicarious_entrapment.pdf (retrieved 2/19/20).

12. https://hbswk.hbs.edu/archive/lessons-from-everest-the-interaction-of-cognitive-bias-psychological-safety-and-system-complexity (retrieved 2/28/2018).

13. https://www.entrepreneur.com/article/283197 (retrieved 2/28/18).

14. Lussier, R. (2019). *Management Fundamentals* (8th ed.). Sage, Thousand Oaks, CA, p. 114–115.

15. http://hrweb.mit.edu/learning-development/learning-topics/meetings/articles/brainstorming (retrieved 3/7/18).

16. Cherrington, D. & Dyer, W. (2009). *Creating Effective Organizations* (5th ed.). Kendall Hunt, Dubuque, Iowa, p. 483.

17. https://hbr.org/2015/03/why-group-brainstorming-is-a-waste-of-time (retrieved 3/22/18).

18. Jones, G. & George, J. (2014). *Contemporary Management* (8th ed.). McGraw-Hill, New York, NY, p. 215.

19. https://www.cdc.gov/healthyyouth/evaluation/pdf/brief7.pdf (retrieved 3/7/18)

20. https://www.rand.org/topics/delphi-method.html (retrieved 3/7/18)

21. Delphi Method, https://www.investopedia.com/terms/d/delphi-method.asp#ixzz58Vms7gXn

22. http://www.mindmapping.com/theory-behind-mind-maps.php (retrieved 3/19/18).

23. https://catalog.flatworldknowledge.com/bookhub/5?e=carpenter-ch11_s03 (retrieved 3/3/18).

24. Janis, I. L. (1982). *Groupthink: Psychological Studies of Policy Decisions and Fiascoes*, Houghton Mifflin Company.

25. Schermerhorn, J. R. (2011). *Organizational Behavior* (12th ed.). Wiley, p. 188.

26. http://www.psysr.org/about/pubs_resources/groupthink%20overview.htm (retrieved 2/19/18).

27. Irving, J. (1972). *Victims of Groupthink. Boston: Houghton Mifflin.* pp. 8–9.

28. https://yalealumnimagazine.com/articles/1947-a-brief-history-of-groupthink (retrieved 3/3/18).

29. Kinicki & Williams, p. 228

CHAPTER 6 ORGANIZATIONS, CULTURE, STRUCTURE AND DESIGN

Key Terms

Introduction

In this chapter, we consider the management function of organizing. Organizing is about arranging tasks and people in order to accomplish the goals of the organization. We will start with the idea of organizational culture, a set of beliefs and assumptions shared by people in an organization. Next, we'll talk about concepts that are common to all organizations and we will examine the various structures that organizations use to group people and tasks. Finally, we'll look at organizational design issues and consider how an organization can fit its structure to the environment.

Learning Outcomes

After reading this chapter, you should be able to:

❑ Remember and understand different types of organizational cultures

❑ Describe the three levels of organizational culture

❑ Identify examples of high performing organizational cultures

❑ Recall the common elements of an organization

❑ Remember and understand the different methods for arranging work and people

Organizational Culture

Earlier in this book, we identified strategies that organizations can use to achieve a competitive advantage. To implement a strategy, managers must determine the right type of organizational culture and organizational structure. Throughout this chapter, we will examine these two issues.

Organizational culture is the system of shared beliefs that guide the behavior of members of an organization.[1] It is the way in which the members of an organization relate to each other, their work, and the outside world. It can support or impede an organization's strategy.[2]

A strong culture helps the organization implement its vision, mission, and strategy. Consider Ritz-Carlton hotels where each employee receives a laminated card listing the company's 12 service values. Each day at each hotel, the company carries out a ceremony, a 15-minute meeting where employees resolve issues and discuss ways to improve service. These meetings, termed "line-ups," keep employees engaged and informed. The focus on the meetings is a "wow story," an account of how a Ritz-Carlton employee lived up to the company's values of extraordinary customer service.[3]

Three Levels of Organizational Culture

Organizational culture appears in three layers: (1) observable artifacts, (2) values, and (3) basic assumptions.[4] Much like an iceberg floating at sea, only a small part of an organization's culture is visible. These are the observable artifacts. Values lie at or just below the waterline, partially visible, whereas attitudes lie deep below the surface and can be imagined but not seen.

Observable artifacts are visible and readily apparent attributes of culture. We can see these artifacts in the way people dress, the way they arrange their work spaces, and how they interact with colleagues and customers.[5] Other examples of visible artifacts include:

- ❏ Acronyms
- ❏ Awards
- ❏ Logos
- ❏ Myths and stories
- ❏ Rites and rituals
- ❏ Symbols

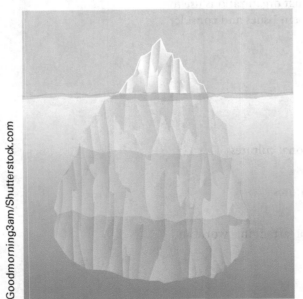

Organizational cultures resemble icebergs, some portions are visible, and others are not.

The online travel agency Kayak.com has a two-foot tall stuffed Elephant named Annabelle in the office. This artifact is a symbol to Kayak's employees, reminding them not to ignore important but difficult topics. The idea is to give staff a place to have the kind of uncomfortable conversations face-to-face instead of hashing them out over email where they tend to escalate and waste time.[6]

At Facebook, the word "hack" is posted around the office, symbolic of the "hacker way" of continuous improvement and pushing boundaries.[7] The "hacker way" is an unconventional path built on the slogan "move fast and break things." The idea is that Facebook would rather make a mistake than get left behind in Silicon Valley. Signs at Facebook provide visitors with tangible evidence of the organization's distributed culture. All of the signs come from people in the organization. There's no sign or motto team.[8]

The second and deeper level of organizational culture consists of an organization's values. Espoused values are the explicitly stated values and norms of the organization. We can see these values in formal statements as part of an organization's mission and vision statements. Southwest Airlines, like many companies, states its values on their website. These values define how to live the "Southwest Way." Southwest values employees who have a warrior spirit, a servant's heart, a fun-loving attitude, and work the Southwest way.[9] These values are further detailed in Table 1.

Enacted values are the values that are actually exhibited by the organization. These are the values we see in action.

Assumptions are the deepest level of culture. Assumptions represent the core beliefs that organizations have about their culture. They are values that are so deeply held that they are taken for granted as being unquestionably true. Because they are taken for

© achinthamb/Shutterstock.com

Organizational culture the system of shared beliefs that guides the behavior of the members of an organization

Observable artifacts visible and readily apparent attributes of culture

Espoused values the explicitly stated values and norms of the organization

Enacted values the values that are actually exhibited by the organization

Assumptions they are values that are so deeply held that they are taken for granted as being unquestionably true

TABLE 1 SOUTHWEST AIRLINES VALUES

Warrior Spirit

❏ Work hard
❏ Desire to be the best
❏ Be courageous
❏ Display urgency
❏ Persevere
❏ Innovate

Fun-LUVing Attitude
❏ Have FUN
❏ Don't take yourself too seriously
❏ Maintain perspective
❏ Celebrate successes
❏ Enjoy your work
❏ Be a passionate team player

Servant's Heart
❏ Follow the Golden Rule
❏ Adhere to the principles
❏ Treat others with respect
❏ Put others first
❏ Be egalitarian
❏ Demonstrate proactive customer service
❏ Embrace the SWA Family

Work the Southwest Way
❏ Safety and reliability
❏ Friendly customer service
❏ Low cost

Adapted from https://www.southwest.com/html/about-southwest/careers/culture.html (retrieved December 31, 2016).

granted, assumptions are difficult to change.[10] For example, employees at AIG Insurance joke that "I'm glad it's Friday because there are only two more working days until Monday." The core assumption being that employees work hard every day.[11]

How Do Employees Learn Culture?

Employees learn about the organization's culture in many ways. At the visible artifact level, the following devices transmit culture to employees and others[12]:

Heroes people whose actions exemplify the organization's values

Stories narratives that are based on true events

Symbols objects such as company logos, pins, jackets, and plaques.

Rites and rituals events and ceremonies that celebrate important occasions and accomplishments of the organization.

1. Heroes are people whose actions exemplify the organization's values. Employees at Walmart have been inspired by founder Sam Walton whose vision of retailing shaped one of the world's largest companies.[13]

2. Stories are narratives that are based on true events. These stories are repeated (and sometimes embellished). A frequently told story at UPS tells how an employee, without authorization, ordered an extra cargo jet to be certain that a load of Christmas presents were delivered on time. Rather than punishing the employee, UPS management rewarded his initiative. This story helps reinforce that the notion that the company values initiative and customer service.[14]

3. Symbols are objects such as company logos, pins, jackets, and plaques. Since 1970, Mary Kay Cosmetics has provided pink Cadillac autos to the company's top performers.[15]

4. Rites and Rituals are events and ceremonies that celebrate important occasions and accomplishments of the organization. For example, employees at the New Belgium Brewery receive a fat tire cruiser bike at their first anniversary and a one-week trip to Belgium after 5 years with the company.[16]

The Competing Values Framework

One method of classifying cultures is known as the competing values framework. Based on a statistical analysis of the major indicators of organizational effectiveness, researchers Quinn and Rohrbaugh discovered two major dimensions underlying conceptions of effectiveness. The first dimension is organizational focus. This dimension ranges from an internal focus on the well-being and development of organizational members to an external focus on the well-being and development of the organization. The second dimension is the organization's preference for structure, ranging from an emphasis on stability and control to a preference for flexibility and change.[17] Figure 1 outlines the two dimensions and the four resulting types of culture.

According to this model, organizational cultures can be classified into four types: (1) clan, (2) adhocracy, (3) market, and (4) hierarchy.[18] Let's review each type.

1. A **clan culture** is focused internally and values flexibility rather than stability and control. Clan cultures encourage collaboration and cohesion between employees. Organizations with clan cultures devote resources to hire and develop employees. They seek to increase commitment through employee involvement and job satisfaction. Southwest Airlines and Zappos are both companies with a clan culture. Zappos encourages employees to spend 10–20 percent of their non-work time with other employees.

2. An **adhocracy culture** has an external focus and values flexibility. This culture encourages innovation, creativity, and a quick response to market changes.

FIGURE 1 COMPETING VALUES MODEL OF ORGANIZATIONAL CULTURE. COURTESY OF JEFFREY ANDERSON.

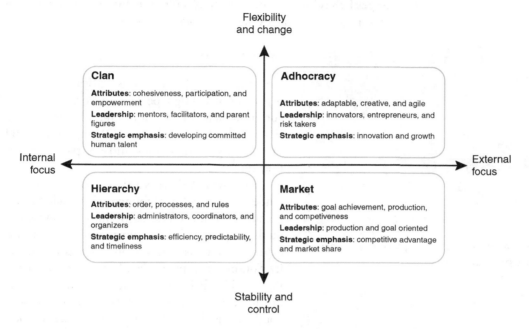

Adhocracy cultures encourage employees to take risks and is appropriate for start-ups and organizations in industries that are going through significant changes. Gore-Tex outerwear manufacturer W.L. Gore is an example of an adhocracy culture.

3. A **market culture** values stability and has a strong external focus. As market cultures focus on the external environment, they are driven by competition and a strong desire to deliver results, customers, productivity, and profits. These goals take priority over employee development and satisfaction. Employees in market cultures are expected to work hard and deliver results on time. Those who deliver are rewarded. Citigroup Inc. is an example of a market culture that pushes managers to maximize profits; those who don't are quickly fired.

4. A **hierarchy culture** values stability and control over flexibility has a strong internal focus. Organizations with a hierarchy culture have formal, structured work environment and rely on control mechanisms to measure efficiency and reliability. Many large organizations such as General Motors, the US Army, and UPS have hierarchy cultures.[19]

The Importance of Culture

Organizational culture can be a powerful force in shaping an organization's long-term success. Research tells us that companies with clan, adhocracy, and market cultures have greater levels of employee satisfaction, innovation, quality, and customer service. Organizational culture serves four functions[20]:

1. **Organizational identity**—Organizational culture helps to give employees a collective identity and helps them relate to the organization.

2. **Collective commitment**—Organizational culture helps create a collective commitment from employees where they view their efforts as part of a larger whole.

3. **Social stability**—Organizational culture can promote social stability by reinforcing a work environment where conflict and change are managed.

4. **Shapes behavior**—An organization's culture helps members make sense of their environment and shapes their workplace behavior.

Southwest Airlines has a high performing organizational culture.

CEO Jack Welch helped establish culture of performance and accountability at General Electric.

Online retailer Zappos creates a culture that values employees.

High Performing Cultures

Creating the right culture is critical for high performing organizations. High performing organizations share two common elements: (1) a unique identity that sets it apart from other organizations and (2) employees who feel a sense of meaning in their jobs and are passionate about what they do.[21]

Southwest Airlines is a classic example of these elements. Under the leadership of founder Herb Kelleher, the company became known for its sense of humor, irreverence, and focus on the employee. This identity made flying Southwest a happy experience for customers. It also increased worker productivity. Southwest employees work to minimize the time between flights. This efficiency translates into lower costs and improved up-time, a key element of Southwest's low-cost strategy. Southwest is the world's largest low-price airline and one of the few airlines to consistently turn a profit in a challenging industry.[22]

Southwest belongs to a unique club of high performing organizations that include Apple, Google, Procter & Gamble, and Coca-Cola. Cultures in these companies are centered on a high performance workplace. The consumer product company Johnson & Johnson has a rich heritage of shared corporate values. Winning is focused on serving the customer. Employees are encourage to work in teams, be open-minded, and think like owners. Under Jack Welch's leadership, General Electric developed a culture where performance and accountability mattered and risks were rewarded. Welch made the connection between cultural values and high performance transforming GE into one of the world's most admired companies.[23]

Zappos, a wholly owned subsidiary of Amazon, is well known for their organizational culture. The company is famous for "delivering wow through customer service," putting customers first and a happy work force second. Collaboration at Zappos is infectious thanks to a culture that encourages everyone to engage. For example, every worker is given the opportunity to issue a $50 coworker bonus for each month as a way to recognize their colleagues. Zappos receives about 30,000 resumes each year for about 300 openings. It's obvious to those who apply that Zappos is a great place to work.[24]

Organizational Structure

Types of Organizations

Recall from Chapter 1 that organizations are collections of people who work together for a common purpose. For our purposes, we can identify three different types of organizations.[25]

1. **For-profit organizations** are formed to make a profit for the organization's owners by offering products or services.

2. **Nonprofit organizations** are created in order to offer some service to the community, rather than make a profit. Examples include hospitals and colleges.

3. **Mutual-benefit originations** exist to advance the cause of its members. Examples include trade associations and unions.

Organization Chart

Organizational charts are diagrams that visually show an organization's work specializations, official positions, and formal lines of authority. The boxes and lines on the diagram resemble a family tree. The chart provides a picture of the reporting relationships (who reports to whom) and the organization's various activities. The organizational chart shows levels of management in horizontal layers. Figure 2 illustrates an organizational chart for a hospital.[26]

> **Organizational charts** diagrams that visually show the organization's work specializations, official positions and formal lines of authority

FIGURE 2 A HYPOTHETICAL ORGANIZATIONAL CHART FOR A HOSPITAL. COURTESY OF JEFFREY ANDERSON.

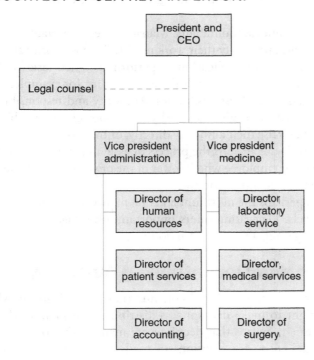

Common Characteristics of Organizations

Let's review some of the common characteristics of organizations. First, organizations are collections of people. Organizations start with groups of two or more people. Organizations have a common purpose. A purpose shared by everyone in the organization. And finally, organizations have a deliberate structure or system to accomplish work.

Members of an organization share a common purpose. That purpose is commonly defined by an organization's mission statement. The purpose of most for-profit companies is to provide a return on the investment of the owners. For nonprofits, the purpose is to provide some value to the society.

Work specialization involves dividing work activities into separate job tasks.[27] Specialized jobs are characterized by simple, easy-to-learn processes, which are highly repetitive. Specialized jobs are easy to learn but can quickly turn boring. These boring, repetitive jobs can lead to low job satisfaction and high absenteeism and turnover.

The **chain of command** is the line of authority that links all employees in the organization. It is associated with two core principles. Unity of command means that each employee is accountable to only one supervisor. The scalar chain defines a line of authority that passes through all employees in the organization.[28]

Authority is the legitimate right to make decisions and to tell people what to do. A manager has the authority to give an order to a subordinate. Managers with authority can hold other people accountable for their actions. Traditionally, authority resides in positions not people. A vice president of a division has authority over that division.[29]

One dimension of authority is the distinction between line and staff authority. **Line authority** is the right to command immediate subordinates in the chain of command. By contrast, **staff authority** is the right to advise others who are not subordinates in the chain of command. For example, a manager in the human resources department might advise another manager on a hiring decision but cannot order that a certain applicant be hired.

With authority comes accountability. Managers are accountable to managers above them and must report and justify their work results. With authority also comes responsibility. Responsibility is the obligation to perform assigned tasks. A factory worker typically has little authority but often little responsibility, for example, to assemble one part. A manager has greater responsibilities. Authority and responsibility go hand in hand. A manager needs to be given authority and responsibility in a balanced fashion.

Managers can exercise their authority directly, or they pass on some of their authority to subordinates. **Delegation** is the process of assigning authority and responsibility to another manager or employee who is lower in the organizational hierarchy. Managers delegate work to become more efficient.

Delegation is perhaps the most fundamental management tactic. It is important at all managerial levels. Delegating offers important advantages, especially when done effectively. By delegating, a manager can do more.[30]

Centralized and Decentralized Authority

One of the important considerations in organizations is the degree to which authority, specifically the right to make decisions, is distributed throughout the organization. **Centralized authority** means that decisions are made at the top management levels. With **decentralized authority**, decisions are made at lower management levels.[31]

Work specialization dividing work activities into separate job tasks

Chain of command the line of authority that links all employees in the organization

Authority the legitimate right to make decisions and to tell people what to do.

Line authority the right to command immediate subordinates in the chain of command

Staff authority right to advise others who are not subordinates in the chain of command

Delegation the process of assigning authority and responsibility to another manager or employee who is lower in the organizational hierarchy

Centralized authority cases where decision-making authority resides with top managers

Decentralized authority organizations where decisions are made at lower levels of management

One advantage of centralized authority is that leads to more uniformity in terms of both processes and products. This is an important consideration for companies such as McDonald's and K-Mart. Companies such as General Motors and Harley-Davidson use decentralized authority as it increases the organization's flexibility and efficiency.[32]

Union Pacific (UP) is one of the biggest railroad freight carriers in the United States. In the early 2000s, the company wasn't able to meet the increased demands for moving freight and they experienced record delays. These delays costs the company millions of dollars in penalty payments. UP had centralized scheduling and route planning. Recognizing that they needed to respond to the needs of the customer, the company reorganized and moved operational decision-making authority to regional managers, decentralizing the company's operations. The move worked and by 2010, UP was recognized as the top rail company for on-time service.[33]

Span of Control

The number of persons who report directly to a single manager is referred to as a span of control. Managers who have a narrow span of control supervise fewer employees than managers with a wide span of control. Narrow spans of control tend to promote taller organizations, with many hierarchical levels. Flat organizations are characterized by wide spans of control that reduces overhead costs and improves agility.[34]

There are several factors that determine the ideal span of control. One is the nature of the work involved. With craftsman, the number can be quite small because the level of supervision required is high. With mass-production jobs, the number can be higher because each worker has a clearly defined task to perform, and little oversight is required. The contemporary view is that spans also depend on both the industry a firm is in and the firm itself.

Tall organizations have a pronounced vertical hierarchy. These organizations have many managerial levels and each manager has a relatively narrow span of control. Flat organizations have fewer levels of management. In flat organizations, managers have a relatively wider span of control. Figure 3 illustrates a tall organization. Organizations that are flat and loosely structured have larger spans of control. GE's guideline was that no managers should supervise more than 10–15 people reporting to them directly. Former GE CEO Jack Welsh wrote: "When there are a lot of layers, it usually means managers have too few people reporting to them."[35]

Organizational Structures

Once managers have planned the organization's vision and strategy, the work must be divided between employees. Organizational design is concerned with creating a structure of reporting relationships, accountability, and responsibility that allow the organization to execute its strategies.[36] In this section, we will outline different types of organizational structures.

In a functional structure, employees are grouped by their job functions. In this structure, employees share technical expertise related to their job function. Consider the example in Figure 4. Here the organization is divided into functional divisions for manufacturing, marketing, finance, and human resources.

By grouping people together by their job functions, the functional approach offers the advantages of efficiency, deep technical knowledge, and skill development within the job function. However, functional structures can produce narrow views and "functional silos" where communication and cooperation between functional areas can be strained.[37]

Span of control the number of persons who report directly to a single manager

Functional structure employees are grouped by their job functions

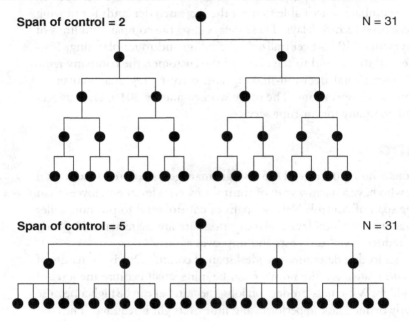

FIGURE 4 A SAMPLE FUNCTIONAL STRUCTURE. COURTESY OF JEFFREY ANDERSON.

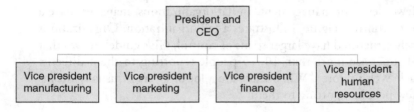

Divisional structures offer an alternative to functional design. Divisional structures divide employees into divisions, often with each operating as a separate business unit. In a divisional structure, job functions are duplicated across each division.[38] Let's examine three common divisional organizations; a product structure, a customer structure, and a geographic structure.

In a **product strucrure**, all functions that contribute to a specific product are grouped together under a product manager. Johnson & Johnson uses this structure. It has more than 250 divisions, each responsible for a separate product line.[39] Figure 5 shows a product structure for a media company, with divisions for film, magazines, the Internet, and music. Time Warner uses a similar structure to organize their media outlets as well as their retail stores, theaters, and amusement parks.[40]

In a **customer structure**, divisions are created around different customer types. Figure 6 shows a prototype organizational chart for a bank with different customer divisions. Bank customers with consumer loans have different needs than commercial

Product structure all functions that contribute to a specific product are grouped together under a product manager

Customer structure divisions are created around different customer types

FIGURE 5 A SAMPLE PRODUCT STRUCTURE FOR A MEDIA COMPANY. COURTESY OF JEFFREY ANDERSON.

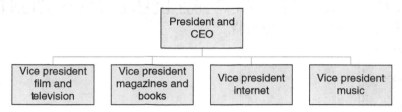

FIGURE 6 A CUSTOMER STRUCTURE. COURTESY OF JEFFREY ANDERSON.

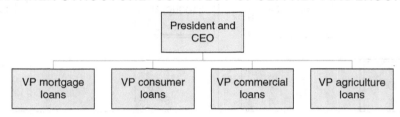

loan customers. Organizing by customer type allows organizations to offer special options and services to meet the needs of their specific customer.

A geographic structure organizes divisions into separate units to serve a particular geographic region. AB InBev, the world's largest beer brewer, used a geographic structure. AB InBev has 151 breweries in 24 countries. The company is divided into six regional groups: North America, Mexico, Latin America North, Latin America South, Europe, and Asia/Pacific.[41]

Geographic structures allow companies to respond to varying demands of different markets. AB InBev has some brands that are sold worldwide, including Heineken, Stella Artois, and Corona, but most of their brands are local. The geographic structure allows them to produce and market beers based on regional preferences and demands.

In a matrix structure, people are arranged simultaneously into two separate groups. Employees are grouped by function, and into product teams. The result is a complex network of multiple reporting relationships and functions that makes the matrix structure very flexible. Each product team member reports to two managers: a functional manager and a product manager.[42] Figure 7 provides an example of a matrix structure.

A matrix structure offers several advantages. The cross-functional product teams are better informed and can be more creative. Decision making in matrix organizations is decentralized and distributed to those with the appropriate knowledge. Employees learn how to work collaboratively with others in a hectic environment and employees are presented with more career options.[43] Table 2 outlines some of the advantages and disadvantages of a matrix structure.

AB InBev uses a geographic structure to sell Jupiler in the Belgian market.

Geographic structure a structure that organizes divisions into separate units to serve a particular geographic region

Matrix structure a structure where employees are grouped by function, and into product teams.

FIGURE 7 A MATRIX STRUCTURE. FROM *CREATING EFFECTIVE ORGANIZATIONS: ESSENTIALS OF ORGANIZATIONAL BEHAVIOR*, FIFTH EDITION, BY DAVID J. CHERRINGTON AND W. GIBB DYER. © 2009. USED BY PERMISSION OF KENDALL HUNT PUBLISHING COMPANY.

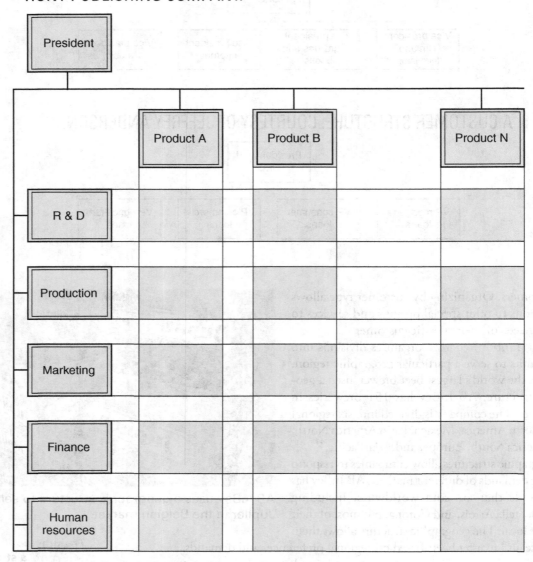

In a **team structure**, all of the work in the organization is done by teams. This type of structure relies on employee empowerment as there is no line of managerial authority from the top to the bottom. Instead, employee teams design and perform their own work in the manner they think is best. In large organizations, the team structure typically complements a functional or divisional structure allowing the organization to have the efficiencies of a bureaucracy with the flexibility of teams. Companies such as Amazon, Boeing, Google, Motorola, and Xerox make extensive use of employee teams to increase productivity.[44]

TABLE 2 ADVANTAGES AND DISADVANTAGES OF A MATRIX STRUCTURE

Matrix Structures	
Advantages	**Disadvantages**
❐ Increased communications and cooperation between functional units ❐ Employee functions and goals are linked at all levels ❐ Cross-functional collaboration promotes creativity ❐ Increased flexibility in staffing; teams can be adjusted to situational demands ❐ Promotes loyalty to the organization rather than a function or unit	❐ The two-supervisor system is subject to power struggles ❐ Responsibilities and priorities compete and can conflict with one another ❐ Accountability is harder to define ❐ Extensive collaboration is needed but rewards are hard to define
Source: Compiled from various sources including Schermerhorn, Management, 13th edition, p. 250 and Bateman, Management, 11th edition, p. 280.	

A network organization is a collection of independent, mainly single-function organizations that work collaboratively to produce a good or a service. Organizations work in a network. These flexible arrangements between suppliers, designers, producers, distributors, and others allow each organization to focus on its core competency. The lines or boundaries between organizations become blurred. Figure 8 provides an example of a network organization.

A very flexible arrangement that the network organization has is a **modular** network or virtual corporation. It is composed of temporary collaborations of members that can be assembled and reassembled based on market conditions. Canadian jet manufacturer Bombardier Aerospace uses a modular network to produce

Bombardier Aerospace uses a modular network to product its jets.

FIGURE 8 A NETWORKED ORGANIZATION. COURTESY OF JEFFREY ANDERSON.

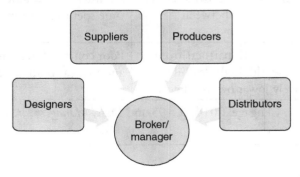

Network organization
a collection of independent, mainly single-function organizations that work collaboratively to produce a good or a service

its jets. The firm has designed its aircraft into 12 "chunks," which are produced by other companies in modules. Bombardier employees assemble the different modules to produce the final aircraft. The modular approach has allowed Bombardier to be agile and efficient, beating the price of its nearest competitor by about $3 million.[45]

In a **learning organization**, everyone in the organization is engaged in identifying and solving problems. The focus is on improving and achieving the organization's goals. Learning organizations are characterized by horizontal team structures and decentralized decision making. Learning organizations openly share information and knowledge and empower employees with a participative strategy. Learning organizations are structured around three building blocks[46]:

1. **A supportive learning environment**—Learning organizations create an environment where employees don't fear being marginalized if they ask naive questions or express a minority viewpoint. Learning organizations promote psychological safety and openness and appreciation for new ideas.

2. **Concrete learning processes and practices**—Learning organizations arise from a series of deliberate and concrete steps that include experimentation, intelligence gathering along with disciplined analysis, and interpretation of problems.

3. **Leadership that reinforces learning**—Organizational learning is strongly influenced by leadership. When people in power demonstrate their willingness to entertain alternative viewpoints, employees are empowered to offer new ideas.

Table 3 outlines the advantages and disadvantages of various organizational structures.

TABLE 3 COMPARING ORGANIZATIONAL STRUCTURES

Organizational Structure	Advantages	Disadvantages
Functional	Resource efficiency, economies of scale, and in-depth skill development in functional areas	Poor communication across division, slow to adapt to the environment and low in innovation
Divisional	Flexible and responsive, customer focused, excellent communication, and coordination across functions	Duplication of effort, lower resource efficiency, and poor communication across divisions
Matrix	Moderately efficient use of resources, highly flexible, and adaptable	Conflicts arising from dual authority structures
Team	Quicker decisions, improved morale, and reduced barriers between departments	Conflict over loyalties and lots of time spent in meetings
Network	Specialized network partners from around the world, high flexibility, and relatively lower overhead costs	Poor control, lower employee loyalty, and unclear boundaries

Source: Adapted from Gulati, Management, Cengage, 2014, p. 195 and Daft, *Management*, 12th edition, Cengage, p. 343.

Job Design

Job design is the process of identifying tasks that employees must complete as part of their job. It is a critical issue as it affects job satisfaction and productivity. Organizations such as GE and Pizza Hut ask employees for suggestions on how to redesign their own jobs. Empowering employees to be involved in job design can motivate workers and increase productivity.[47]

Job simplification is the process of eliminating or combining tasks in the work sequence. Job simplification is based on the idea of division of labor and Taylor's scientific management.

Job rotation involves performing different jobs for a set period of time. For example, employees at GM auto factories rotate between different jobs. By being trained on different production tasks, employees develop a greater conceptual knowledge.

Job enrichment is the process of building intrinsic motivators into a job to make it more interesting and challenging. A simple way to enrich jobs for managers is to delegate authority.

Organizational Design

When managers are considering organizational structures, they must consider a number of contingencies. These contingencies ask the question "what is the best approach to use in this situation?" Managers need to consider four factors in designing the best structure for their organization. These factors are the organization's environment, differentiation vs. integration, the organization's life cycle, and the link between strategy and structure.[48]

Mechanistic vs. Organic

British behavioral scientists Tom Burns and G.M. Stalker identified two extreme types of organizational environments: stable and unstable. Next, they examined the designs of organizations in each of these environments. Their research identified two types of organizational designs; mechanistic and organic.[49]

Mechanistic organizations are similar to the traditional bureaucratic model. These designs are found most frequently in stable environments. In mechanistic organizations, authority is centralized, procedures and rules are clearly outlined, and employees are closely supervised. In mechanistic organizations, communication is typically top-down. This type of structure is important at companies such as McDonalds as the market demands uniform quality, cleanliness, and service.[50]

Organic organizations tend to work best in unstable or changing environments. In an **organic organization**, authority is decentralized. There are fewer rules and policies. Employees are expected to be flexible and respond quickly to changes in the environment. Technology companies such as Apple and Motorola use organic designs in order to adapt to a rapidly changing technological environment. At Motorola, for example, employees are given considerable discretion over how work is performed and how problems can be solved.[51]

Table 4 outlines some of the differences between mechanistic and organic organizations.

Mechanist organizations where authority is centralized, procedures and rules are clearly outlined, and employees are closely supervised.

Organic organizations where authority is decentralized and there are fewer rules and policies

TABLE 4 MECHANISTIC VS. ORGANIC ORGANIZATIONS

Mechanistic	Organic
❏ Highly specialized jobs ❏ Centralized authority with a clear chain of command ❏ High degree of formalized communication ❏ Narrow spans of control	❏ Cross-functional teams and shared tasks ❏ Decentralized authority ❏ Informal communication with a free flow of information ❏ Wide spans of control

Source: Courtesy of Jeffrey Anderson.

Differentiation vs. Integration

The ideas of mechanistic vs. organic were extended by Harvard researchers Paul Lawrence and Jay Lorsch. They proposed a differentiation vs. integration dimension. **Differentiation** is the tendency of different parts of the organization to be broken down into subunits. An organization that is highly differentiated will have many subunits. This dispersal and fragmentation is a result of technical specialization and division of labor. For example, a company with different product lines might have different divisions each with its own production and sales staff.

Integration is the tendency of subunits to work together in a coordinated fashion. In highly integrated organizations, specialists work together to achieve a common goal. This means adopting a formal command structure and standardized processes and rules and the use of cross-functional teams.[52]

The Organizational Life Cycle

Many organizations progress through a four-stage life cycle. This life cycle follows the natural sequence of birth, youth, midlife, and maturity. Each stage offers unique challenges.[53]

1. **The Birth Stage** is non-bureaucratic. There are no written rules and little administrative support. For Apple computer, this stage started when Stephen Wozniak and Steve Jobs built computers in Wozniak's parents' garage in Paulo Alto, California.

2. **The Youth Stage** is pre-bureaucratic. This is a stage of expansion and growth. During this stage, division of labor and rules is instituted. For Apple computer, this occurred from 1978 through 1981 as they produced the Apple II product line.

3. **The Midlife State** is bureaucratic. This is a period where growth transitions to stability. The organization has evolved with staff of specialists, decentralization of functional divisions, and many rules. Apple became a large company in the 1980s. They hired John Sculley as the CEO and Jobs and Wozniak left the company.

© Joe Ravi/Shutterstock.com

Apple computer has evolved through each of the steps of the organizational life cycle.

4. **The Maturity Stage** is very bureaucratic. The organization becomes very large and mechanistic. When Jobs was fired in 1985, Apple entered a period of missteps including the launch of the Newton PDA. Overall Apple lost a significant market share. Two CEOs followed Scully and it wasn't until 1997 when Steve Jobs returned to Apple that the company saw the beginnings of the successes it enjoys today.

The Link between Strategy and Structure

An organization's structure should enable goal achievement. Goals are an important part of an organization's strategy and should be linked closely with its structure. Research has shown that some structural designs work best with certain strategies. For example, an organic structure works best with organizations that are pursuing unique innovations. Mechanistic organizations, with efficiencies, stability, and tight controls, work best for companies that want to control costs.[54]

Summary of Learning Outcomes and Key Points

❐ **Remember and understand different types of organizational cultures**

Organizational culture is the set of shared values and assumptions common to members of an organization. According to the competing values framework, organizational cultures can be classified into four types: (1) clan culture, which has an internal focus and values flexibility, (2) adhocracy which values flexibility and has an external focus, (3) market, which has an external focus and values stability, and (4) hierarchy, which has an internal focus and values stability.

❐ **Describe the three levels of organizational culture**

Organizational culture exists at three levels. The first level is observable artifacts that are physical manifestations of culture. The second level is values. Espoused values are those that are explicitly stated by the organization. Enacted values are those that are exhibited by the organization's actions.

❐ **Identify examples of high performing organizational cultures**

Creating the right culture is critical for high performing organizations. High performing organizations share two common elements: (1) a unique identity that sets it apart from other organizations and (2) employees who feel a sense of meaning in their jobs and are passionate about what they do. Companies such as Southwest Airlines, General Electric, and Zappos have created organizational cultures that help their organizations excel.

❐ **Recall the common elements of an organization**

Organizations are collections of people who share a common purpose. They have a deliberate structure with a chain of command and a vertical hierarchy. Managers in organizations have authority to make decisions and give directions. They can delegate authority to subordinates. In centralized organizations, decisions are made by top managers. In decentralized organizations, decisions are made at lower management levels.

❏ **Remember and understand the different methods for arranging work and people**

Organizations divide their activities to achieve a division of labor. In a functional structure, employees with common skills and job responsibilities are grouped together. In divisional structures, employees are grouped by product, customer, or geographic location. Matrix organizations combine a functional and divisional approach with a dual-authority network. Team structures rely on autonomous cross–functional groups of employees, and network organizations are collections of companies that collaborate in different portions of the value chain.

Closing Case*

What a Long Strange Business Plan It's Been
The Organizational Culture of the Grateful Dead

The Grateful Dead were an American rock band formed in 1965 in Palo Alto, California. The band was known for its unique and eclectic style, which fused elements of a wide range of musical genres. They were ranked 57th in the issue The Greatest Artists of All Time by Rolling Stone magazine. They were inducted into the Rock and Roll Hall of Fame in 1994 and their Barton Hall Concert at Cornell University (May 8, 1977) was added to the Library of Congress's National Recording Registry. The Grateful Dead have sold more than 35 million albums worldwide.

Northfoto/Shutterstock.com

The Grateful Dead toured constantly throughout their career, playing more than 2,300 concerts. They promoted a sense of community among their fans, who became known as "Deadheads," many of whom followed their tours for months or years on end.

Oddly enough, the Dead's influence on the business world may turn out to be a significant part of its legacy. Without intending to—while intending, in fact, to do just the opposite—the band pioneered ideas and practices that were subsequently embraced by corporate America. One was to focus intensely on its most loyal fans. The band established a telephone hotline to alert fans to their touring schedule ahead of any public announcement, reserved for them some of the best seats in the house, and capped the price of tickets, which the band distributed through its own mail-order house. Fans could get really good tickets, without even camping out. The Dead were masters of creating and delivering superior customer value. Treating customers well may sound like common sense. However, it represented a break from the top-down ethos of many organizations in the 1960s and 1970s. Only in the 1980s, faced with competition from Japan, did American CEOs and management theorists widely adopt a customer-first orientation.

The Dead, one of the most profitable bands of all time, incorporated early on, complete with a board of directors. They established a lucrative merchandising division and took legal action against copyright violators. Instead of selling a lot of records and doing limited touring as most bands did, the Dead reversed that model and toured year round—playing 80 plus shows per year. This new business model made them not only one of the most profitable but also most enduring bands of all time.

The Dead were well ahead what is now a common business practice—insourcing. Insourcing involves bringing as many business functions as possible in-house—increases creative control, keeps customers happier, and boosts profitability. Now, most firms that insource are simply reversing bad outsourcing decisions. The Dead, by contrast, found that they could take better care of their employees (by ensuring good jobs), create a

---

*Adapted from Wikipedia http://en.wikipedia.org/wiki/Grateful_Dead, Businessweek Executive Summaries http://www.businessweek.com/stories/2010-02-23/executive-summary and Management Secrets of the Grateful Dead by HYPERLINK "http://www.theatlantic.com/doc/by/joshua_green" Joshua Green The Atlantic Monthly, March 2010

higher-quality product (such as records), and provide a higher quality of service to their customers (through ticket sales) by doing it themselves rather than counting on outside contractors. "The Dead have always poured money back into the scene in the form of sound and lights and musical instruments," said Dan Healy, the band's legendary sound man. Unlike most rock bands, the Dead wanted their shows to be not merely loud but also precise—to blow listeners away with subtlety as well as power. When they discovered they couldn't buy such equipment, they worked to develop the technology themselves, creating the Wall of Sound, which was state-of-the art sound system used in the late 1973 and 1974.

People attending a Grateful Dead concert for the first time were often surprised to see the forest of professional-grade microphones rising to the sky from the audience. Tapers, as these Dead Heads were known, (lawfully) recorded Dead shows using their own equipment. Rather than banning taping, the band innovated by setting up designated taping sections at concerts. In return for sanctioning taping, the band requested that tapers refrain from selling tapes to other fans or using them for other commercial purposes—but it did encourage them to make copies to give away to their friends. By allowing fans to tape their shows, the band sacrificed a potential revenue source. Writing in Wired magazine in 1994, the band's lyricist, John Perry Barlow, noted that "the best way to raise demand for your product is to give it away."

As Barlow explained, "Adam Smith taught that the scarcer you make something, the more valuable it becomes. In the physical world, that works beautifully. But we couldn't regulate [taping at] our shows, and you can't online. The Internet doesn't behave that way. But here's the thing: if I give my song away to 20 people, and they give it to 20 people, pretty soon everybody knows me, and my value as a creator is dramatically enhanced." This approach directly contradicted standard practice in the music industry. It makes sense only if Barlow is correct in his two central theses—that their product was a community of listeners and that music dissemination, not scarcity, can be the heart of the value proposition.

"The product is not the music and not even the band. Their product is the audience. Belonging to that audience is their brand."

The notion that C-suite executives may have something to learn from Jerry Garcia, a man who preferred tie-dyed over tailored, may seem a tad trippy. While the band has long been a subject of academic inquiry, recently business theorists have weighed in. Recent business books about the band include Everything I Know About Business I Learned from the Grateful Dead by Barry Barnes and Marketing Lessons from the Grateful Dead by David Scott.

Questions for Discussion

1. What are some of the visible artifacts of the Grateful Dead's organizational culture?
2. How would you describe the espoused and enacted values of the Grateful Dead as an organization?
3. How did the Dead translate their values into business strategy and operations?

End Notes

1. Kinicki, A. & Williams, B. (2013). *Management: A Practical Introduction* (6th ed.). McGraw-Hill, New York, NY, p. 228.

2. Retrieved December 30, 2013, from https://geert-hofstede.com/organisational-culture.html.

3. Bateman & Snell (2013). *Management* (11th ed.). McGraw-Hill, New York, NY, p. 69 and retrieved April 4, 2017, from https://www.forbes.com/sites/carmine-gallo/2011/02/23/wow-your-customers-the-ritz-carlton-way/#37b5a669da32.

4. Kinicki, A. & Williams, B. (2013). *Management: A Practical Introduction* (6th ed.). McGraw-Hill, New York, NY, p.231.

5. Schermerhorn, J. & Bachrach, D. (2015). *Management* (13th ed.). John Wiley & Sons, New York, NY, p. 269.

6. Retrieved April 4, 2017, from https://www.bloomberg.com/news/articles/2012-12-06/inside-the-elephant-room-at-kayak-dot-com.

7. Kinicki, A & Fugate, M. (2016). *Organizational Behavior.* McGraw-Hill, New York, NY, p. 482.

8. Retrieved April5, 2017, from https://www.fastcompany.com/3053776/how-facebook-keeps-scaling-its-culture.

9. Retrieved December 31, 2016, from https://www.southwest.com/html/about-southwest/careers/culture.html.

10. Lussier. (2017). *Management Fundamentals* (7th ed.). Los Angeles, CA, p. 39.

11. Kincki, A. & Williams, B. (2016). *Management: A Practical Introduction* (7th ed.). McGraw-Hill, New York, NY, p. 232.

12. Kinicki, A. & Williams, B. (2013). *Management: A Practical Introduction* (6th ed.). McGraw-Hill, New York, NY, p. 231.

13. Retrieved December 31, 2016, from http://www.biography.com/people/sam-walton-9523270#building-an-empire.

14. Daft R. & Marcic, D. (2015). *Understanding Management* (9th ed.). Cengage, Stamford, CT, 2015, p. 78.

15. Retrieved December 31, 2016, from http://www.roadandtrack.com/car-culture/news/a29271/mary-kays-pink-cadillacs-were-nearly-lincolns/.

16. Retrieved December 31, 2016, from http://www.newbelgium.com/Brewery/company/benefits.

17. Retrieved April 7, 2017, fromhttp://www.valuebasedmanagement.net/methods_quinn_competing_values_framework.html.

18. Kincki, A. & Williams, B. (2016). *Management: A Practical Introduction* (7th ed.). McGraw-Hill, New York, NY, p. 229.

19. Kincki, A. & Williams, B. (2016). *Management: A Practical Introduction* (7th ed.). McGraw-Hill, New York, NY, p. 230.

20. Retrieved April 7, 2017, from http://highered.mheducation.com/sites/0071051406/student_view0/chapter11/key_concept_summaries.html.

21. Retrieved December 31, 2016, from https://hbr.org/2013/12/the-definitive-elements-of-a-winning-culture.

22. Retrieved January 1, 2017, from http://www.businessinsider.com/southwest-airlines-puts-employees-first-2015-7.

23. Daft. (12th ed.). pp. 99–100.

24. Retrieved April 3, 2017, from https://www.forbes.com/sites/danpontefract/2015/05/11/what-is-happening-at-zappos/#55061a294ed8.

25. Kinicki, 7th, p. 238.

26. Bateman, Snell, & Konopaske. (2016). *Management* (5th ed.). McGraw-Hill, New York, NY, 2016, p. 144.

27. Robbins & Coulter (2016). *Management* (13th ed.). Pearson, Upper Saddle River, NJ, p. 290.

28. Daft. (12th ed.). p. 330.

29. Bateman, T. & Snell,S. (2013). *Management* (3rd ed.). McGraw-Hill, New York, NY, p. 153.

30. Bateman & Snell. (2013). *Management* (11th ed.). McGraw-Hill, New York, NY, pp. 270–271.

31. Daft (12th ed.). p. 330.

32. Kincki, A. & Williams, B. (2016). *Management: A Practical Introduction* (7th ed.). McGraw-Hill, New York, NY, p.244.

33. Jones, G. &George, J. (2014). *Contemporary Managemen t*(8th ed.). McGraw-Hill, New York, NY, p. 317.

34. Schermerhorn, J. & Bachrach, D. *Management* (13th ed.). Wiley, New York, NY, p. 257.

35. Retrieved April 7, 2017, from http://www.economist.com/node/14301444.

36. Kincki, A. & Williams, B. (2016). *Management: A Practical Introduction* (7th ed.). McGraw-Hill, New York, NY, p. 245.

37. Schermerhorn, J. & Bachrach, D. (2015). *Management* (13th ed.). Wiley, New York, NY, pp. 245–246.

38. Bateman, T. & Snell,S. (2013). *Management* (3rd ed.). McGraw-Hill, New York, NY, p. 158.

39. Bateman & Snell. pp. 159–160.

40. Kinicki & Williams (7th ed.). p. 246.

41. Williams, C. (2016). *Management* (8th ed.). Cengage, 2016, p. 184.

42. Jones, G. &George, J. (2014). *Contemporary Management* (8th ed.). McGraw-Hill, New York, NY, p. 310.

43. Bateman & Snell. *Management* (3rd ed.). p. 160.

44. Robbins, DeCenzo, & Coulter. *Fundamentals of Management* (9th ed.).

45. Bateman, Snell & Konopaske. (2016). *Management* (5th ed.). McGraw-Hill, New York, NY, p. 157.

46. Retrieved April 7, 2017, from https://hbr.org/2008/03/is-yours-a-learning-organization.

47. Lussier. (2015).*Management Fundamentals* (6th ed.). Los Angeles, CA, p. 197.

48. Kinicki, A. & Williams, B. (2013). *Management: A Practical Introduction* (6th ed.). McGraw-Hill, New York, NY, p. 251.

49. Griffin, R. (2016).*Fundamentals of Management* (8th ed.). Cengage, Boston, MA, p. 175.

50. Kinicki, A. & Williams, B. (2013). *Management: A Practical Introduction* (6th ed.). McGraw-Hill, New York, NY, p. 252.

51. Griffin, R. (2016).*Fundamentals of Management* (8th ed.). Cengage, Boston, MA, p. 175.

52. Kinicki, A. & Williams, B. (2013). *Management: A Practical Introduction* (6th ed.). McGraw-Hill, New York, NY, p.

53. Kinicki, A. & Williams, B. (2013). *Management: A Practical Introduction* (6th ed.). McGraw-Hill, New York, NY, p. 252.

54. Robbins & Coulter. (2016). *Management* (13th ed.). Pearson, Upper Saddle River, NJ, p.301.

CHAPTER 7 HUMAN RESOURCE MANAGEMENT

Key Terms

Base compensation
Collective bargaining
Development
Equal employment opportunity
External recruiting
Human capital
Human resource management
Human resource management
   process

Human resource planning
Internal recruiting
Job analysis
Job description
Job specification
Labor unions
Onboarding
Orientation
Performance appraisal

Realistic job preview
Recruiting
Reliability
Selection
Sexual harassment
Socialization
Training
Validity

Introduction

This chapter is all about how organizations manage their people. For many organizations, people are their most valuable resources. We will explore the set of processes that organizations use to attract, develop, and retain qualified people for jobs in the organization. First, we will explore the legal environment of human resource management. Then we will examine the ways that organizations recruit and select people. Next, we will look at ways that organizations develop and retain employees. Finally, we will examine the unique set of circumstances that comprise organizations with union employees.

© Shutterstock.com

Learning Outcomes

After reading this chapter, you should be able to:

❑ Describe the purpose of and activities of human resource management

❑ Remember and understand the legal framework of human resource management

❑ Identify the various ways that managers attract and develop a qualified workforce

❑ Understand the role of unions and the labor management process

Human Resource Management

Human resource management includes all organizational activities managers perform to attract, develop, and maintain a talented workforce.[1] These activities include planning, recruiting, selecting, developing, and compensating the organization's employees. We'll explore each of these activities throughout this chapter. Organizations succeed through the efforts of talented people and organizations that can't manage people

well are less likely to be successful. Organizations also operate in an environment with many legal restraints. We'll look at these complicated legal issues also in this chapter.

Human capital refers to the knowledge, skills, and abilities of employees that add economic value to an organization. The term is often used nowadays to describe the strategic value of employee knowledge and skills. Managing human capital to sustain a competitive advantage is perhaps the most important part of human resource management. Conceptually, human capital recognizes that not all labor is equal and that the quality of employees can be improved by through human resource management activities.[2]

The Legal Environment

General environmental forces, described in Chapter 2, have a major impact on an organization's human resource practices. Organizational strategy is shaped by these forces. This is particularly true with regard to the Political or Legal environment. Organizations aren't free to hire and fire whoever they want, but rather must comply with a number of employment laws.[3] As a manager, you should be aware of U.S. laws in four areas as follows

Laws Protecting Employees from Discrimination

Operating within legal limitations, U.S. managers are not completely free to choose who they will hire, promote or fire. While employment laws have tended to reduce discrimination in the workplace, they have also reduced management's discretion over some human resource decisions.[4]

Title VI of the Civil Rights Act of 1964 is the cornerstone of U.S. employment laws designed to protect employees from discrimination. This act has been amended in 1972 and 1991. At its core, the Civil Rights Act is the provision of equal employment opportunity. The Civil Rights Act established the Equal Employment Opportunity Commission (EEOC). The EEOC has the authority to file civil lawsuits against organizations that do not provide timely resolution to charges of discrimination.[5]

Affirmative Action was enacted by Executive Order 11246.[6] Many U.S. organizations have affirmative action plans to ensure that employment decisions and practices support protected groups.[7]

Sexual harassment is a form of workplace discrimination against individuals because of their sex. According to the EEOC, sexual harassment includes unwelcome sexual advances, requests for sexual favors, and other verbal or physical conduct of a sexual nature. While the law doesn't prohibit simple teasing, offhand comments, or isolated incidents that are not very serious, harassment is illegal when it is so frequent or severe that it creates a hostile or offensive work environment or when it results in an adverse employment decision (such as the victim being fired or demoted).[8]

Sexual harassment
Is a form of workplace discrimination against individuals because of their sex.

There are two types of sexual harassment which violate the Civil Rights Act of 1963. First, in *quid pro quo* harassment, a person's job is put in jeopardy unless they acquiesce to unwanted sexual attention.[9] For example, a man may imply that a date is a condition of employment for a woman applicant. The most typical form of harassment though is the *hostile work environment*, where individuals experience offensive or intimidating behavior in workplace. This behavior can include sexual innuendo, taunts or offensive jokes.[10]

Laws Concerning Compensation and Benefits

The Social Security Act of 1935 established the U.S. retirement system. Passed in 1938, the Fair Labor Standards Act provided a minimum wage for workers involved in interstate commerce. The Fair Labor Standards Act also provided for a maximum workweek of 40 hours. After 40 hours worked, workers must be paid overtime, a rate of one and half times their regular hourly wage. Salaried executive, administrative, and professional employees are exempt from over-time rules.[11]

Laws Concerning Health and Safety

Many jobs like mining and factory work are performed under dirty and dangerous conditions. The Occupational Safety and Health Act (OSHA) established a body of law that requires organizations to provide nonhazardous working conditions to employees. Subsequent laws extended health coverage including the 2010 health care reform legislation that requires employers with more than 50 employees to provide health insurance.[12]

Laws Concerning Labor Relations

Union activities and management's behavior toward unions are heavily regulated issues. The National Labor Relations Act (also known as the Wagner Act) was passed in 1935 and provides a procedure for employees to vote on union representation. The Wagner Act established the National Labor Relations Board (NLRB) to enforce the act's provisions. In 1946, the Labor-Management Relations Act (also known as the Taft-Hartley Act) was passed to provide a limitation on union power after a series of severe strikes. Taft-Hartley increased management rights during a union organizing campaign and established the National Emergency Strike provision which allows the U.S. president to prevent or end a strike that threatens national security. Together, these two laws balance union and management power.[13]

Selected Major U.S. Employment Laws		
National Labor Relations Act (also known as the Wagner Act)	1935	Establishes procedures by which employees can establish labor unions and requires employers to bargain collectively with unions
Fair Labor Standards Act	1938	Established a federal minimum wage and maximum workweek of 40 hours
Labor Management Relations Act (also known as the Taft-Hartley Act)	1946	Limits union powers and specifies management rights during union campaigns
Equal Pay Act	1963	Requires that men and women be paid equally for equal work
Civil Rights Act, Title VII	1964 (amended in 1972)	Prohibits discrimination on the basis of race, color, religion, national origin or sex
Age Discrimination in Employment Act	1967	Prohibits discrimination against workers over the age of 40
Occupational Safety and Health Act	1970	Establishes safety and health standards for employers
Vietnam-era Veteran's Adjustment Act	1972	Prohibits discrimination against Vietnam-era veterans.
Pregnancy Discrimination Act	1978	Prohibits employment discrimination against woman on the basis of pregnancy
Americans with Disabilities Act (ADA)	1990	Prohibits discrimination against individuals with disabilities and requires employers to make reasonable accommodations for such workers to perform their jobs.
Family Medical Leave Act	1993	Provides up to 12 weeks of unpaid leave for medical and family reasons

Courtesy of Jeffrey Anderson.

The Human Resource Management Process

Human resource management process
Includes those activities aimed at attracting, developing, and retaining a qualified workforce.

The goal of human resource management is to support the organization by aligning talented people with organizational strategies and goals. The human resource management process includes those activities aimed at attracting, developing, and retaining a qualified workforce.[14]

Human Resource Planning

Human resource planning includes all of the activities that managers use in order to project current and future human resource needs. Part of human resource planning involves the forecasting demand and supply. Managers estimate the demand, or need for the qualifications and number of employees in the future, based on the organization's strategy. Supply forecasts estimate the availability of qualified current employees and the future supply of the labor market.[15]

Job Analysis is a systematic study to determine the basic elements of a job. In job analysis, specialists interview and observe job holders and develop job descriptions and job specifications. A job description summarizes the duties of a job. A job specification lists the minimum qualifications a person must have to perform the job successfully.[16] Information from job analysis is used for a number of human resource activities including selection, performance appraisal, and compensation decisions.[17]

Recruiting

Organizations must attract a pool of qualified applicants to meet job requirements. Recruiting is the process of locating and attracting qualified applicants for open jobs.[18] People need to know about job openings before they can apply and that's the purpose of recruiting.[19]

Internal recruiting is the process of making those already employed by the organization aware of job openings. Most vacant positions are filled through internal recruiting tactics like job postings on bulletin boards, newsletters, and the organization's web intranet.[20] The college internship is another form of internal recruiting that brings a student to the workplace on a temporary basis and allows both parties an experience based opportunity to consider one another for future long-term employment.[21]

External recruiting involves attracting job applicants from outside the organization. Traditionally, organizations have relied on newspapers, employment agencies, recruiting firms, and college placement offices for external recruiting. Today, increasing

Job analysis A systematic study to determine the basic elements of a job.

Job description Summarizes the duties of a job.

Job specification Lists the minimum qualifications a person must have to perform the job successfully.

Recruiting The process of locating and attracting qualified applicants for open jobs.

Internal recruiting The process of making those already employed by the organization aware of job openings.

External recruiting Involves attracting job applicants from outside the organization.

FIGURE 1 THE HR PROCESS. COURTESY OF JEFFREY ANDERSON.

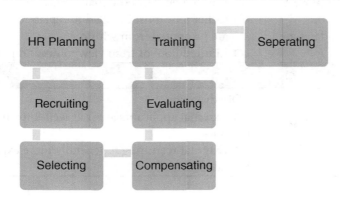

Linked in™

numbers of companies use social media as recruiting tools.[22] Through social recruiting, employers browse social media sights like LinkedIn, Facebook, Reddit, and Twitter, looking for prospective job candidates whose online profiles show potential leadership, special skills, and networks.[23]

In traditional recruiting, the emphasis is on selling the job and the organization to applicants. The focus on this case is on the positive aspects of the job, minimizing the negative aspects. This can create unrealistic expectations that result in turnover when new employees become disillusioned and leave a job. In a realistic job preview, applicants are given complete, undistorted information before being selected. Rather than "selling" an individual on a job, realist job previews are more balanced information about both the positive and negative aspects of a job.[24]

Selection is the process of choosing the most qualified applicants among those recruited for a given job.[25] In this section, we will explore three types of selection tools; background information, interviewing, and employment tests.

Background checks are used to verify the accuracy and truthfulness of applicants. Application forms and resumes contain background information such as education, work experience, and certifications. Many organizations use services like InfoLink Screening Services to conduct background checks to eliminate applicants who have lied or overstated their qualifications. References cause problems because many employers don't give candid assessments of former employees. Many employers fear that they will be sued by former employees if they say anything negative. Others fear that they may be sued by future employers for endorsing an applicant that didn't work out.[26] Background checks verify the honesty of applicants and can eliminate those who lie about their qualifications. Most companies today conduct an online search for job candidates. Most hiring managers check social media sites like Facebook and LinkedIn. Many companies have chosen not to extend job offers to candidates whose online image is unprofessional.[27]

The interview is the most commonly used selection technique. Interviews may take place, by phone, videoconference or the internet. Face to face interviews have been

Realistic job preview Applicants are given complete, undistorted information before being selected.

Selection The process of choosing the most qualified applicants among those recruited for a given job.

TABLE 1 OUTLINES THE ADVANTAGES AND DISADVANTAGES OF INTERNAL AND EXTERNAL RECRUITING.

Internal Recruitment	
Advantages	Disadvantages
❏ Less expensive Increased morale of employees motivated by career opportunities ❏ Less risk as the skills of internal candidates are already known	❏ Limited pool of potential applicants ❏ Other jobs must be filled to replace employees who are promoted from within ❏ Limited pool of fresh viewpoints and perspectives
External Recruitment	
Advantages	Disadvantages
❏ Applicants bring fresh perspectives and ideas ❏ Applicants may have specialized experiences and knowledge	❏ External applicants aren't as well-known as internal ones ❏ External recruiting is generally more expensive and takes longer

Courtesy of Jeffrey Anderson.

perceived as more fair than lead to higher job acceptance than videoconferencing and telephone interviews.[28] Typically, the interview is the most heavily weighted step in the selection process as the interviewer has a chance to assess things about a candidate that can't be learned from a resume or application.[29]

© Shutterstock.com

There are several kinds of interviews; unstructured, semi-structured, and structured. In **unstructured interviews**, interviewers are free to ask any questions they want. In these types of interviews, different interviewers tend to ask different questions. By contract, in **structured interviews**, each interviewee is asked questions from a standardized lists of questions so that all job applicants are asked the same set of questions for the same job. The structured interview allows different interviewers to compare interview results against a common standard. The structured interview also prevents interviewers from asking questions that aren't related to the job.[30]

Finally, organizations can use selection tests to predict who will likely perform well in a particular job. **Selection tests** are intended to measure skills and abilities related to doing well on the job.[31] In a **performance test,** the test taker performs a sample of the job. Most companies use some type of performance test for administrative assistant and clerical jobs. The typing test is the most widely used performance test although performance tests have been developed for almost every occupation including management.[32]

For jobs that require physical abilities, such as firefighting, package delivery, and garbage collection, managers use **physical ability** tests to measure physical strength and stamina. Typically, autoworkers are tested for dexterity as that physical ability is important for job performance at many auto plants.[33]

Drug testing is now being used frequently as a screening tool. Since the passage of the Drug-Free Workplace Act of 1998, applicants and employees of federal contractors have been subject to testing for illegal drugs. Drug testing is more complicated for employers in the states that have legalized marijuana for medical or recreational purposes. So far though, most state medical marijuana laws do not include employment protections for workers. Because these laws are new and vary from state to state, employers are caught in a legal grey area for the time being.[34]

Selection methods are prediction exercises. Reliability and validity are important concerns with selection tools. Reliability means that a selection method delivers consistent results with regard to what it measures. A method is reliable if it delivers the same results over time. As an example, a test would be reliable if the same individual received a similar score when taking the test on two different occasions. Validity means that there is a clear and direct relationship between what the method measures and future job performance. For example, a method would be reliable if there is evidence that individuals with a high score perform better on the job than individual with a low score.[35]

Reliability
Means that a selection method delivers consistent results with regard to what it measures.

Validity Means that there is a clear and direct relationship between what the method measures and future job performance.

Orienting

Orientation Same as onboarding.

Onboarding The process of introducing a new employee to the organization and the job.

Socialization The process by which new members learn and adapt to the ways of the organization.

Once an individual is selected for a position, he or she must learn about the organization and the job. Orientation or Onboarding is the process of introducing a new employee to the organization and the job. Onboarding is a socialization process that is designed to give new employees the information they need to be successful on the job. After orientation, employees should understand information in three areas. First, employees should learn what is required of their job, how they will be evaluated, and who are their co-workers and managers. Also, managers need to know the organization's mission, its purpose, products, services, operations, and history. Finally, employees should learn about the organization's work rules and benefits.[36]

Socialization is the process by which new members learn and adapt to the ways of the organization. Socialization begins with onboarding and continues through the first six months or so of employment. How well an employee will perform and fit with the organization usually becomes clear during this period. When done well, socialization sets the basis for high performance and job satisfaction. When done poorly, it leaves an individual's performance and integration into the organization up to chance.[37]

Training and Developing

Training The set of activities that provide learning opportunities for employees to acquire and improve job-related skills.

Training is the set of activities that provide learning opportunities for employees to acquire and improve job-related skills. Training refers to educating technical and operational employees on how to better perform their current jobs.[38]

Organizations that value their human resources often invest heavily in training programs. On-the-job training takes place on the job site. The employee learns while performing the job. One common approach is job rotation, where employees spend time working in different jobs or locations. Another approach is coaching, where an experienced employee gives advice to a new or less experienced co-worker. Mentoring is a form of coaching where new employees are assigned as a protégé to a senior or veteran employee. Some organizations, such as Cisco and MasterCard, use reverse mentoring. In reverse mentoring, younger employees mentor senior ones to improve their technology skills.[39]

Development Ongoing education, designed to improve the skills employees need for future jobs.

Training and development are different processes. Training is designed to teach employees the skills that they need to perform their current job. Development is ongoing education, designed to improve the skills employees need for future jobs.[40] Jobs in fields like medicine, accounting, law, and management require ongoing education and development, not just so employees can do their job now, but also so that they develop the skills needed for the future.[41]

Evaluating

Performance appraisal A formal assessment of how well an employee is performing in his or her job.

A performance appraisal is a formal assessment of how well an employee is performing in his or her job.[42] Performance appraisal is an on-going process of evaluating employee performance so it is an important part of a manager's job.[43] More than 70 percent of managers admit they find it difficult to give a critical performance review to an underperforming employee.[44] Nearly 60 percent of HR managers report that they dislike their organization's performance appraisal system, citing that appraisals aren't done often enough and neglect pathways to improvement.[45]

Objective performance measures are easily and directly quantified or counted. Common measurements might include output, sales, customer complaints, waste, and rejection rates. Often though, objective measures aren't available and subjective measures must be used instead. **Subjective performance appraisals** require that someone make a judgment when assessing employee performance.[46] Traits like initiative, leadership and attitude require the rater to make judgments about employee performance. Behavioral appraisals, while still subjective, focus on observable aspects of an employee's performance. With **Behaviorally Anchored Rating Scales (BARS),** scales are developed that focus on evaluating specific job behaviors making performance less ambiguous.[47] Table 2 outlines the observable behavior and resulting rating scale for customer service dimensions of a retail clerk.

Traditionally, managers and supervisors observe employee performance for appraisal information. Increasingly, peers and team members have been used to provide appraisal information and provide performance feedback. In a process known as **360-degree appraisal**, feedback is obtained multiple stakeholders like peers, subordinates, and supervisors. The 360-degree appraisal offers a much more complete picture of an employee's strengths and weaknesses. The approach can lead to significant improvements for employees who are motivated to improve their ratings. However, employees are often unwilling to rate their colleagues critically resulting in a kind of uniformity amongst ratings. Additionally, 360-degree appraisal may be less useful than objective criteria when measuring performance.[48]

Compensating

One of the most important work issues is pay. Base compensation is the salary or hourly wages paid to employees.[49] There are three basic forms of compensation and an organization might use all three. (1) A **salary** is paid to individuals for their total contribution, not hours worked. (2) **Wages** are hourly compensation, typically for operating

Base compensation
The salary or hourly wages paid to employees.

TABLE 2 BEHAVIOR OBSERVATION SCALE FOR CUSTOMER SERVICE.

	Almost Never				Almost Always
Greets customer with a 'hello" and smile	1	2	3	4	5
Calls other stores to find out of stock merchandise	1	2	3	4	5
Handles customer complaints and concerns promptly	1	2	3	4	5

Sample BARS Appraisal Form

employees. (3) **Incentives** represent compensation tied to performance, such as a sales commission or a bonus.[50]

Benefits are additional forms of compensation paid fully, or in part by the organization. Examples of these benefits include; health insurance, dental insurance, vision insurance, life insurance, disability protection, paid holidays, sick time, vacation time, discounts on products or services, educational benefits, and more.[51] By law, employers must provide workers' compensation, to cover job-related injuries, unemployment compensation for employees who are laid off or terminated, Medicare for health insurance and Social Security for retirement.[52] Other benefits are provided, at least partly, to make the organization competitive in the job market. The average organization spends more than one-third of their cash payroll on these types of benefits.[53]

Employee Separations

Employee separation is a broad term that describes the loss of an employee for any reason. Voluntary separation occurs when employees retire or quit. Involuntary separation occurs when employers terminate or lay off employees.[54]

Employment is terminated for three main reasons; attrition, layoffs, and firings. Attrition is voluntary turnover, layoffs, and firings are involuntary.

Attrition occurs when employees leave the organization for other jobs, decide to stop working for a time, or retire. Human resource planning needs to account for new positions created through attrition. Often, employees who leave the organization voluntarily are interviewed by human resources staff in what's termed an exit interview. These exit interviews can help identify problems that lead to turnover.

Layoffs are an involuntary separation as part of organizational downsizing, typically due to poor economic conditions, mergers and acquisitions or poor organizational performance. Layoffs have been described as one of the most ineffective and expensive forms of reducing a workforce as morale typically drops and many employees leave voluntarily as a result.[55]

As a result of restructuring in American industry brought on by mergers, divestiture and increased competition, many organizations have been downsizing or laying off large numbers of management and non-management employees. Victims of restructuring, face difficulties like loss of self-esteem, challenging searches for new employment, and the stigma of being unemployed. Some employers help people who have been dismissed by offering **outplacement,** services aimed at helping people who have been dismissed find employment outside the organization. In many cases, how managers deal with layoffs can impact the attitudes and performance of those employees who remain at the organization. A well thought out layoff process can prevent disenchantment, distrust, and lethargy among employees who remain with the organization.[56]

The Union Environment

In recent years, union membership in the United States has declined from a peak of 33 percent at the end of World War II to approximately 12 percent in 2010. Increased automation has eroded union jobs in manufacturing, formerly a union stronghold. Employees in office jobs seem less interested in joining unions and are harder for unions to organize. Increasing global competion has made managers less willing to give in to union demands and the benefits of union membership are less clear to many workers, especially skilled ones who no longer stay with the same employer all of their career.[57]

Even though union membership is declining, managers need to be aware of the different regulations and processes of a union environment, particularly if they work in that environment. **Labor relations** is the term that encompasses all of the interactions between organizations and employees who are represented by a labor union.[58]

Labor unions are organizations of employees that are formed to protect and advance the interests of their members through collective bargaining on job-related issues. Unions helped grow the American and European middle-class, bringing benefits to many in society, whether union members or not.[59]

There are five steps in the union organizing process which are outlined in Figure 1. When workers in a particular organization decide that they want to form a union, they must get workers to sign authorization cards designating a certain union as their bargaining agent. When at least 30 percent of workers sign cards, the union can ask for official recognition. Most organizations refuse to issue that recognition so the union then petitions the National Labor Relations Board (NLRB) to determine which workers should become bargaining unit employees, represented by that union. Once the NLRB determines the composition of the bargaining unit, an election is held. If 50 percent or more of employees in that bargaining union vote for unionization, the NLRB certifies the union as those workers' exclusive representative.[60]

Collective bargaining is the negotiation process that results in a contract between employees and management concerning working conditions. The most common issues in that negotiation include wages, working hours, benefits, and working conditions.[61] The process of negotiating a labor contract may take months and involve many proposals and counter-proposals. Once an agreement is reached, the labor contract must be ratified by the union membership. In cases where an agreement is not reached or not ratified, unions may threaten to strike to put pressure on management to make concessions.[62]

Organizations generally prefer that employees not belong to unions because unions limit management freedoms. Often management may wage its own campaign to convince employees to vote against a union. Experts agree that the best way to avoid a union

Labor unions
Organizations of employees that are formed to protect and advance the interests of their members through collective bargaining on job-related issues.

Collective bargaining
The negotiation process that results in a contract between employees and management concerning working conditions.

FIGURE 2 THE UNION ORGANIZING PROCESS. COURTESY OF JEFFREY ANDERSON.

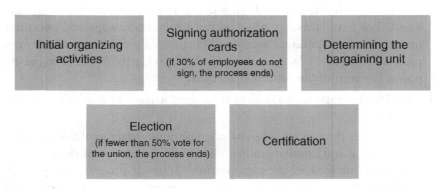

FIGURE 3 UNION MEMBERSHIP.[64] © KENDALL HUNT PUBLISHING COMPANY.

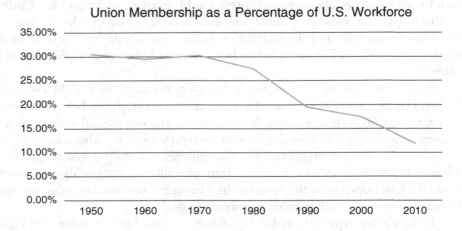

Union Membership as a Percentage of U.S. Workforce

is to practice good labor relations. Fair treatment and clear standards with regard to pay, promotions, layoffs, and discipline can make a union unnecessary from an employee's perspective.[63]

Summary of Learning Outcomes and Key Points

❏ **Describe the purpose of and activities of human resource management**

Human resource management is the set of activities aimed at attracting, developing, and retaining qualified employees for jobs in the organization. Human resource management is an important function as people are the most valuable resources in most organizations.

❏ **Remember and understand the legal framework of human resource management**

Employment is an area that is regulated by government. A series of federal laws are in place to; (1) protect employees from discrimination, (2) Regulate wages and benefits, (3) Promote health and safety standards, and (4) Balance union and management power. The Civil Rights Act of 1964 and other acts prohibit discrimination, including sexual harassment, in the workplace. The Fair Labor Standards Act provides for a minimum wage and overtime payments. The Occupational Safety and Health Act provides standards for workplace safety and the Wagner Act and the Taft-Hartly Act seek to balance the power between unions and management

❏ **Identify the various ways that managers attract and develop a qualified workforce**

Recruiting is the process whereby organizations attract qualified workers from both internal and external groups. Selection is the process of choosing qualified applicants for jobs in the organization. Training programs help employees develop skills for their current jobs and development programs help employees develop skills for future jobs. Employees receive feedback on their job performance through performance appraisals.

❏ **Understand the role of unions and the labor management process**

Unions are employee organizations that bargain collectively with management regarding wages, benefits, and working conditions. Unions form through a process involving authorization cards and an election. The National Labor Relations Board oversees the union organizing process.

Questions for Review

1. Describe the steps in the human resource management process.
2. Describe common selection methods. How do reliability and validity ensure the legitimacy of those methods?
3. Compare the advantages and disadvantages of internal and external recruiting.
4. Describe the union organizing process.

End Notes

1. Kinicki & Williams. (2013). *Management: A Practical Introduction* (6th ed.). McGraw-Hill, Burr Ridge, IL, p. 264.
2. Retrieved April 16, 2016, from http://www.investopedia.com/terms/h/humancapital.asp
3. Lussier. (2017). *Management Fundamentals* (7th ed.). Los Angeles, CA, p. 265.
4. Lussier, p. 200.
5. Schermerhorn & Bachrach. (2015). *Management* (13th ed.). Wiley, New York, NY, p. 295.
6. Retrieved April 26, 2016, from http://www.archives.gov/federal-register/codification/executive-order/11246.html
7. Robins & Coulter. (2016). *Management* (13th ed.). Pearson, Upper Saddle River, NJ, p. 342
8. Retrieved April 24, 2016, from https://www.eeoc.gov/laws/types/sexual_harassment.cfm
9. Lussier, p. 267.
10. Kinicki (6th ed.). p. 271.
11. Kincki, p. 268.
12. Kinicki, p. 268.
13. Griffin, p. 230.
14. Schermerhorn, (7th ed.). p. 292.
15. Jones and Jones, p. 374.
16. Kinicki (7th ed.). p. 265.
17. Griffin, pp. 320–231.
18. Kinicki (6th ed.)
19. Lussier, p. 271.
20. Kinicki, p. 272.
21. Schermerhorn, p. 299.
22. Kinicki, p. 272.
23. Schermerhorn, p. 299.
24. Shermerhorn, p. 300.
25. Lussier, p. 273.
26. Kinicki, p. 275.
27. Bateman & Snell. (2013). *Management* (11th ed.). McGraw-Hill, New York, NY, p. 336.
28. Kinicki, p. 277.
29. Lussier, p. 275.
30. Williams, C. (2016). *Effective Management* (7th ed.). Cengage, Boston, MA, p. 316
31. Williams, p. 313.

32. Bagteman, p. 33.

33. Jones G. & George, J. (2014). *Contemporary Management* (8th ed.). McGraw-Hill, New York, NY, p. 381.

34. Bateman, p. 337.

35. Schermerhorn, p. 301.

36. Kinicki, pp. 280–281

37. Schermerhorn, p. 304.

38. Kinicki, p. 280.

39. Schermerhorn, p. 304.

40. Lussier, p. 278.

41. Kinicki, p. 281.

42. Griffin, p. 237.

43. Robbins, p. 280.

44. Robbins, p. 352.

45. Schermerhorn, p. 305.

46. Williams, p. 323.

47. Bateman, p. 347.

48. Bateman, p. 350.

49. Schermerhorn, p. 308.

50. Griffin. (2016). *Fundamentals of Management* (8th ed.). Cengage, Boston, MA, p. 240.

51. Kinicki, p. 288.

52. Lussier, p. 285.

53. Griffin, p. 243.

54. Williams, p. 329.

55. Lussier, p. 288.

56. Bateman, p. 340.

57. Bateman, p. 360.

58. Lussier, p. 288.

59. Kinicki, p, 292.

60. Kinicki, p. 292.

61. Lussier, p. 288.

62. Griffin, p 248.

63. Griffin, p. 248.

64. Huffington Post. Retrieved April 26, 2016, from http://www.huffingtonpost.com/2013/01/23/union-membership-rate_n_2535063.html

CHAPTER 8 MANAGING DIVERSE INDIVIDUALS

Key Terms

Attitude	Halo effect	Selective perception
Burnout	Job satisfaction	Self-efficacy
Causal attribution	Locus of control	Self-esteem
Diversity	Machiavellianism	Self-fulfilling prophecy
Emotional intelligence	Organizational commitment	Self-serving bias
Emotional stability	Perception	Stereotyping
Employee engagement	Personality	Stress
Fundamental attribution error	Recency effect	Values

Introduction

People are constellations of multiple identities. This includes personal identities like age, height, weight, gender, race, country of origin, religious affiliation, familial status, and level of education. People have work identities including the industry they work in, the size of their organization, and their job, department, or position level. Other individual differences like personality, values, attitudes, preferences, biases, and opinions combine to make each person unique.

The many factors describe above lists suggest that a "one size fits all" management approach won't work when managing diverse individuals. Understanding individual differences allows managers to create situations that engage employees in their job and make the organization more productive. In this chapter, we will explore the many ways that people are different and the same.

Learning Outcomes

After reading this chapter, you should be able to:

- ❏ Describe the various personality theories and core self-evaluations that affect behavior in the workplace
- ❏ Understand emotional intelligence and other personality characteristics
- ❏ Discuss individual values and attitudes
- ❏ Describe the perceptual process and perceptual biases

□ Explain the value of diversity to modern organizations

□ Discuss the impact of stress in the workplace

Personality

Personality
The unique combination of an individual's emotional, thought, and behavior patterns

An individual's personality is the unique combination of their emotional, thought, and behavior patterns. Personality affects how a person reacts to situations and interacts with others. Our personality reflects our natural way of doing things and relating to other people. An individual's personality is often described in measurable quantifiable terms. Like attitudes, personality affects how and why people behave the way that they do. Over the years, researchers have sought to identify those traits that best describe personality. The two best known approaches are the Myers Briggs Type Indicator (MBTI) and the Big Five Personality Dimensions Model.[1]

MBTI

A popular approach to classifying personality traits is the assessment instrument known as the MBTI. The MBTI is a 100 question survey that asks people how they would typically feel or act in different situations. Based on their answers, individuals are classified as having a preference in four categories; (1) extraversion or introversion (E or I), (2) sensing or intuition (S or N), (3) thinking or feeling (T or F), and (4) judging or perceiving (J or P). Here are the definitions for these terms:

□ **Extraversion vs. Introversion.** People with a preference for extraversion are social, outgoing, and assertive. They prefer a work environment that gives them variety and is action oriented. Individuals with a preference for introversion are quiet and shy. They prefer a work environment that allows them to concentrate and explore new experiences in depth.

□ **Sensing vs. Intuition.** People with a preference for sensing like quiet and order. They have a strong need for closure and dislike new problems unless there is a standard solution. They show patience with routine and tend to be good at details. Individuals with a preference for intuition largely rely on unconscious processes to solve problems. They like new problems and are impatient with routine details.

□ **Thinking vs. Feeling.** Thinking types use logic and reason to solve problems. They are unemotional and unconcerned with people's feelings. Thinking types like analysis and prefer to put things in a logical order. They sometimes appear hard-hearted and relate best to other thinking types. Feeling types by contrast, rely on their personal values and emotions. They are aware of other's feelings, prefer harmony, and relate well to most other people.

□ **Judging vs. Perceiving.** Judging types like to control. They prefer a world of order and structure. They're good planners because they are decisive, purposeful, and exacting. They focus on quick decisions and only want the information needed to make a decision. Perceiving types are spontaneous and flexible. They are curious, tolerant, and adaptable. They focus on finding out all that they can about a problem before making a decision.

Table 1 Summarizes the four MBIT categories of personality traits.

TABLE 1 SUMMARY OF MBTI PERSONALITY TRAITS.

Dimension	Explanation	
EI	**Extraversion**: Those who derive their energy from other people and objects	**Introversion**: Those who derive their energy from inside
SN	**Sensing**: Those who rely on their five senses to perceive the external environment	**Intuition**: Those who rely on their intuition and hunches to perceive the external environment
TF	**Thinking**: Those who use their logic to arrive at solutions	**Feeling**: Those who use their values and ideas about right and wrong to arrive at solutions
JP	**Judging**: Those who are organized, systematic, and like to have clarity and closure	**Perception**: Those who are curious, open minded, and prefer to have some ambiguity

Combining the four preferences produces 16 personality types. It's important to note that no combination of personality types is better than another, they are just different. More than 2 million people a year take the MBTI assessment and it is used by companies like Apple, GE, AT&T, and 3M to match people to certain jobs.

While a very popular tool, there is no scientific evidence that the MBTI is a valid measure of personality.[2]

The Big Five Personality Traits

The big five personality traits is a model that is based on the findings of several independent researchers and dates to the late 1950s. The model we know today began to take shape in the 1990s and is credited to Lewis Goldberg, a researcher at the Oregon Research Institute, who named the model "The Big Five." This model is now considered to be an accurate and respected personality scale, which is routinely used by businesses and in psychological research.[3]

The big five model measures five key dimensions of an individual's personality. A popular acronym for the Big Five is "OCEAN." The five factors are presented in that order here.

Openness: Sometimes called "intellect" or "imagination." This dimension measures an individual's creativity and desire for knowledge and new experiences. Openness to experience relates to an individual's willingness to try to new things, to be vulnerable, and the ability to think outside the box.

Conscientiousness: This dimension considers the level of care that an individual takes in his or her life and work. People who score high on conscientiousness tend to be organized and thorough, and know how to make plans and follow them through. People who score low, are likely to be lax and disorganized. Conscientious people excel in their ability to delay gratification and work within the rules. They plan and organize effectively.

Extraversion/Introversion: This dimension measures an individual's level of sociability. This factor has two familiar ends of the spectrum: extroversion and introversion. It includes how an individual draws their energy and how they interact with others. Is a person outgoing or quiet, for instance? Do they draw energy from a crowd, or find it difficult to work and communicate with other people?

People who are high in extroversion be likely to seek out opportunities for social interaction, they are often the "life of the party." They are comfortable with others, sociable, and prone to action rather than contemplation. People low in extroversion are more likely to be people "of few words" people who are quiet, introspective, reserved, and thoughtful.

Agreeableness: This is a measurement of how well a person gets on with other people. Are they considerate, helpful, and willing to compromise? Or do they tend to put their needs before others'?

People who are high in agreeableness are often well-liked, respected, and sensitive to the needs of others. They likely have few enemies, are sympathetic, and affectionate to their friends and loved ones, as well as sympathetic to the plights of strangers. People on the low side of the agreeableness spectrum are less likely to be trusted and liked by others. They may be callous, blunt, rude, ill-tempered, antagonistic, and sarcastic. Although not everyone who is low in agreeableness is cruel or abrasive, they are not likely to leave others with a warm fuzzy feeling.

Neuroticism, (sometimes called emotional stability). Neuroticism is the one Big Five factor where a high score indicates negative traits. This dimension measures emotional reactions. Does the person react negatively or calmly to bad news? Do they worry obsessively about small details, or are they relaxed in stressful situations?

People who are high in neuroticism are generally given to anxiety, sadness, worry, and low self-esteem. They may be temperamental or quick to anger and they tend to be self-conscious and unsure of themselves. Individuals who score on the low end of neuroticism tend to feel confident, sure of themselves, and adventurous. They may also be brave and free from worry and self-doubt.

These five factors do not represent an exhaustive explanation of personality, but they are known as the "Big Five" because they include a large portion of personality-related terms. The Big Five factors are not necessarily traits in and of themselves, but are factors in which many related traits and characteristics fit. Table 2 describes some of the characteristics of persons with high scores in these five dimensions.

Table 2 Characteristics of persons with high scores in the Big Five Personality Dimensions.

TABLE 2 CHARACTERISTICS OF PERSONS SCORING HIGH ON THE FIVE DIMENSIONS.

Big Five Personality Dimension	Characteristics of persons with a high score
Openness to experience	Intellectual, imaginative, curious, open-minded
Conscientiousness	Dependable, responsible, persistent, goal-oriented
Extroversion	Outgoing, sociable, talkative, assertive
Agreeableness	Trusting, good-natured, cooperative, softhearted
Neuroticism	Anxious, insecure, nervous

Core Self-Evaluations

A core self-evaluation is a group of broad personality traits consisting of four positive individual traits: (1) self-efficacy, (2) self-esteem, (3) locus of control, and (4) emotional stability. Managers should understand these traits as they influence the workplace behavior of employees.

1. **Self-efficacy** is the personal belief that one has in their ability to perform a task. It is the individual's belief about how successful they will be on a particular assignment. General self-efficacy refers to our overall belief in our ability to succeed. Self-efficacy reflects confidence in one's ability to exert control over their own motivation, behavior, and social environment. One's cognitive self-/evaluations influence all manner of their experience, including the goals for which they strive, the amount of energy they expended toward goal achievement, and likelihood of attaining particular levels performance.[4]

   Self-efficacy
   The personal belief that one has in their ability to perform a task

2. **Self-esteem** is a person's overall opinion of themselves—how they feel about their own abilities and limitations. It is an indicator of the extent to which someone likes or dislikes themselves. When people have healthy self-esteem, they feel good about themselves and feel deserving the respect of others. When people have low self-esteem, they put little value on their opinions and ideas. People with low self-esteem might constantly worry that they aren't good enough.[5]

   Self-esteem
   A person's overall opinion of themselves

3. **Locus of control** indicates how much people believe that they control their outcomes through their own efforts. People with an internal locus of control believe that that they control their own destiny while people with an external locus of control believe that they are controlled by external forces.

   Locus of control
   Is the degree to which people believe that they control their outcomes through their own efforts

   Figure 1 contrasts an internal vs. an external locus of control. It is also important to note that locus of control is a continuum. No one has a 100 percent external or internal locus of control. Rather, most people lie somewhere on the continuum between these two extremes.

   Locus of control has important implications for the workplace. People with an internal locus of control have less anxiety, greater motivation, and higher expectations that their efforts will lead to performance. An internal locus of control can be improved by giving people more autonomy in the job.[6]

FIGURE 1 LOCUS OF CONTROL.

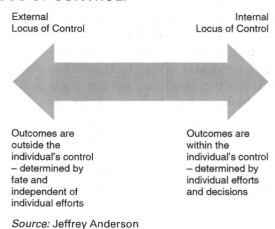

External
Locus of Control

Internal
Locus of Control

Outcomes are outside the individual's control – determined by fate and independent of individual efforts

Outcomes are within the individual's control – determined by individual efforts and decisions

Source: Jeffrey Anderson

Table 3 outlines factors associated with an internal and external locus of control.

4. **Emotional stability** is the extent to which people feel secure and unworried and how they are to experience negative emotions during stressful situations. Individuals with low emotional stability are more likely to be anxious and view the word in a negative frame. People who are high in emotional stability are likely to be better performers on the job.

TABLE 3 INTERNAL VS. EXTERNAL LOCUS OF CONTROL.

People with an Internal Locus of Control	People with an External Locus of Control
❏ Are more likely to take responsibility for their actions	❏ Often blame outside forces for their circumstances
❏ Are less likely to be influenced by the opinions of other people	❏ Often credit luck or chance for any successes
❏ Often perform at tasks when they are allowed to work at their own pace	❏ Don't believe that they can change their situation by their own efforts
❏ Generally, have a strong sense of self-efficacy	❏ Frequently feel hopeless or powerless in when facing difficult situations
❏ Tend to work hard to achieve their personal goals	❏ Are more likely to experiencing learned helplessness
❏ Are confident in the face of challenges	
❏ Tend to be healthier	
❏ Report being happier and more independent	
❏ Often achieve greater personal success in the workplace	

Other Personality Insights

Emotional Intelligence

An emotion is a mental state that occurs spontaneously, rather than through conscious effort. People experience both positive emotions such as happiness, pride, love, and relief as well as negative ones such as anger, anxiety, sadness, envy, and disgust. Emotional intelligence is one's ability to notice and manage emotional signals and cues. Emotional intelligence includes four components which are outlined in Figure 2.[7]

Self-awareness is ability to be aware of what you are feeling. This component describes how aware an individual is of their feelings and emotions. People with self-awareness are in touch with their emotions and can assess their own strengths and weaknesses. They have a healthy sense of self-confidence.

Self-management is our ability to manage our emotions and impulses. It includes our ability to control disruptive or harmful emotions and balance one's mood so that worry, fear, anxiety, and anger don't cloud thinking and interfere with what needs to be done. Individuals with strong self-management skills are able to remain optimistic and hopeful even when faced with set-backs and obstacles. This ability is critical in pursuing long-term goals.

FIGURE 2 FOUR COMPONENTS OF EMOTIONAL INTELLIGENCE.

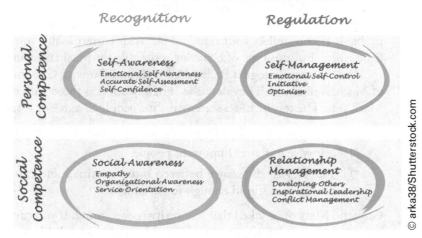

Social awareness is our ability to understand others and practice empathy, which is the ability to put yourself in the shoes of another. Social awareness allows us to recognize what others are feeling without being told. People with social awareness are able to understand different points of view. They are able to interact effectively with many different types of people.

Relationship management is the ability to connect to others, to build positive relationships and to respond to the emotions of others. People with relationship management skills are good listeners and effective communicators. They treat others with compassion and respect and can influence others in positive ways.

Studies point to a positive relationship between high job performance and high emotional intelligence. Having high emotional intelligence is an important skill, especially for jobs in sales which require a high degree of social interaction. High emotional intelligence is also important for managers as they are responsible for influencing others, building positive attitudes and relationships in the organization.

Machiavellianism
A personality type which tends to deceive and manipulate others

Machiavellianism

Machiavellianism refers to a personality type that is a master manipulator. The term describes the extent to which individuals adhere to the political philosophy of Italian writer Niccolò Machiavelli, who advocated views involving cunning, deceit, and the notion that "means justify the ends."

Machiavellians (or "High Machs") are temperamentally predisposed to be calculating, conniving, and deceptive. They are essentially amoral and use other people as stepping stones to reach their goals. From a Machiavellian's perspective, if one allows themselves to be used, then they probably deserve it. P. T. Barnum expressed this sentiment as "There's a sucker born every minute."

Machiavellianism derives from the Italian philosopher Machiavelli who advocated cunning and deceit.

Everyone can all be deceitful at times, depending on the need or circumstances. If you've ever called in sick when you were well or lied to your spouse about what you were doing, you have demonstrated the human capacity to manipulate others. These instances probably do not reflect your standard behavior patterns, and you may have even felt a little guilty. But this type of behavior is the rule for Machiavellians.

In 1970, psychologists Richard Christie and Florence Geis introduced the first test of Machiavellianism. They describe "High Machs" as those with elevated scores on the Mach test. The test includes statements for people to agree or disagree with such as:

❏ "The best way to handle people is to tell them what they want to hear."

❏ "It is wise to flatter important people."

❏ "The biggest difference between most criminals and other people is that the criminals are stupid enough to get caught."

Groucho Marx once joked that "Sincerity is everything. If you can fake that, you've got it made." He was joking, but to a High Mach, this sounds like practical advice.

How can you spot a High Mach? Here are five traits to watch for:

1. They work best in jobs and social situations where the rules and limitations are ambiguous.

2. An emotional detachment and cynical outlook enable them to control their impulses and be careful, patient opportunists.

3. Their tactics include charm, friendliness, self-disclosure, guilt, and (if necessary) pressure.

4. They prefer to use subtle tactics (charm, friendliness, self-disclosure, guilt), when possible, to mask their true intentions and provide a basis for plausible denial if they are detected. However, they can use pressure and threats when necessary.

5. They tend to be preferred by others in competitive situations (debating, negotiations), but are *not* preferred as friends, colleagues, or spouses.

Values Attitudes and Behavior

Values are abstract ideals that guide a person's thinking and behavior. Values dictate life-long behavior patterns that are generally established by the time a person reaches their early teens. Values can be reshaped by significant life events, such as having a child or surviving the death of a loved one.

Values are abstract ideals. They are global beliefs and feelings that are directed toward objects, people or events. Values generally are consistent over time and across similar situations.

Managers who understand the values of employees are better suited to assign them to meaningful work projects and are better able to help avoid conflicts between work activities and personal values.

An attitude is a relatively enduring set of beliefs, feelings, and behavioral tendencies towards socially significant objects, groups, events, or symbols. It is a learned predisposition toward and a given object. It is important to understand the components of attitudes because attitudes directly influence individual behavior.

Attitudes can be described in terms of three components. This model is known as the **ABC model of attitudes**.[8]

Values
Global beliefs and feelings that are directed toward objects, people or events

Attitude
A learned predisposition towards and a given object

- **The Affective component**: this involves a person's feelings and emotions about a person, object or situation. For example: "I am afraid of spiders."
- **The Behavioral component**: this is the way that a person intends to act or behave. For example: "I will avoid spiders and scream if I see one."
- **The Cognitive component**: this involves a person's belief and knowledge about an object. For example: "I believe spiders are dangerous."

Figure 3 outlines the three components of attitudes.

FIGURE 3 THE THREE COMPONENTS OF ATTITUDE.

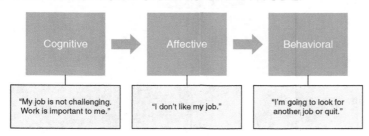

Source: Jeffrey Anderson

In 1957, psychologist Leon Festinger proposed the term cognitive dissonance to label the psychological discomfort that a person experiences when one's ideas, beliefs, or behaviors contradict each. Cognitive dissonance theory suggests that we have an inner drive to hold all our attitudes and behavior in harmony and avoid disharmony (or dissonance). When there is an inconsistency between attitudes or behaviors (dissonance), something must change to eliminate the dissonance. Exactly *how* we choose to resolve the dissonance (and its accompanying discomfort) is a good reflection of our mental health. In fact, cognitive dissonance can be a great opportunity for growth.

Values and attitudes are usually in harmony. Together, they influence people's behavior in the workplace.

Perception

Perception may be defined as the analysis of sensory information within the brain. It is the process we use to interpret and understand our environment. As we go through our day, we are surrounded by the rich stimuli of modern life and we rely heavily on our insight to apprise us of where we are placed within this world. Perception allows us to understand our surroundings and what they mean.

The perceptual process is complex but can be summarized in four steps as illustrated in Figure 4.

Perception
The analysis of sensory information within the brain

FIGURE 4 THE FOUR STEPS IN THE PERCEPTUAL PROCESS.

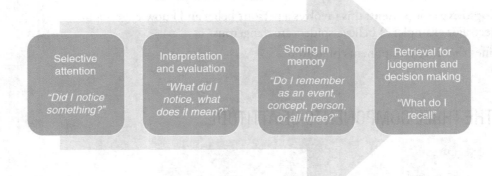

Selective attention

"Did I notice something?"

Interpretation and evaluation

"What did I notice, what does it mean?"

Storing in memory

"Do I remember as an event, concept, person, or all three?"

Retrieval for judgement and decision making

"What do I recall"

Source: Jeffrey Anderson

Perceptual process is the phenomena that explains how we group smaller objects into larger ones as part of the perceptual process. For example, flashing lights can create the illusion of movement. The principles of perceptual organization are much like heuristics, which are mental shortcuts for solving problems.

Let's consider four principles of the perceptual process.

Similarity. Stimuli that have common physical characteristics are more likely to be grouped together than those that do not. In the image at right, for example, you probably see the rows of black and white circles as rows rather than just a collection of dots.

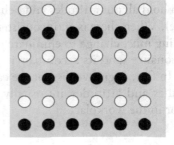

Figure-ground. People tend to perceive objects that stand against a background. Depending on your perception, you may see two silhouetted faces or a candlestick in the image at the left.

Proximity. Things that are near each other seem to be grouped together. In image at the right, the circles on the left appear to be part of one grouping while those on the right appear to be part of another. Because the objects are close to one another, we group them together.

Closure. Things are grouped together if they seem to complete some entity. Our brains habitually ignore contradictory information and fill in gaps in information. In the image at the left, you may see a triangle because your because your brain fills in the missing gaps in order to create a meaningful image.

Managers needn't be overly concerned about the theoretical steps in perception but should understand perception can be distorted as it has significant implications for their job. Perceptual errors can occur at any stage of the process and these errors can be damaging to individuals and their organization.

While there are other types of perceptual distortion we will consider the following: (1) selective perception, (2) stereotyping, (3) implicit bias, (4) the halo effect, (5) the recency effect, and (6) causal attributions. These perceptual errors form a screen that filters our responses to information we receive as outlined in Figure 5.

FIGURE 5 PERCEPTUAL DISTORTIONS IN COMMUNICATION.

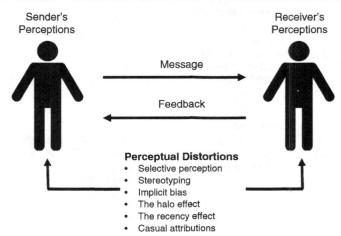

Selective perception
Tendency to focus on aspects of a situation or person that are consistent with and reinforce our existing beliefs and ignore those that are inconsistent with those beliefs

Stereotyping
The tendency to attribute characteristics of a group to an individual that belongs in that group

Selective perception is the tendency to focus on aspects of a situation or person that are consistent with and reinforce our existing beliefs and ignore those that are inconsistent with those beliefs. Selective perception is a defense mechanism that allows us to screen out information that is uncomfortable.

Here's an example of selective perception: You buy a new car, a cool hybrid that you love. As you drive it for the first few days and weeks, then you begin to notice similar hybrid cars everywhere you go. Question: Did all those people buy their hybrids the same day you did? Answer: Of course not. They were there all along—you just didn't notice them before because they weren't relevant to you. That particular car simply wasn't on your perceptual radar until you bought one.

Stereotyping is the tendency to attribute characteristics of a group to an individual that belongs in that group. Stereotypes are overgeneralizations where we infer that a person has a whole range of characteristics and abilities that we assume all members of that group have. For example, assuming that a tall African American male is skilled at basketball, or thinking that a Jewish person is motivated by money. These stereotypes can be positive or negative.

Figure 6 contrasts selective perception and stereotyping.

Researchers have found that stereotypes exist of different races, cultures, or ethnic groups. The most famous study of racial stereotyping was published by Katz and Braly when they reported the results of a questionnaire completed by students at Princeton University. The study found that most students held clear negative stereotypes; they viewed Jews as shrewd, Japanese as sly, African-Americans as lazy and Americans as hard-working. Not surprisingly, stereotypes favor the race of the beholder and belittle other races.[9]

FIGURE 6 SELECTIVE PERCEPTION AD STEREOTYPING.

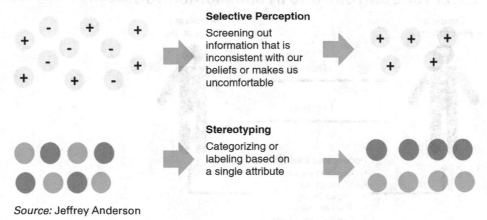

Selective Perception
Screening out information that is inconsistent with our beliefs or makes us uncomfortable

Stereotyping
Categorizing or labeling based on a single attribute

Source: Jeffrey Anderson

Sex-role stereotypes are beliefs in differing traits and abilities for men and women that make them more suitable for different roles. For example, women sometimes are not perceived as effective leaders compared to makes. Age stereotypes include the belief that older workers are less motivated and more resistant to change. Race and ethnic stereotypes are reflected in racial discrimination with regard to hiring.

The halo effect is an impression that is formed based on a single trait. For example, some may have the impression that an overweight person is lazy, incompetent, and lacks discipline. The halo effect can be reflected with both positive and negative traits. In the workplace, this bias is most likely to show up on a performance appraisal. For example, if an associate comes off as negative to the manager, he or she could receive a poor review because the manager may see everything they do as negative, even if they actually have a lot of job knowledge and skill.

The recency effect is the tendency to remember recent information more than earlier information. This misperception can be seen with investors who are more likely to buy a stock if they see something recent in the news.

Causal attribution is the process of trying to determine the causes of people's behavior. Correctly or incorrectly, we constantly create cause-and-effect explanations for our behavior and the behaviors of others. For example, we might say that "Bill drinks too much because he lacks willpower, but I need a couple of drinks after work because I am under a lot of pressure."

Even if causal attributions are self-serving and incorrect, it's important to understand how people make these attributions as they are a significant influence on behavior at work. For example, a manager may think that an employee's poor performance is due to laziness and reprimand that person. Whereas another manager may attribute the same poor performance to a lack of ability and schedule training.

Managers should understand two attributional tendencies that can distort one's interpretation of observed behavior. These are the fundamental attribution error and the self-serving bias.

The fundamental attribution error describes the tendency to overestimate the effect of personality and underestimate the effect of the situation in explaining a person's behavior." In other words: When we see someone doing something, we tend to think it relates to their personality rather than the situation the person might be in. For example, if someone cuts in front of you in traffic, your immediate reaction is, "This person is a complete jerk!" But in reality, maybe he never cuts into traffic and is doing it this time only because he late to the airport to fly to see his great aunt, who is ill. Consider the person who doesn't return your call, you may think that his is inconsiderate but maybe he is going through personal issues.

The self-serving bias describes the tendency of people to attribute positive events to their own character but attribute negative events to external factors. With the self-serving bias, people tend to take more responsibility for success than failure. For example, a star quarterback credits the hard work of his team after a victory. The next week, after a loss, he says "It just wasn't our night. This is a common cognitive bias that has been extensively studied in social psychology.[10]

Figure 7 contrasts the fundamental attribution error and the self-serving bias.

Halo effect
An impression that is formed based on a single trait

Recency effect
The tendency to remember recent information more than earlier information

Causal attribution
The process of trying to determine the causes of people's behavior

Fundamental attribution error
The tendency to overestimate the effect of personality and underestimate the effect of the situation in explaining a person's behavior

Self-serving bias
The tendency of people to attribute positive events to their own character but attribute negative events to external factors

FIGURE 7 COMPARING THE FUNDAMENTAL ATTRIBUTION ERROR AND SELF-SERVING BIAS.

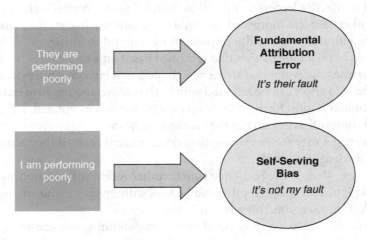

Source: Jeffrey Anderson

Self-fulfilling prophecy

A self-fulfilling prophecy is a belief that comes true because one acts as if it is already true. Also called the Pygmalion effect, it is the phenomena that people's expectations lead them to behave in ways that makes the expectation come true. The expectation that one will see a particular outcome changes their behavior, which shapes the way others see them. In turn, others provide the feedback the individual is expecting up to get, which serves to reinforce their original belief.

For example, let's say that I'm going to a party where I don't know many people. If I believe I don't make a good first impression, or I worry that nobody will talk to me, I will probably enter the party acting awkward, anxious, and standoffish. In turn, people are likely to interact with me with less enthusiasm, or they may ignore or shun me. This serves to reinforce my belief that I'm not good with people I don't know. If, instead I enter the party believing that I'm good at interacting with people I don't then I'm likely to be outgoing, engaging, and less likely to take a cold shoulder personally. As a result, people will likely respond pleasantly to my friendliness and I may indeed make new friends.[11]

The lesson for managers is that if you expect employees to perform poorly, they likely will. When you expect them to perform well they also likely will. Managerial expectations can have a powerful influence on employee behavior and performance. Effective managers recognize that everyone has the potential to increase their performance. Helping employees visualize their success can help them master key skills.[12]

Job Satisfaction

Job satisfaction is an attitude that reflects the extent to which an individual feels positively about a job and work experiences. People hold attitudes about many things in the workplace including their supervisor, organizational policies, performance goals, pay and more. Job satisfaction is a comprehensive term that encompasses those attitudes.

Most organizations strive for employee satisfaction, but not all reach this goal. That's why it's important for managers to know more about the factors that can increase employee satisfaction, and how job satisfaction can increase an organization's overall success.

Job satisfaction takes more than just good pay and benefits. Here are some of the key job satisfaction aspects cited by employees in a 2016 study from the Society for Human Resource Management (SHRM):[13]

Employees who are satisfied with their jobs are generally more productive than those who are dissatisfied.

- ❐ **Respect**—Employees rate respectful treatment of all employees as the single most important factor in job satisfaction.

- ❐ **Trust**—Possibly because of the workplace uncertainty in the years following the Great Recession, employees indicated that trust between themselves and senior management was an extremely important satisfaction factor.

- ❐ **Security**—Employees who go to work each day wondering whether your job is secure face a great deal of anxiety. Organizations can provide a sense of security by communicating honestly and being transparent about the organization's health and long-term viability.

- ❐ **Healthy Environment**—Workplaces that are free from stress, morale issues, harassment, and discriminatory practices create a positive and healthy environment for all employees.

- ❐ **Career Path**—Employees are more likely to excel when they can see an upward track, with the opportunity to earn higher pay and take on greater responsibilities.

- ❐ **Pay and Benefits**—While good pay isn't the only reason employees find satisfaction in their jobs, it does rank high on the list. Competitive pay generally makes employees feel valued, and gives them less reason to look for other work.

It's well known that talented employees are an organization's greatest resource. Keeping workers happy provides many positive outcomes including:

- ❐ **Lower Turnover**—Turnover can be a significant cost to the organization. Retaining employees helps to create a better work environment, and makes it easier to recruit new employees. Satisfied employees are typically much less likely to leave.

- ❐ **Higher Productivity**—Regardless of job title and pay grade, employees who report high job satisfaction tend to perform with higher productivity.

- ❐ **Increased Profits**—Safe and happy employees can lead to higher sales, lower costs, and a stronger profit margin.

- ❐ **Loyalty**—When employees feel that the organization has their best interests at heart, they generally support its mission and work harder to help achieve its objectives. They are also more likely to tell their friends, which helps spread goodwill.

Organizational commitment

Organizational commitment
Psychological attachment that an employee has with their organization

Organizational commitment is a psychological attachment that an employee has with their organization. Organizational commitment plays a big role in establishing the bond that an employee shares with the organization. It also helps in determining the value of an employee to an organization. Employees with higher organizational commitment are generally more productive and proactive in their jobs.[14]

Researchers John Meyer and Natalie Allen developed a Three Component Model of Commitment. The model explains that commitment to an organization is a psychological state, that has three distinct components which affect how employees feel about their organization. Figure 8 outlines these three components:[15]

1. **Affective commitment** refers to an employee's positive emotional attachment to the organization. Individuals with a high affective commitment strongly identify with the goals of the organization. They are committed to the organization because they "want to belong."

2. **Continuance commitment** is an employee's commitment to an organization due to the fact that one calculates the cost of losing organizational membership. These considerations include economic costs (for example, pension accruals) and social costs (relationships and friendships with colleagues that might end) as well. Individuals feel that they "have to" commit to the organization. The severity of this commitment often increases with age and experience. People are more likely to experience continuance commitment if they're in an established, successful role, or if they've had several promotions within one organization.

3. **Normative commitment** is an individual's commitment to an organization they feel obligated. These feelings might occur if the organization has invested resources when employing the person (trainings, courses, etc.). These investments make the employee feel obliged to put considerable effort into the job and stay with the organization in order to "repay the debt." This type of obligation can also result from one's upbringing. For instance, your family might have stressed

FIGURE 8 THREE COMPONENTS OF ORGANIZATIONAL COMMITMENT.

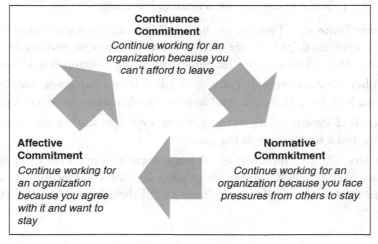

Source: Jeffrey Anderson

that you should stay loyal to your organization. In this case, employees stay with an organization because "it's the right thing to do."

Job Satisfaction Influences Work Behaviors

Researchers identify a link between job satisfaction and organizational citizenship behaviors (OCB). Organizational citizenship behaviors are the things that people do to go "above and beyond the call of duty." A person who is a good organizational citizen will do things that, while not required, advance the organization's performance. This might include extra service for a customer or working late to meet a deadline. Organizational citizenship behaviors are voluntary and not part of a person's job.

Organizations need people who will do more than is required and companies that have these types of employees outperform those which don't. But the drawback of OCB occurs when employees experience work overload, stress, and work-life conflicts.[16]

Job satisfaction is also linked to employee engagement. Organizations want employees who are connected to, satisfied with, and enthusiastic about their jobs. Employee engagement is a strong sense of belonging and connection to one's work and employer. When employees are engaged, they are passionate about their work. Disengaged employees have "checked out" and are indifferent to their jobs. They show up late for work and have no energy or passion.

Employee engagement
A strong sense of belonging and connection to one's work and employer

A number of benefits result from having highly engaged employees. Engaged employees are two and a half times more likely to be top performers. Highly engaged employees result in higher employee retention which keeps recruiting and training costs low. Both of these outcomes contribute to high organizational performance.[17]

A survey of American workers by the Gallup Organization suggests that the things that counted most in employee engagement was the belief that one has the opportunity to do their best every day. Also high on the list were the belief that one's opinions are valued, believing that fellow workers are committed to quality and the belief that there is a direct link between one's work and the organization's mission.[18]

Diversity and Inclusion

Diversity can be defined as the range of human differences, including but not limited to race, ethnicity, gender, gender identity, sexual orientation, age, social class, physical ability or attributes, religious or ethical values system, national origin, and political beliefs. Workplace diversity includes both employees and customers.

Diversity
The range of human differences, including but not limited to race, ethnicity, gender, gender identity, sexual orientation, age, social class, physical ability or attributes, religious or ethical values system, national origin, and political beliefs

To help distinguish the ways in which people differ, diversity experts Lee Gardenswartz and Anita Rowe have identified a "diversity wheel" which is pictured in Figure 9. The wheel depicts four diversity layers: (1) personality, (2) internal dimensions, (3) external dimensions, and (4) organizational dimensions.[19]

Internal dimensions are those differences that exert a powerful, sustained effect throughout each stage of a person's life and include gender, age, ethnicity, race, sexual orientation, and physical abilities. These are considered primary dimensions of diversity because they are, for the most part, out of one's control. These dimensions strongly influence our attitudes and assumptions about others which influence our behavior.

Diversity refers to the variety of people with different group identities in the workplace.

FIGURE 9 THE DIVERSITY WHEEL.

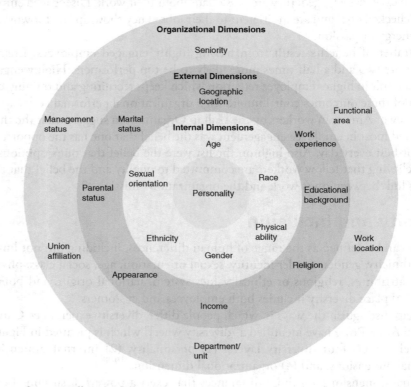

Source: Jeffrey Anderson

External dimensions include some element of choice. These are personal characteristics that people acquire, discard, and modify throughout their lives. External dimensions include educational background, marital status, appearance, income, geographic location, work experience, and religion. These dimensions are secondary as we are much more able to influence them than internal dimensions.

Finally, organizational dimensions include work-related classifications such as position, union affiliation, work location, and division or department.

Inclusion is involvement and empowerment, where the inherent worth and dignity of all people are recognized. An inclusive organization promotes and sustains a sense of belonging; it values and practices respect for the talents, beliefs, backgrounds, and ways of living of its members.[20]

Industry leaders are recognizing that increase diversity and inclusion are a crucial remaining competitive. In a PWC's survey of 410 financial services CEOs, almost 80% said that encouraging greater diversity and inclusion was a critical component of organizational success.

But why does diversity and inclusion matter? Simply put, it's good for business. A 2015 McKinsey study found that there is a direct, linear relationship between racial and ethnic diversity and better financial performance. Companies in the top quartile for gender diversity are 15% more likely to have profits above industry average, and those with racial and ethnic diversity are 35% more likely to have higher profits.[21]

So, much like the evolution of socially responsible investing, what started as simply the right thing to do has evolved into providing better returns, and is becoming a baseline for today's top companies.

Barriers to Diversity

When we speak of barriers to diversity, we are referring to people in the organization, those people who are resistant to making the organization more diverse. Resistance to change is an issue that most managers face. Resistance to diversity is one variation of that resistance to change. Here are six ways that resistance to diversity may be expressed:[22]

1. **Stereotypes and Prejudices.** Ethnocentrism is the belief that one's own culture is superior to another. When differences are viewed as a weakness this may be expressed as a concern that diversity in hiring will sacrifice quality.

2. **Fear of Discrimination against Majority Members.** Some employees may fear that diversity is achieved at the expense of the majority group. Reverse discrimination is the notion that minorities are favored at the expense of the majority.

3. **Resistance to Diversity Programs.** Some companies including PepsiCo., IBM, and Deloitte & Touche have aggressive diversity programs and offer special classes on how to get along. Some employees may see those programs as distracting and they may be resentful if those programs are reinforced through the organization's performance review system.

4. **A Negative Diversity Climate.** The diversity climate is viewed as positive when view the organization as being fair to all employees. The diversity climate is negative when employees perceive that harassment and discrimination are tolerated.

5. **Lack of Support for Family Demands.** More and more, women are moving between participating in the workforce and being stay at home mothers. When organizations aren't' supportive in offering flexible hours, these women may find it difficult to work evenings, or take business trips.

6. **A Hostile Work Environment for Diverse Employees.** Hostile work environments are characterized by sexual, racial, and age harassment and potentially are in violation of the Civil Rights Act. Whether directed against women, men, older individuals or LGBTQ people, hostile work environments are demeaning and unethical.

Trends in diversity

How will the workforce become more diverse in the twenty-first century? Let's consider five categories of internal dimensions.

1. **Age.** The workforce will be older people in the workforce. In the United States, workers of age 55 and older are expected to take more 25% of the labor force by 2024.
2. **Gender.** Numbers of women in the workforce will continue to increase. Women are expected to account for 47% of the labor force by 2024.
3. **Race and ethnicity.** There will be more people of color in the workforce. The non-Hispanic while population is projected to peak by 2024 and then decrease thereafter.
4. **Sexual orientation.** LGBTQ people will become more visible. Americans have become more tolerant of differences in sexual orientation.
5. **Physical abilities.** About 20% of the workforce have a physical or mental disability.

It is estimated that workplace stress causes $190 billion in health care costs each year.

Stress
A state of tension experienced by people who face situations that require change or some type of response

Stress

Stress is a state of tension experienced by people who face situations that require change or some type of response. It is the body's reaction to any change that requires some adjustment or response. People can react to stressful changes with physical, mental, and emotional responses. Stress is a normal part of our lives and we can experience stress from our environment. Even positive changes such as buying a new home, the birth of a child, or a promotion can cause stress.

Workplace stress is the harmful physical and emotional response that can occur when there is conflict between and employee's job demands and his or her amount of control over meeting these demands. Generally, the combination of high job demands and a low amount of control over the situation can lead to stress.

Secretaries, waitresses, middle managers, police officers, editors, and medical interns are some of the most stressful occupations as they require the jobholder to respond to the demands and timetables of others, with little control over events. Complaints of too much responsibility and too little authority, unfair labor practices and inadequate job descriptions are common complaints in these jobs. Employees can respond to these pressures through workers' unions or other organizations, grievance, or personnel offices or, more commonly, by direct negotiations with their immediate supervisors.[23]

Stress in the workplace can originate from many sources or come from just one single event. Workplace stress can impact employees and employers alike. In general, it is believed that some stress is okay (sometimes referred to as "challenge" or "positive stress") but when stress occurs in amounts that a person can't handle, both mental and physical changes may occur.[24]

Continuing stress can wear down the body's natural defenses, which leads to a variety of physical symptoms. These symptoms are outlined in Table 4:[25]

TABLE 4 PHYSICAL SYMPTOMS OF STRESS.

Physical Symptoms of Stress	
❏ Dizziness or a general sense of "being out of it"	❏ Sleep problems
❏ General aches and pains	❏ Elevated heart rate
❏ Grinding teeth, clenched jaw	❏ Cold and sweaty palms
❏ Headaches	❏ Tiredness, exhaustion
❏ Indigestion or acid reflux symptoms	❏ Trembling/shaking
❏ Changes in appetite	❏ Changes in weight
❏ Muscle tension in neck, face, or shoulders	❏ Upset stomach, diarrhea
	❏ Sexual difficulties

Some of the factors that can cause workplace stress include work hours, management style, and interpersonal relationships. To combat stress in the workplace, employers should assess their employees to determine the common stressors and work toward mitigating stressful elements of the workplace.[26]

Type A and Type B behavior is a theory of personality that describes two ends of a spectrum of personality which is linked to stress levels. Individuals often have elements of both personalities. The theory was developed from work by cardiologists Freidman and Rosenman.

Type A behavior is demonstrated by being ambitious, organized, impatient, and a desire to be punctual. People with a Type A personality can be irritable. They are hard workers and career orientated.

Type B behavior is basically the opposite from Type A. Type B personalities are relaxed, not competitive, and generally not as ambitious as their Type A counterparts.

Individuals with a Type B personality are less likely to experience high levels of stress and generally score lower on stress levels measurement. This is because they don't experience the urgency and competitive pressure that someone who is Type A will feel.[27]

Burnout is a state of chronic stress that leads to physical and emotional exhaustion, cynicism, and detachment, feelings of ineffectiveness, and lack of accomplishment.

Excessive workplace stress causes an astounding 120,000 deaths and results in almost $190 billion in healthcare costs each year. This accounts for 5–8% of national healthcare spending, which is derived primarily from high demands at work ($48 billion), lack of insurance ($40 billion), and work–family conflict ($24 billion).[28]

Many employers recognize that they have a duty to ensure that employees do not become ill and an economic interest to prevent stress, as stress is likely to lead to high staff turnover, an increase in satisfaction.

Some general organizational strategies for reducing stress include:

❏ Employee assistance programs aimed at helping employees cope with stress

❏ Holistic wellness programs that include nutritional awareness, relaxation techniques, and physical fitness

Burnout
A state of chronic stress that leads to physical and emotional exhaustion, cynicism and detachment and feelings of ineffectiveness and lack of accomplishment

- Creating a supportive environment with a personal and supportive management style
- Making jobs interesting
- Making career counseling available

Summary of Learning Outcomes and Key Points

- **Describe the various personality theories and core self-evaluations that affect behavior in the workplace**

An individual's personality is the unique combination of their emotional, thought, and behavior patterns. There are two personality theories that attempt to classify personality traits. (1) The MBTI suggests that individuals have a preference in four categories; extraversion or introversion (E or I), sensing or intuition (S or N), thinking or feeling (T or F), and judging or perceiving (J or P). The big five personality factors identify five traits; Openness, Agreeableness, Conscientiousness, Extroversion and Neuroticism. Each trait represents a continuum of behavior and preferences.

Core self-evaluations represent four broad positive traits; (1) self-esteem, (2) self-efficacy, (3) locus of control, and (4) emotional stability. Self-esteem is the extent to which people like or dislike themselves. Self-efficacy is the belief in one's own personal ability to perform a task. Locus of control indicates who much people believe that they can control their own outcomes through their own efforts. Emotional stability concerns how secure or insecure one is when experiencing pressure.

- **Understand emotional intelligence and other personality characteristics**

Emotional intelligence is the ability to monitor yours' and others' feelings and use this information to guide your thinking and actions. Emotional intelligence includes self-awareness, self-management, social awareness, and relationship management.

Other personality characteristics include Machiavellianism, which is one's desire to manipulate others.

- **Discuss individual values and attitudes**

Values are abstract ideals that guide a person's thinking and behavior. They are global beliefs and feelings that are directed toward objects, people, or events. Values generally are consistent over time and across similar situations.

An attitude is a relatively enduring set of beliefs, feelings, and behavioral tendencies toward socially significant objects, groups, events, or symbols. It is a learned predisposition toward and a given object.

Attitudes can be described in terms of three components; the affective component involves a person's feelings and emotions. The behavioral component is the way that intend to act or behave and the cognitive component: involves a person's belief and knowledge about an object.

❏ **Describe the perceptual process and perceptual biases**

Perception may be defined as the analysis of sensory information within the brain. It is the process we use to interpret and understand our environment. The perceptual process is the phenomena that explains how we group smaller objects into larger ones as part of the perceptual process. The chapter presented four examples; similarity, figure-ground, proximity, and closure.

While there are other types of perceptual distortion we will consider the following: (1) selective perception, (2) stereotyping, (3) implicit bias, (4) the halo effect, (5) the recency effect, and (6) causal attributions.

Selective perception is the tendency to focus on aspects of a situation or person that are consistent with and reinforce our existing beliefs and ignore those that are inconsistent with those beliefs.

Stereotyping is the tendency to attribute characteristics of a group to an individual that belongs in that group. Implicit bias is the attitudes or beliefs that affect our understanding.

The halo effect is an impression that is formed based on a single trait.

The recency effect is the tendency to remember recent information more than earlier information.

The fundamental attribution error describes the tendency to overestimate the effect of personality and underestimate the effect of the situation in explaining a person's behavior. The self-serving bias describes the tendency of people to attribute positive events to their own character but attribute negative events to external factors.

A self-fulfilling prophecy is a belief that comes true because one acts as if it is already true.

❏ **Explain the value of diversity to modern organizations**

Diversity is the range of human differences, including but not limited to race, ethnicity, gender, gender identity, sexual orientation, age, social class, physical ability or attributes, religious or ethical values system, national origin, and political beliefs. The diversity wheel depicts four diversity layers: (1) personality, (2) internal dimensions, (3) external dimensions, and (4) organizational dimensions. Research has shown a direct, linear relationship between racial and ethnic diversity and better financial performance.

❏ **Discuss the impact of stress in the workplace**

Stress is a state of tension experienced by people who face situations that require change or some type of response. Workplace stress is the harmful physical and emotional response that can occur when there is conflict between and employee's job demands and his or her amount of control over meeting these demands. Excessive workplace stress causes an astounding 120,000 deaths and results in almost $190 billion in healthcare costs each year. Many employers recognize that they have a duty to ensure that employees do not become ill and an economic interest to prevent stress, as stress is likely to lead to high staff turnover, an increase in satisfaction.

Questions for Review

1. What are some of the different dimensions of personality?
2. How can emotional intelligence help you cope with difficult situations?
3. What are the benefits of a diversity in the workplace?
4. How does the perceptual process influence communication with others?

End Notes

1. Robbins, S. and Coulter, M., Management, 13th edition, Pearson, Boston, MA, 2016, p. 437.

2. Ibid, p. 438–439.

3. https://positivepsychologyprogram.com/big-five-personality-theory/, retrieved 9/19/18.

4. http://www.apa.org/pi/aids/resources/education/self-efficacy.aspx, retrieved 9/23/18.

5. https://www.mayoclinic.org/healthy-lifestyle/adult-health/in-depth/self-esteem/art-20047976, retrieved 9/24/18.

6. Kinicki, A. and Williams, B., Management, A Practical Introduction, 8th edition, McGraw-Hill, New York, NY, 2018, p. 359.

7. Daft, R. and Marcic, D., Understanding Management, 10th edition.

8. https://www.simplypsychology.org/attitudes.html, retrieved 9/24/18.

9. https://www.simplypsychology.org/katz-braly.html, retrieved 9/29/18.

10. https://psychcentral.com/encyclopedia/self-serving-bias/, retrieved 9/27/18.

11. https://www.psychologytoday.com/us/blog/psychology-writers/201210/using-self-fulfilling-prophecies-your-advantage, retrieved 9/24/18.

12. Kinicki, A. and Williams, B., Management, A Practical Introduction, 8th edition, McGraw-Hill, New York, NY, 2018, p. 372.

13. https://www.villanovau.com/resources/hr/importance-of-job-satisfaction-in-the-workplace/#.W6kNt_YpDb0, retrieved 9/124/18.

14. https://www.mbaskool.com/business-concepts/human-resources-hr-terms/15453-organizational-commitment.html, retrieved 9/24/18.

15. https://www.mindtools.com/pages/article/three-component-model-commitment.htm retrieved 9/24/18.

16. Schermerhorn, J. and Bachrach, D., Exploring Mangement, 6th edition, Wiley, New York, NY, 2018, p. 231.

17. Robbins, S. and Coulter, M., Management, 13th edition, Pearson, Boston, MA, 2016, p. 434.

18. Schermerhorn, J. and Bachrach, D., Exploring Mangement, 6th edition, Wiley, New York, NY, 2018, p. 231.

19. Kinicki, A. and Williams, B., Management, A Practical Introduction, 8th edition, McGraw-Hill, New York, NY, 2018, p. 378–379

20. https://ferris.edu/HTMLS/administration/president/DiversityOffice/Definitions.htm, retrieved 9/24/18

21. http://www.investmentnews.com/article/20180922/FREE/180929973/making-diversity-intentional-is-first-step-to-boosting-inclusion, retrieved 9/14/18

22. Kinicki, A. and Williams, B., Management, A Practical Introduction, 8th edition, McGraw-Hill, New York, NY, 2018, p;. 382

23. http://www.apa.org/helpcenter/workplace-stress.aspx, retrieved 9/27/18

24. https://www.ccohs.ca/oshanswers/psychosocial/stress.html, retrieved 9/27/18

25. https://my.clevelandclinic.org/health/articles/11874-stress, Retrieved 9/27/18

26. https://www.safetyandhealthmagazine.com/articles/stress-in-the-workplace-2, retrieved 9/27/18

27. https://www.tutor2u.net/psychology/reference/type-a-and-type-b-behaviour, retrieved 9/29/18

28. http://workplacementalhealth.org/Mental-Health-Topics/Workplace-Stress, retrieved 9/27/18

Key Terms

Content theories	Instrumentality	Negative reinforcement
Continuous reinforcement	Intermittent reinforcement	Outputs
Distributive justice	Interval reinforcement	Physiological needs
Esteem needs	Intrinsic rewards	Positive reinforcement
Expectancy	Job enlargement	Procedural justice
Extinction	Job enrichment	Punishment
Extrinsic rewards	Job rotation	Safety needs
Flexible working hours	Motivation	Self-actualization needs
Hygiene factors	Motivators	Social needs
Inputs	Need	Valence

Introduction

In their role as leaders, managers must motivate individuals to perform those actions that are necessary for the organization to reach its goals. In this chapter, we will explore three different perspectives on motivation. First, we will examine content theories of motivation that includes Maslow's hierarchy of needs, Alderfer's ERG theory, and McClelland's learned needs theory. Next, we will explore the process theories that examine the thought processes behind motivation including Equity Theory, Expectancy Theory and Goal Setting Theory. Then we will discuss how reinforcement theory is used as a tool to modify behavior. Finally, we will examine job design and the use of compensation as a motivational tool.

Learning Outcomes

After reading this chapter, you should be able to:

- ❏ Define motivation and explain the difference between intrinsic and extrinsic rewards
- ❏ Identify and describe the various content theories of motivation
- ❏ Identify and describe the various process theories of motivation
- ❏ Describe reinforcement theory and how it can be used to motivate employees
- ❏ Discuss major approaches to job design and its influence on motivation
- ❏ Describe various approached to motivating employees through compensation

© ajt/Shutterstock.com

Extrinsic rewards are provided by others.

Motivation

Motivation may be defined as the psychological processes that stimulate and direct goal-directed behavior. It is imperative that managers understand the processes of motivation so that they are able to guide employees toward accomplishing organizational goals.[1]

Employee motivation affects productivity and understanding motivation is an important component of leading and influencing others.

Rewards

Motivation The psychological processes that stimulate and direct goal-directed behavior

Extrinsic rewards Tangible rewards given to employees by managers, and include pay raises, bonuses, and benefits.

Intrinsic rewards The psychological rewards that employees get from performing important work and doing it well.

Extrinsic rewards are the tangible rewards given to employees by managers, and include pay raises, bonuses, and benefits. They are called "extrinsic" because they are external to the work itself and granted (or not) by others. Intrinsic rewards, by contrast, are the psychological rewards that employees get from performing important work and doing it well. Intrinsic rewards include personal achievement, a sense of pleasure and personal accomplishments. Extrinsic rewards are as significant as pay is an important consideration for most workers and unfair pay can be strong demotivator. However, day-to-day motivation is more strongly driven by intrinsic rewards.[2]

"The reward of a thing well done is to have done it."

—Ralph Waldo Emerson

© Prostock-studio/Shutterstock.com

Intrinsic rewards are internal, such as the feeling of satisfaction that comes doing a good job.

Content Perspectives on Motivation

Content theories Motivation theories that emphasize the needs that motivate people.

Need A physiological or psychological deficiency that arouses behavior

Content theories, also known as need-based perspectives, emphasize the needs that motivate people. Content theories ask the question, "what kind of needs motivate employees in the workplace"? A Need may be defined as a physiological or psychological deficiency that arouses behavior.[3] In addition to McGregor's Theory X/Theory Y (see Chapter 1), content perspectives include the following theories:

- ❏ Maslow's hierarchy of needs theory
- ❏ Alderfer's ERG theory
- ❏ McClelland's acquired needs theory
- ❏ Herzberg's two-factor theory

Maslow's Hierarchy of Needs

Perhaps the most famous content theory was developed by Abraham Maslow. Maslow's **hierarchy of needs** theory proposes that people are motivated by multiple needs that they seek to fulfill in a hierarchical order. Maslow identified five general types of needs, listed here from the most basic to the highest level.[4] These five levels of needs are illustrated in Figure 1.

1. **Physiological needs.** These are the most fundamental human physical needs and include food, water, and oxygen.
2. **Safety needs.** These needs include a safe and protected physical and emotional environment and freedom from threats.
3. **Social needs.** These needs reflect the desire to be accepted by one's peers, to have friendships, be part of a group and be loved by others.
4. **Esteem needs.** These needs reflect the individual's desire for a positive self-image and to receive attention, recognition, appreciation, and respect from others.
5. **Self-actualization needs.** These needs include the need for self-fulfillment. They represent the need to develop one's full potential.

FIGURE 1 MASLOW'S HIERARCHY OF NEEDS.

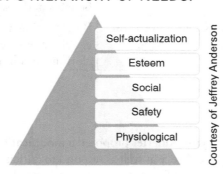

Courtesy of Jeffrey Anderson

According to Maslow's theory, people seek to satisfy their needs in a sequence. Lower-level needs take priority and must be satisfied before higher-level needs cause arousal. A person who has physiological needs will seek to satisfy those needs before satisfying safety needs and so on. In this progression principle, people seek to satisfy lower-level needs first. Once a lower-level need is satisfied, it is no longer a motivator and the next higher-level need is activated.

Although Maslow's theory identifies that needs that are likely to be important sources of motivation, research does not support Maslow's contention that there is a need hierarchy or his notion that people are only motivated by one need at a time. Nonetheless, a key conclusion may be drawn from the theory; people try to satisfy different needs at work. To have motivated employees, managers must determine which needs employees are seeking to satisfy and make sure that people receive outcomes that satisfy those needs. By doing so, managers align the interests of individual employees with the interests of the organization. By doing what is good for the organization, employees receive outcomes that satisfy their individual needs.[5] Table 1 provides some examples of how managers can satisfy the various needs of employees in the workplace.

TABLE 1 MASLOW'S HIERARCHY OF NEEDS.

	Needs	Description	Examples of How Managers Can Help Employees Satisfy These Needs at Work
Highest-level needs	Self-Actualization	The need to realize one's full potential	By providing opportunities for people to use their skills and abilities to the fullest extent possible
	Esteem needs	The need to be respected by others and to receive recognition and appreciation	By granting promotions and recognizing accomplishments
Lowest-level needs	Social needs	Need for social interactions, friendship, love and affection	By promoting good interpersonal relationships and social interactions such as company picnics and holiday parties
	Safety needs	Needs for security, stability and safety	By providing job security, medical benefits and a safe workplace
	Physiological needs	Basic human survival needs for things such as food, water, shelter	By providing a level of pay that enables employees to buy food, clothing and housing

ERG Theory

American psychologist Clayton Alderfer proposed a modification to Maslow's hierarchy in an attempt to simplify the theory as well as respond to criticism of its lack of empirical evidence. His ERG theory identified three categories of needs[6]:

1. **Existence needs**. The need for physical well-being
2. **Relatedness needs**. The need for satisfactory interpersonal relationships
3. **Growth needs**. Needs that focus on the desire for personal growth and increased competence

Like Maslow's theory, the ERG model is hierarchical. Existence needs have priority over relatedness needs which have priority over growth needs. Unlike Maslow's model, ERG theory allows for different needs to be pursued simultaneously. ERG theory acknowledges that if a higher need remains unfulfilled, a person may regress to lower-level needs which are easier to satisfy. This is known as the frustration–regression principle.[7] Figure 2 compares ERG theory to Maslow's hierarchy.

Maslow's theory is better known to American managers than Alderfer's, but ERG theory has more scientific support. Both are valuable as they remind managers of the types of reinforcers or rewards that can be used to motivate employees. Regardless of whether a manager prefers Maslow or Alderfer theory, he or she can motivate employees by helping satisfy their needs, particularly by providing opportunities for self-actualization and growth.[8]

FIGURE 2 ALDERFER'S ERG THEORY ALIGNED WITH MASLOW'S HIERARCHY OF NEEDS.

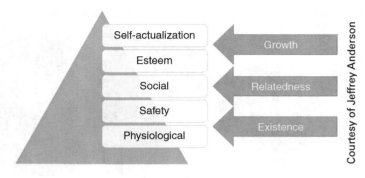

Acquired Needs

Building on Maslow's work, David McClelland identified three motivators that he believed we all have; a need for power, a need for affiliation, and a need for achievement. According to his Acquired Needs Theory, people will have different characteristics, depending on their dominant need. This dominant need is largely dependent on our culture and life experiences. Here are the characteristics of the three needs:

Need for Achievement (nAch)

- ❐ Has a strong need to set and achieve challenging goals
- ❐ Takes calculated risks to realize goals
- ❐ Likes to have feedback on progress and accomplishments
- ❐ Often likes to work alone

Need for Affiliation (nAff)

- ❐ Wants to belong to the group
- ❐ Wants to be liked and will often go along with the group
- ❐ Prefers collaboration to competition
- ❐ Doesn't like risk and uncertainty

Need for Power (nPow)

- ❐ Wants to influence and control others
- ❐ Likes to win arguments
- ❐ Enjoys competition and likes to win
- ❐ Enjoys status and recognition

McClelland believed that these motivators are not inherent; we develop them through our culture and life experiences. Achievers like to solve problems and realize goals. Those with a high need for affiliation don't like to stand out or take risk, and they value relationships above anything else. People with a strong power motivator like to control others and be in charge. Managers can use this knowledge to lead, praise, and motivate their team more effectively, and to better structure team member roles.[9] Figure 3 shows different levels or intensities of the three needs.

FIGURE 3 MCCLELLAND'S THREE NEEDS.

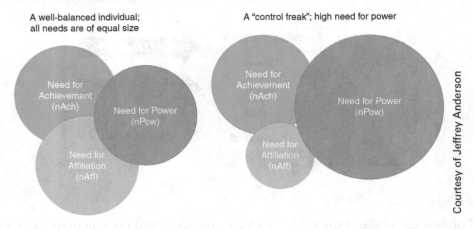

A well-balanced individual; all needs are of equal size

A "control freak"; high need for power

Courtesy of Jeffrey Anderson

Motivators Factors that provide positive satisfaction, arising from intrinsic conditions of the job itself

Hygiene factors Factors that do not provide satisfaction or motivation though dissatisfaction results from their absence

Herzberg's Two Factor Theory

In order to better understand employee attitudes and motivation, Frederick Herzberg interviewed employees and asked what pleased and displeased them. His research found that the factors that caused job satisfaction (and presumably motivation) were different from those caused job dissatisfaction. He developed the motivation-hygiene theory to explain these results. He called the satisfiers motivators and the dissatisfiers hygiene factors, He used the term "hygiene" as these are considered maintenance factors that are needed to avoid dissatisfaction but that by themselves do not cause satisfaction.

The factors that govern whether there is dissatisfaction or no dissatisfaction are not part of the work itself, but rather, are external factors. These are factors that provide extrinsic rewards to meet lower-level needs. Motivators are intrinsic, because the motivation comes from the work itself rather than carrot and stick incentives.

Table 2 presents the leading factors causing dissatisfaction and dissatisfaction.

TABLE 2 HERZBERG'S HYGIENE AND MOTIVATOR FACTORS.

Hygiene Factors	Motivator Factors
❑ Salaries, wages, & other benefits	❑ Sense of personal achievement
❑ Company policies	❑ Status
❑ Good interpersonal relationships	❑ Recognition
❑ Quality of supervision	❑ Challenging/stimulating work
❑ Job security	❑ Responsibility
❑ Working conditions	❑ Opportunity for advancement
❑ Work–life balance	❑ Promotion
	❑ Growth
When in Place, These Factors Result in...	**When in Place, These Factors Result in...**
❑ General satisfaction	❑ High motivation
❑ Prevention of dissatisfaction	❑ Hi satisfaction
	❑ Strong commitment

Herzberg reasoned that because the factors causing satisfaction are different from those causing dissatisfaction, the two emotional states cannot simply be treated as opposites of one another. The opposite of satisfaction is not dissatisfaction, but rather, no satisfaction. Correspondingly, the opposite of dissatisfaction is no dissatisfaction.

While this distinction between the two opposites may sound like a play on words, Herzberg argued that there are two distinct human needs portrayed. First, there are physiological needs that can be fulfilled by money, for example, to purchase food and shelter. Second, there is the psychological need to achieve and grow, and this need is fulfilled by activities that cause one to grow. Figure 4 shows how Herzberg's view of motivation differs from the traditional view.

According to the two-factor theory, management not only must provide hygiene factors to avoid employee dissatisfaction, but also must provide factors intrinsic to the work itself in order for employees to be satisfied with their jobs.[10]

FIGURE 4 CONTRASTING VIEWS OF SATISFACTION AND DISSATISFACTION.

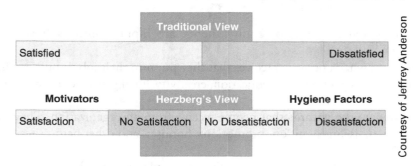

Courtesy of Jeffrey Anderson

Process Perspectives

While content perspectives examine the question of "what" motivates individuals, the process or cognitive perspectives address the issue of how the process of motivation works and sustains itself over time. Process perspectives examine such the factors that determine the degree of effort, the continuation of effort, the modification of effort, etc.

Process perspectives examine motivation from the perspectives of the thought processes by which people decide how to act. Three process perspectives on motivation are (1) equity theory, (2) expectancy theory, and (3) goal setting theory.[11]

Equity Theory

Imagine that your friend Mary is paid $12 working as an office assistant. She has worked in this role for six months, doing a very good job. She is a good colleague who is willing to help others. She stays late when needed and is flexible if asked to rearrange her priorities or her work hours.

According to Equity Theory, people are motivated to correct perceived inequities in the workplace.

© MilousSKShutterstock.com

Now imagine that Mary finds out her manager is hiring another employee, John, who is going to work with her, who will hold the same job title and will perform the same type of tasks. John has more advanced computer skills, but it is unclear whether these will be used on the job. The starting pay for John will be $14 an hour.

How would Mary feel? Would she be as motivated as before, going above and beyond her duties?

If your reaction to this situation is to think "Mary would think it's unfair," your feelings may be explained using equity theory. According to equity theory, individuals are motivated by their sense of fairness. This sense of fairness is a result of the social comparisons we make, specifically when we compare our inputs and outputs with someone else's inputs and outputs. We perceive fairness if we believe that the input-to-output ratio we are bringing into the situation is similar to the input/output ratio of a comparison person, or a referent. Perceived inequity creates tension within us and drives us to action that will reduce the perceived inequity.[12] This process is illustrated in the Figure 5.

Elements of Equity Theory

The fundamental elements of equity theory are inputs, outputs (rewards) and comparisons.[13]

Inputs are what a person perceives that they put into their job. Inputs can include time, effort, training, experience, education, creativity, intelligence, seniority, status, and so on.

Outputs are the rewards that people receive from an organization. They include pay, benefits, praise, recognition, promotions, bonuses, and other perquisites such as a corner office.

Comparison—According to equity theory, people compare the ratio of their own outputs to inputs against the ratio of a referent other. When employees compare these ratios, they make a judgment about fairness. If they are satisfied with the comparison, they don't change their behavior. If they perceive inequity or unfairness, they are motivated to change their behavior to change the inequity.

Equity theory suggests that a person who feels that they are being under rewarded will respond to the perceived inequity in one or more ways including:

❒ Reducing inputs ("I'm just going to do the minimum required")

❒ Increasing the outputs ("I'm going to ask for a raise")

Inputs Factors that an employee contributes to his or her job including education, skill, experience, work ethic and training

Outputs Factors that an employee receives from his or her job including salary, perks, bonus, and recognitions in the form of awards

FIGURE 5 THE EQUITY FORMULA.

Person		Referent Other	Employee Assessment
$\dfrac{Inputs}{Outputs}$	$=$	$\dfrac{Inputs}{Outputs}$	Equity
$\dfrac{Inputs}{Outputs}$	$<$	$\dfrac{Inputs}{Outputs}$	Inequity (under rewarded)
$\dfrac{Inputs}{Outputs}$	$>$	$\dfrac{Inputs}{Outputs}$	Inequity (over rewarded)

- Changing the comparison ("I compare much better with Bob than Jim")
- Changing the situation ("I'm going to look for another job")

Originally, equity theory research concentrated on distributive justice, which is the perceived fairness of the amount and allocation of rewards between individuals. More recent research has focused on procedural justice, the perceived fairness of the process used to determine reward distribution. Recent research shows that while procedural justice tends to affect and employee's level of organizational commitment and trust in one's boss and intention to quit, distributive justice has a greater impact on employee satisfaction.

What are implications for managers? Five practical lessons can be drawn from equity theory[14]:

Equity theory suggests that people compare the ratio of their outputs to inputs against the outputs and inputs of others. How would you deal with someone you perceive to be a slacker who gets promoted over you?

1. **Employee perceptions count.** No matter how fair management considers reward allocation, each employee's perception is what matters.

2. **Employees want a voice in decisions that impact them.** Managers benefit by allowing employees to participate in decisions about work outcomes. Generally, employee perceptions of procedural justice are enhanced when they have a voice.

3. **Allow for appeals.** Giving employees an appeal process enhances their perceptions of procedural justice.

4. **Leader behavior matters.** Employee perceptions of procedural justice are influenced by leadership behavior. For example, employees at Honeywell felt better about being asked to take unpaid leaves when they learned that CEO David Cole did not take a $4 million bonus.

5. **A climate for justice.** Managers who create a climate of justice and fairness generally experience better team performance and customer service interactions.

Distributive justice The perceived fairness of the amount and allocation of rewards between individuals

Procedural justice The idea of fairness in the processes that resolve disputes and allocate resources

Expectancy An individual's perception of his or her ability to accomplish an objective

Expectancy Theory

Expectancy theory proposes that motivation is a function of an individual's expectations about their ability to perform tasks and receive desirable rewards. Expectancy theory is not concerned with identifying needs but instead looks at the thinking process that individuals use to realize rewards.[15]

Expectancy theory is based on the relationship between an individual's effort, performance, and the desirability of outcomes associated with high performance. There are three variables:

Expectancy refers to an individual's perception of his or her ability to accomplish an objective. Expectancy would be high if an individual had confidence that effort would produce desired results.

Expectancy theory suggests that belief in one's ability to perform a task is an important component of motivaton.

Instrumentality the perception of the relationship between performance and the likelihood of receiving a desired outcome or reward

Valence the importance that an individual places on the potential outcomes or rewards that can be achieved on the job

Instrumentality is the perception of the relationship between performance and the likelihood of receiving a desired outcome or reward. Expectancy is the degree to which the individual believes that performing at a particular level is instrumental for attaining the desired outcome. For example, if an employee believes that he or she would receive a bonus for a meeting a sales goal, instrumentality would be high.

Valence is the importance that an individual places on the potential outcomes or rewards that can be achieved on the job. If the rewards that are available from effort and performance are not valued, motivation will be low.

To maximize expectancy, people must have confidence in their abilities. They must believe that if they put forth the effort, they will perform. This is an issue of perceived competency. Managers can build expectancy by selecting the right workers for the job, training, developing and supporting them so that jobs can be achieved. Figure 6 outlines the process of Expectancy Theory.

To maximize instrumentality, people must see the link between high performance and outcomes. Managers can increase instrumentality by clarifying rewards and allocating them fairly and contingent on performance. To maximize valence, people must value the outcomes associated with high performance. This is a matter of individual preferences. Managers can use the content theories to help understand different individual needs and then link those needs with outcomes having positive valences which can be earned through high performance.[16]

FIGURE 6 THE PROCESS OF EXPECTANCY THEORY.

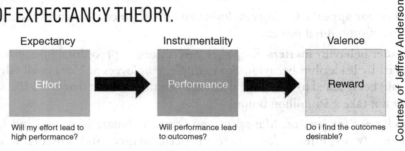

Courtesy of Jeffrey Anderson

© sergey causelove/Shutterstock.com

Reaching organizational and individual goals is an important motivational factor for many employees.

Goal-Setting Theory

Researchers Ed Lock and Gary Latham suggested that the goals organizational members strive to attain are prime determinants of their motivation and subsequent performance. Goal setting theory proposes that people are motivated by goals that are specific, challenging, and attainable. According to Lock and Latham, it is natural for people to set and work toward goals; however, the goal-setting process is only useful if employees understand and accept their goals.[17]

The motivational benefits of goal-setting happen when mangers and team leaders work with others to set the right goals. Participation is a key part of the process. When managers and employees work together to set goals, employees are likely to experience greater motivation and job satisfaction. Participation increases the understanding of goals as well as acceptance and commitment to those goals. It's not always possible to jointly set goals with employees and in those cases, research suggests that workers respond positively to supervisor assigned goals if they trust in their supervisor to deliver adequate resources and support.[18]

Reinforcement Theory

Reinforcement theory was pioneered by Edward Thorndike and B.F. Skinner and is concerned with how the consequences of certain behavior affect that behavior in the future. Derived from operant conditioning, reinforcement theory and suggests that behavior with favorable consequences is likely to be repeated, whereas behavior with negative consequences tends not to be repeated. The use of reinforcement theory to change behavior is called behavior modification.[19]

Reinforcement theory proposes that the consequences of their behavior will motivate employees to behave in certain ways. It's about teaching and learning. Employees learn what is desired and what is not desired behavior as a result of consequences to that behavior. Employees engage in specific behaviors to meet their needs and self-interests. As Former White House chief of staff Donald Rumsfeld put it: "If you make something more (or less) attractive, people will do more (or less) of it.[20]

Four Types of Reinforcement

Reinforcement is anything that causes a behavior to be repeated or inhibited. There are four types of reinforcement; positive reinforcement, negative reinforcement, extinction, and punishment.[21] Figure 7 outlines the four different types of reinforcement.

Positive reinforcement is the use of positive consequences to strengthen a desired behavior. For example, a manager might praise an employee for showing up on time for a meeting. If a desired behavior is not positively reinforced, it may decrease or stop over time.

Positive reinforcement The use of positive consequences to strengthen a desired behavior

FIGURE 7 DIFFERENT TYPES OF REINFORCEMENT.

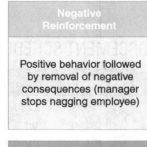

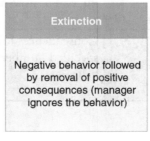

Courtesy of Jeffrey Anderson

Positive Reinforcement	Negative Reinforcement
Positive behavior followed by positive consequences (manager praises the employee)	Positive behavior followed by removal of negative consequences (manager stops nagging employee)
Punishment	**Extinction**
Negative behavior followed by negative consequences (manager demotes employee)	Negative behavior followed by removal of positive consequences (manager ignores the behavior)

Negative reinforcement The withdrawal of a negative consequence for desired behavior

Punishment Negative consequence undesired behavior

Extinction Withholding reinforcement when undesired behavior occurs

Negative reinforcement strengthens behavior by withdrawing a negative consequence for desired behavior. For example, a supervisor who had been nagging an employee to meet production goals stops nagging the employee when those goals are reached.

Punishment involves the use of a negative consequence to decrease undesired behavior. A manager could reprimand an employee for showing up late to a meeting. The employee is less likely to repeat the behavior so as to avoid the negative consequence.

Extinction involves withholding reinforcement when undesired behavior occurs. Extinction decreases the likelihood that undesired behavior will occur again by ignoring that behavior. For example, a manager might ignore an employee who arrives late for a meeting.

Reinforcement Schedules

The timing of the reinforcement also influences the reoccurrence of the behavior. Reinforcers are most effective when they immediately follow the behavior, but not necessarily after each occurrence of the behavior. Delayed reinforcement loses its effectiveness and if delayed too long may be associated with some other behavior. Immediate reinforcement is especially important when teaching new behaviors. When a behavior has been learned, intermittent schedules of reinforcement are often more effective in maintaining those behaviors. Three major reinforcement schedules are continuous, intermittent, and interval.[22]

Continuous reinforcement A consequence follows every occurrence of the behavior

Intermittent reinforcement Consequences are delivered after so many occurrences of the behavior

Interval reinforcement Consequences follow behavior after different times, some shorter and some longer, varying around a specified average time

With continuous reinforcement, a consequence follows every occurrence of the behavior. For example, employees paid on piece rate earn money for every part they produce. The more they produce, the more they earn.

With intermittent reinforcement, consequences are delivered after so many occurrences of the behavior. For example, a salesperson may receive a bonus after selling groups of five subscriptions.

With interval reinforcement, consequences follow behavior after different times, some shorter and some longer, varying around a specified average time. For example, reinforcements such as promotion are awarded intermittently.

Table 3 outlines the different schedules for variable reinforcement.

TABLE 3 INTERMITTENT REINFORCEMENT SCHEDULES.

	Fixed	Variable
Interval (time)	Consequences follow behavior after a fixed interval of time has occurred	Consequences follow behavior after different time intervals, some shorter, some longer that vary around an average time.
Ratio (behavior)	Consequences follow a specified number of behaviors	Consequences follow after differing numbers of behaviors that vary around a specified average numbers of behaviors

Practical Application

Although each type of reinforcement is appropriate in certain circumstances, many studies have concluded that positive reinforcement is more closely linked to improved performance. The reason? With positive reinforcement, people see a clear link with desired performance. In the best seller "The One Minute Manager", Blanchard and Johnson describe the management style of "catch them doing something right". This is the opportunity for managers to give one-minute praisings. One-minute praisings are so called because it takes a minute or less to tell someone that he or she did a good job. There is no need to elaborate when once can simply say that he or she he did something good it was noticed. One-minute praisings include praising people immediately, telling them what they did right, how and encouraging them to do more of the same.

In his 1937 book "How to Win Friends and Influence People", Dale Carnegie put it another way; "Any fool can criticize, condemn, and complain—and most fools do." Carnegie explained that leaders should acknowledge when a follower is not meeting expectations, but do so in a way that acknowledges what is working, avoiding resentment and encouraging improvement.

"Abilities wither under criticism; they blossom under encouragement," Carnegie wrote. Be lavish with praise, but only in a genuine way, he advised.

"Remember, we all crave appreciation and recognition, and will do almost anything to get it," he said. "But nobody wants insincerity. Nobody wants flattery."[23]

Figure 8 provides an example of the four types of reinforcement in a work context.

FIGURE 8 EXAMPLES OF FOUR TYPES OF REINFORCEMENT.

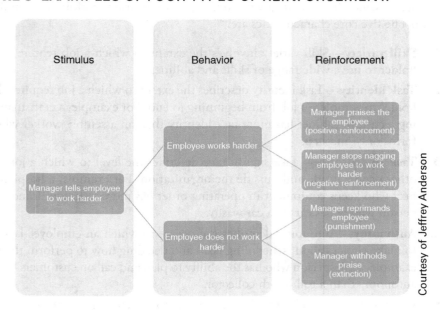

Courtesy of Jeffrey Anderson

Designing Motivating Jobs

Job Design is a **psychological theory of motivation** that is defined as the systematic and purposeful allocation of task to groups and individuals within an organization. Three tactics for designing motivating jobs include job rotation, job enlargement, and job enrichment.

Job rotation The practice of moving employees between different tasks to promote experience and variety.

Job enlargement Increasing the scope of a job through extending the range of its job duties

Job enrichment The vertical expansion of a job's scope by adding planning and evaluation responsibilities

With **job rotation**, employees can move from one task to another instead of spending all of their time on one routine task. For example, at a cafeteria restaurant, an employee might move from serving pasta to salads, then to vegetables or dessert. Job rotation is intended to alleviate boredom by giving people a variety of job activities at various times.

On one hand, people are moving from one boring job to another. But job rotation can provide multiple benefits if implemented with employee interests in mind. Harrah's Entertainment uses job rotation for IT workers, giving them a broad knowledge of the business that enhances their value to the company and provides options for career development.

Job enlargement is similar to job rotation as employees are given multiple tasks. Although job rotation involves doing one job at a time and changing tasks, job enlargement means doing multiple tasks at the same time. In a study of job enlargement at financial institutions, enlarged jobs resulted in higher job satisfaction, better error detection and improved customer service.[24]

Job enrichment is a vertical expansion of a job's scope by adding planning and evaluation responsibilities. Job enrichment increases job depth, that is, the degree of control that an employee has over his or her work. In other words, employees in job enrichment assume some of the responsibilities of management giving them increased freedom, independence, and responsibility. Although job enrichment may improve the quality of life for employees, research evidence is inconclusive as to its usefulness.[25]

Researchers J. Richard Hackman and Greg Oldham developed the job characteristics model of job design which is an outgrowth of job enrichment. The job characteristics model consists of five core characteristics that affect three psychological states of an employee which in turn affect work outcomes, motivation, performance, and satisfaction. The five core characteristics are:[26]

1. **Skill variety**—Skill variety involves the extent to which a job requires the job holder to use a wide range of skills and abilities.

2. **Task identity**—Task identity describes the extent to which a job requires the job holder to complete a job from beginning to end. For example, a craftsman making a custom cabinet has more task identity than an assembly worker who performs only one step.

3. **Task significance**—Task significance describes the level to which a job affects other people inside and outside the organization. For example, a hospital engineer who keeps equipment in operating order has more task significance than a person who wipes cars at a car washy.

4. **Autonomy**—Autonomy describes the degree to which an employee is allowed to make choices about scheduling tasks and deciding how to perform them. For example, a salesperson who has the ability to plan and call on customers has more autonomy than a toll-booth collector.

5. **Feedback**—Feedback describes the extent to which workers receive clear and direct information about how well they are performing their job.

According to the job characteristics model, these five core characteristics affect an employee's motivation because they affect three critical psychological states; meaningfulness of work, responsibility for results and knowledge of results. In turn, these psychological states can result in higher motivation, performance, satisfaction and lower absenteeism.

The most effective job enrichment addresses all five core job dimensions. A person's growth need strength is the degree to which a person wants personal and psychological development. Job enrichment is more effective for people with high growth need strength but few people respond negatively to job enrichment.

Figure 9 illustrates the job characteristics model.

FIGURE 9 THE JOB CHARACTERISTICS MODEL.

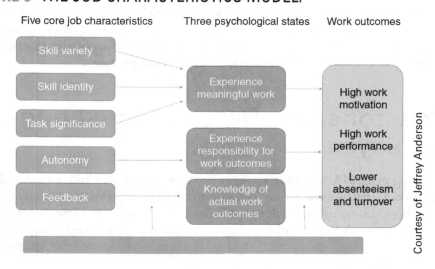

Motivation and Compensation

Most people are paid an hourly wage or a salary. Both of these types of compensation are easy for an organization to manage. But by itself, a wage or salary provides little incentive for an employee to work hard. Incentive compensation plans attempt to do this, but no single plan will boost the performance of every employee.

In accordance with many of the motivation theories discussed earlier in this chapter, incentive plans must meet the following criteria to be effective:[27]

1. Rewards must be based on measurable performance
2. Rewards must satisfy individual needs
3. The employee and manager must agree upon the rewards
4. Rewards must be believable and achievable by employees

How would you like to be rewarded for your efforts? Some of the most well-known compensation plans include *pay for performance, bonuses, gain sharing, pay for knowledge, and stock options.*

Pay for performance—Also known as merit pay, pay for performance rewards individuals in proportion to their contributions. For example, many farm workers are paid according to how much fruit they pick. Another example is sales representatives who work on commission.

Bonuses—Rewards employees with a one-time cash payment based on performance. For example, retailer Neiman-Marcus pays its salespeople a percentage of the earnings from the goods they sell.

Gain sharing—Rewards all employees in a unit when predetermined performance targets for cost reduction or productivity are met. One version, the Scanlon plan, provides employees with two-thirds to three-fourths of the total cost savings achieved.

Pay for knowledge—Connects employee salary with task skills acquired. Employees are motivated to learn the skills for multiple jobs, thus increasing organizational flexibility and efficiency. For example, in K–12 education, teachers are encouraged to increase their salary by earning further college credit.

Stock options—Allows certain employees the right to purchase stock at a future price for a predetermined amount. The idea is that the employee will work harder to increase the value of their benefit. Along with other benefits, Starbucks gives stock options to all employees who work more than 25 hours per week.

Nonmonetary Ways of Motivating Employees

According to a 2013 Accenture survey, more than half of men and women indicated that work–life balance was the key determinant of their career success, ahead of money, recognition, autonomy, and making a difference. According to the Pew Research Foundation, Millennials in particular are apt to say the most important things in life are "being a good parent" (52 percent) and having a successful marriage (30 percent) rather than "having a high-paying career" (15 percent).[28]

Some of the employer programs designed to cater to the desire for work–life balance include flexible working hours, vacations, and sabbaticals.

Flexible working hours The practice of allowing employees some choice in their daily work schedules

Flexible working hours, also called flextime, allows employees some choice in their daily work schedules. A typical flextime schedule offers choices for starting and ending times, allowing employees to start earlier or leave later depending upon their preference. This flexibility allows employees to honor personal commitments such as parenting, elder car, medical appointments, and other emergencies. All top 100 companies on Working Mother magazine's best employers list offer flexible working hours. Flextime can reduce employee stress and turnover.[29]

Putting it All Together

We began this chapter by defining motivation and distinguishing between two types of rewards. We discussed needs and process based theories as well as reinforcement theory. We outlined different ways to motivate employees through job design and compensation. Which model is the best? The answer to that question will likely be different for each employee. The question of motivation is much like the parable of the blind men feeling the elephant. There are different parts, each with their own unique characteristics. The best motivational tool is the one that fits best with each individual employee.

Summary of Learning Outcomes and Key Points

❑ **Define motivation and explain the difference between intrinsic and extrinsic rewards**

Motivation may be defined as the psychological processes that stimulate and direct goal-directed behavior. Extrinsic rewards are the tangible rewards given to employees by managers, and include pay raises, bonuses, and benefits. Intrinsic rewards, by contrast, are the psychological rewards that employees get from performing important work and doing it well.

❑ **Identify and describe the various content theories of motivation**

Content theories, also known as need-based perspectives, emphasize the needs that motivate people. Content theories include Maslow's hierarchy of needs theory, Alderfer's ERG theory, McClelland's acquired needs theory, and Herzberg's two-factor theory.

Maslow's Hierarchy of Needs suggests that people seek to satisfy needs in a specific order starting with the most basic psychological needs to the highest-level need, self-actualization. Alderfer's ERG theory condenses Maslow's five-needs into three needs; existence, relatedness, and growth. McClelland's acquired needs theory says that people are motivated by three learned needs; affiliation, achievement, and power. Finally, Herzberg's two-factor theory outlines two sets of needs; motivators and hygiene factors. Hygiene factors don't motivate people but reduce dissatisfaction.

❑ **Identify and describe the various process theories of motivation**

Process perspectives examine motivation from the perspectives of the thought processes by which people decide how to act. Three process perspectives on motivation are (1) equity theory, (2) expectancy theory, and (3) goal setting theory.

According to equity theory, people compare their inputs and outputs to the inputs and outputs of other and are motivated when there is inequity in that comparison. With expectancy theory, people are motivated by three factors; (1) expectancy, which is the belief in one's ability to perform a task, (2) instrumentality, which is their belief that successful performance will result in a reward, and (3) the perceived value of that reward. Goal setting theory proposes that people are motivated by setting goals that are specific, challenging, and attainable.

❑ **Describe reinforcement theory and how it can be used to motivate employees**

Reinforcement theory is concerned with how the consequences of certain behavior affect that behavior in the future. Derived from operant conditioning, reinforcement theory suggests that behavior with favorable consequences is likely to be repeated, whereas behavior with negative consequences tends not to be repeated. The use of reinforcement theory to change behavior is called behavior modification.

There are four types of reinforcement; positive reinforcement, negative reinforcement, extinction, and punishment.

❑ **Discuss major approaches to job design and its influence on motivation**

With **job rotation**, employees can move from one task to another instead of spending all of their time on one routine task. **Job enlargement** is similar to job rotation as employees are given multiple tasks. But while job rotation involves doing one job at a time and changing tasks, job enlargement means doing multiple tasks at the same time. **Job enrichment** is a vertical expansion of a job's scope by adding planning and evaluation responsibilities. Job enrichment increases job depth, that is, the degree of control that an employee has over his or her work.

The job characteristics model of job design which is an outgrowth of job enrichment. The job characteristics model consists of five core characteristics that affect three psychological states of an employee which in turn affect work outcomes, motivation, performance, and satisfaction. The five core characteristics are skill variety, task identity, task significance, autonomy, and feedback.

❐ **Describe various approaches to motivating employees through compensation**

Some of the most well-known compensation plans include *pay for performance, bonuses, gain sharing, pay for knowledge, and stock options.*

According to a 2013 Accenture survey, more than half of men and women indicated that work–life balance was the key determinant of their career success, ahead of money, recognition, autonomy, and making a difference. Some of the employer programs designed to cater to the desire for work–life balance include flexible working hours, vacations, and sabbaticals.

End Notes

1. Kinicki, A. & Williams, B. (2018). *Management: A Practical Introduction* (8th ed.). McGraw-Hill, New York, NY, p. 397.

2. https://iveybusinessjournal.com/publication/the-four-intrinsic-rewards-that-drive-employee-engagement/ (retrieved 12/4/17).

3. Kinicki & Williams, p. 399.

4. Daft, R. & Marcic, D. (2017). *Understanding Management* (10th ed.). Cengage Learning, Boston, MA, p. 521–523.

5. Jones, G. & George, J. (2014). *Contemporary Management* (8th ed.). McGraw-Hill, New York, NY, p. 413.

6. Daft & Marcic, p. 523.

7. http://www.netmba.com/mgmt/ob/motivation/erg/ (retrieved 12/3/17).

8. Bateman, T. & Snell, S. (2015). *Management* (11th ed.). McGraw-Hill, New York, NY, p. 452.

9. https://www.mindtools.com/pages/article/human-motivation-theory.htm (retrieved 12/3/17).

10. http://www.netmba.com/mgmt/ob/motivation/herzberg/ (retrieved 12/3/17).

11. http://highered.mheducation.com/sites/0077330439/student_view0/chapter12/index.html (retrieved 2/29/18).

12. http://open.lib.umn.edu/principlesmanagement/chapter/14-4-process-based-theories (retrieved 12/4/17).

13. Kinicki & Williams, p. 407.

14. Ibid., p. 408.

15. Daft, R. & Marcic, D. (2017). *Understanding Management* (10th ed.). Cengage Learning, Boston, MA.

16. Schermerhorn, J. & Bachrach, D. (2015). *Management* (13th ed.). John Wiley & Sons, p. 374.

17. Kinicki & Williams, p. 411.

18. Schermerhorn & Bachrach, p. 376.

19. Kinicki & Williams, p. 417.

20. Lussier, R. (2019). *Management Fundamentals* (8th ed.). Sage, Los Angeles, CA, p. 378.

21. Kinicki & Williams, p. 417.

22. Cherrington, D. & Dyer, W. (2009). *Creating Effective Organizations* (5th ed.). Kendall-Hunt, Dubuque, Iowa, p. 204.

23. http://www.businessinsider.com/lessons-from-how-to-win-friends-and-influence-people-2015-4 (retrieved 2/9/18).

24. Bateman & Snell, p. 454.

25. Robbins, S. & Coulter, M. (2016). *Management* (13th ed.). Pearson, Boston, MA, p. 469.
26. Kinicki & Williams, p. 415.
27. Ibid., p. 421.
28. Ibid., p. 423.
29. Schermerhorn, J. & Bachrach, D. (2018). *Exploring Management* (6th ed.). John Wiley and Sons, New York, NY, p. 153.

CHAPTER 10 MANAGING TEAMS

Key Terms

Agile team
Conflict
Cross-functional teams
Group
Group cohesiveness

Interest-Based Relational (IBR)
    approach
Norms
Scrum
Self-managed teams

Social loafing
Team
Team building
Virtual team

Introduction

Much of what is accomplished today in organizations is not the result of individual work, but rather work performed by teams. In this chapter, we will examine the various characteristics of effective teams. We will outline the team development process and discuss team roles, norms, and the effects of teams on individual behavior. We will also discuss the conflict that occurs with teams and review strategies for resolving conflict.

Learning Outcomes

❏ Understand the differences between groups and teams
❏ Remember and understand different types of teams
❏ Understand the team development life cycle and team member roles
❏ Describe how factors such as conformity, cohesiveness, and team size influence team effectiveness
❏ Understand the nature of conflict in teams and methods to resolve conflict.

Groups vs. Teams

What is the difference between a group of employees and a team? Often the terms are used as synonyms and both groups and teams share some common characteristics, but there are

A team is a small group with complementary skills who hold themselves mutually accountable for performance goals.

© Rena Schid/Shutterstock.com

Group two or more two or more freely acting individuals who share collective norms, collective goals, and have a common identity.

Team a small group of people with complementary skills who are committed to a common purpose, performance goals, and approach for which they hold themselves mutually accountable.

also some key differences. Not all groups are teams. A group is two or more two or more freely acting individuals who share collective norms, collective goals, and have a common identity. A team is a small group of people with complementary skills who are committed to a common purpose, performance goals, and approach for which they hold themselves mutually accountable.[1] Table 1 gives an example of a group vs. a team.

Performance goals and mutual accountability are two of the key differences between groups and teams. Teams often create synergies, producing more than the sum of the individual team members.

You are likely familiar with teams, especially if you have watched or participated in team sports. Work teams differ from work groups and have their own unique characteristics. Work groups often interact to share information and make decisions to help each member perform their job more effectively or efficiently. Work groups offer little opportunity for collective work. Work teams by contrast have members that are work intensively on a common goal. Members of group teams have complementary skills and hold each other mutually accountable.

Table 2 contrasts work groups and work teams.

TABLE 1 GROUPS VS TEAMS.

Here we see a **group** people waiting to board a bus. They have a common purpose (ride the bus) and a common identity.	Here we see a pit crew working as a **team**. They have complementary skills, performance goals and approach. They hold each other mutually accountable.

TABLE 2 WORK GROUPS VS. WORK TEAMS.

Work Groups	Work Teams
There is one leader in charge	Leadership is shared among the team
Each person is accountable only to themselves	Members are accountable to each other
Work is done individually	Work is done collectively
Meetings are efficient with no collaboration or open-ended discussion	Meetings feature open-ended discussions and collaborative problem solving
Work is decided by a group leader who and delegated to group members	Work is decided and performed collaboratively

The Power of Teams

Used effectively, teams can have a powerful effect as a building block for organizational structure. Companies like Whole Foods, 3M and W.L. Gore are structured around teams. Many of 3M's breakthrough products are a result of teams that function as an entrepreneurial business unit within the larger corporation.[2]

Teams have become the fundamental building-blocks of organizations. Routinely, employers are looking for "team players. While teams are as old as civilization a new report by Deloitte, "Global Human Capital Trends," suggests that the fashion for teamwork has reached a new high. Nearly half of those surveyed said their companies were either in the middle of restructuring or about to embark on it; and in most cases, this restructuring meant putting more emphasis on teams.[3]

Teams are essential to solving complex business problems.

As the operating environment of business continues to increase in complexity, organizations are looking more to leveraging the power of teams to move and react faster. Business performance isn't based upon the individual efforts of a few but rather the collective efforts of teams that comprise each business unit.

Teams facilitate the transfer of understanding, and in today's knowledge economy, knowledge may by powerful but sharing knowledge is the true source of power as it enables others to act.

According to a report by Ernst & Young, "almost nine out of ten companies agree that the problems confronting them are now so complex that teams are essential to provide effective solutions. To achieve superior performance, companies need to tap into the full range of skills and expertise at their disposal."[4]

The new organizational reality of today is that team performance drives organizational performance.

Types of Teams

Different types of teams have different characteristics and attributes. We can distinguish between different types of teams according to their purpose, duration, and level of member commitment.

First, we should distinguish between formal groups and informal groups. **Formal groups** are those that are established to achieve to achieve organizational goals. **Informal groups** are formed for the individual needs of the members, for example, the need for social interaction. Five coworkers who have lunch together every Friday would be an example of an informal group.[5]

Here are a few types of formal groups in an organization:

Work teams have a clear purpose that all members share. Work teams work collectively on a specific common goal. For example, work teams at Chipotle perform interrelated tasks to prepare food for customers. **Project teams** are work teams that are

Formal groups are established to achieve organizational goals.

Cirque de Soleil makes extensive use of teams to plan, design, and execute its elaborate shows.

Cross-functional teams Teams that include members from different functional areas of the organization, such as finance, sales and operations.

Self-managed teams Groups of workers who are empowered and have responsibility for administrative oversight of their tasks.

assembled to solve a particular problem or complete a specific task. For example, many retailers form project teams to open new store locations. At the end of the project, these teams are disbanded.[6]

Cross-functional teams are set up to include members from different functional areas of the organization, such as finance, sales, and operations. Cross-functional teams can break down functional silos that limit communication and cooperation between different departments. Retailer Target uses cross-functional teams from merchandising, marketing, design, communications, and supply chain to create new limited edition fashions.[7]

One type of cross-functional team is a task force, which is a group of employees from different departments formed to deal with a specific activity. A task force exists only until the task is completed. Some organizations also use employee involvement teams. These teams meet regularly with the goal of using their experience and expertise for continuous improvement. The quality circle is an example of an employee involvement team.

Self-managed teams are groups of workers who are empowered and have responsibility for administrative oversight of their tasks. On a day-to-day basis, team members decide what the team will do, how it will do it and what specific tasks each team member will perform. Managers often form self-managed teams to improve quality, increase motivation and satisfaction and lower costs. Some experts estimate that about 80% of Fortune 1,000 companies use self-managed teams.[8]

Typically, self-managed teams schedule work and assign tasks, with managers present to serve as facilitators. Self-managed teams come in many different forms, with varying degrees of autonomy. It is important to know that using self-managed teams does not mean that workers are left to do their own thing but it is important that organizations who use self-managed teams are prepared to undergo changes in management philosophy, structure, training, and staffing practices. The traditional notion of management authority is turned on its head and some managers perceive self-managed teams as a threat to their job security. Nonetheless, self-managed teams are used with increasing frequency in organizations today.

Are self-managed teams effective? Research results are mixed. Self-managed teams have been found to improve work-life quality, customer service, and productivity. Multiple studies suggest that self-managed teams have a positive effect on productivity and certain attitudes like responsibility and control but no significant effect on absenteeism or turnover. While research results don't present a sweeping endorsement, experts say that the trend toward self-managed teams will continue upward in North America because of a strong cultural preference for direct participation.[9]

A virtual team is a team whose members rarely meet face-to-face but instead interact using various forms of information technology such as e-mail, computer networks, telephone, fax, and video conference. Virtual teams are typically geographically or organizationally dispersed. Virtual teams offer the flexibility in that

Virtual teams interact electronically.

membership is not limited by time and location. Virtual teams can reduce the costs of office space and travel expenses although virtual meetings present challenges with work satisfaction and trust. Given technological advances and increasing globalization, virtual teams are growing in popularity, particularly with multinational organizations.[10]

However, virtual teams do pose some drawbacks. Team members must learn to work together in new contexts. The natural give and take of face-to-face meetings is much more difficult to attain through video-conferencing or other methods. Some studies have demonstrated that physical proximity enhances information processing. As a result, some organizations try to bring virtual team members together on a regular basis to try and minimize these problems.[11]

Virtual team A team whose members rarely meet face-to-face but instead interact by using various forms of information technology such as e-mail, computer networks, telephone, fax and video conference.

Agile Teams

Until recently, Agile was viewed as a set of management practices for software development. That's because Agile's initial advocates were software developers who followed the document titled Manifesto for Software Development published in 2001. Now, after endorsements from Harvard Business Review, McKinsey & Company and the 2015 Learning Consortium Project, Agile is spreading quickly to all parts of organizations.

The emergence of Agile as a global movement extending beyond software is driven by the need for organizations to cope with today's turbulent customer-driven marketplace. Agile enables organizations to manage continuous change and permits organizations to flourish in a world that is increasingly volatile, uncertain, complex, and ambiguous.[12]

An Agile team is a cross-functional group of people that have the personnel and resources needed to produce a working, tested incremental version of a product. These people are dedicated to the team and as a rule, do not move them between or across teams as demands ebb and flow.[13]

Agile team A cross-functional group of people that have the personnel and resources needed to produce a working, tested incremental version of a product.

Scrum is an agile methodology to manage a project. In Scrum, the focus is on a self-organizing, cross-functional team. The scrum team is self-organizing as there is no overall leader who assigns tasks and decides how a problem will be sold. These issues are decided by the entire team.

Scrum An agile methodology to manage a project.

Scrum teams are cross-functional, meaning everyone is needed to take a feature from idea to implementation.

Scrum teams are supported by two defined roles. First, the ScrumMaster, who can be thought of as a coach for the team, helping team members use the Scrum process to perform at the highest level.

The second role is the product owner (PO). He or she represents the business, customers, or users, and guides the team toward solving the customer's needs.[14]

Team Development Life Cycle

Each team, as it develops, passes through distinct stages. Research findings suggest that team development is not

Scrum teams are self-organizing and cross-functional.

random, but evolves over a series of definitive stages. Psychologist Bruce Tuckman described the path that most teams follow on their way to high performance.[15] That process is outlined in Figure 1.

FIGURE 1 TEAM DEVELOPMENT LIFE CYCLE.

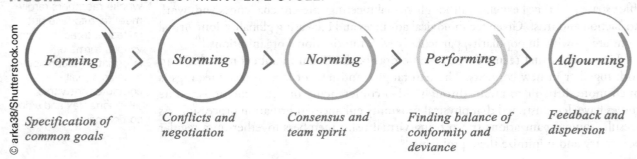

Forming — Specification of common goals

Storming — Conflicts and negotiation

Norming — Consensus and team spirit

Performing — Finding balance of conformity and deviance

Adjourning — Feedback and dispersion

© arka38/Shutterstock.com

Forming

The forming stage is a period of orientation where team members get to know one another. In this stage, members first get together. As individuals, they consider questions such as, "Why am I here?", "Who else is here?" and "Who am I comfortable working with?" This stage is an important opportunity for members to get involved with each other, including introducing themselves to the team. In the forming stage, individual behavior is driven by a desire to be accepted by the others, and avoid controversy or conflict.

Uncertainty is high in the forming stage because members are unsure of issues such as "Will I fit in?" and "What is expected of me?" During this stage, a team leader should give members time to get acquainted and encourage informal discussions.

Storming

The storming phase is marked by conflict. Different ideas compete for consideration. The team addresses issues such as what problems they are really supposed to solve, how they will function independently and together and what leadership model they will accept. During this stage, members begin to voice their individual differences, join with others who share the same beliefs and jockey for position in the group.

If teams can't move beyond the storming phase, they likely will become bogged down and never achieve a level of high performance. During this phase, members should be encouraged to participate and propose ideas, disagree with one another, and work through the uncertainties and conflict of team tasks and goals. Being able to express one's ideas helps build camaraderie and a shared understanding.

Norming

In the norming stage, members are beginning to share a common commitment to the purpose of the group, including its overall goals and how each of the goals can be achieved. The team develops norms, or standards on how they will operate, make decisions, and who will lead the team.

In this stage, members settle into their role on the team and know what to expect from one another. Minor differences are resolved and friendships have developed that will make the team more cohesive. During this stage, members feel that things are starting to come together. However, teams may cycle back and forth between storming and norming several times before finally moving to the performing stage.

Performing

In the performing stage, teams are able to function as a unit as they find ways to get the job done smoothly and effectively without inappropriate conflict or the need for external supervision. During this stage, the team is working effectively and efficiently toward achieving its goals.

At this point of the team development process, team members should be fully committed to the team and think of themselves as part of a team, not just as employees. Team members often become very loyal to one another at this stage and feel mutual accountability for the success or failure of the team. At this phase, a lot of work gets done and it is fun to be a part of the team.

Adjourning

In the adjourning stage, the task is complete and the team is disbanded. During this stage, the emphasis is on wrapping up and gearing down. Task performance may no longer be the top priority and members may feel heightened emotions, strong cohesiveness, and potential regret over the disbanding of the team. During this phase, leaders may wish to signify the disbanding of the team with a ritual or ceremony that provides the potential to give members closure and a sense of completeness.

These five stages generally occur in sequential order but in time-pressured situations they may occur quite quickly. These stages may be accelerated even more in the case of virtual teams. Table 3 outlines some of the issues facing individuals and teams throughout the development lifecycle.

TABLE 3 INDIVIDUAL AND TEAM ISSUES ACROSS THE GROUP DEVELOPMENT LIFECYCLE.

	Forming	Storming	Norming	Performing	Adjourning
Individual Issues	How do I fit in?	What is my role on the team?	What do others expect from me?	How can I best perform my role?	What's next?
Team Issues	Why are we here?	Why are we fighting over who is in charge and who does what?	Can we agree on roles and work together as a team?	Can we do the job together?	Can we help members transition out of the team?

Team Roles

Roles are socially determined expectations of how team members should act in a specific position. A role is a tendency to behave, contribute, and interrelate with others in a particular. Members develop their own roles based on their own expectations and those of the team and the organization. For example, some people assume leadership roles, others might focus on work tasks and others on communications within the team.[16]

Early research on teams found that teams tend to have two categories of roles; task and maintenance.

Task roles are those behaviors that concentrate on completing the team's tasks. Task roles help keep the team on track and get the work done. There are five task roles:

1. The **contractor** role includes those behaviors that organize the team's work, such as producing timelines and schedules.
2. The **creator** role deals with changes in the team's task process structure, such as reframing the team's goals.
3. The **contributor** role shares information and expertise with the team.
4. The **completer** roles are those behaviors associated with transforming ideas into action, such as gathering information or summarizing ideas into a report.
5. The **critic** role includes "devil's advocate" behaviors which challenge the assumptions being made by the team.

Maintenance roles are those behaviors that foster constructive relationships between team members. Maintenance roles focus on keeping people engage with the team. Research has identified three maintenance roles:

1. The **cooperator role** includes supporting those with expertise toward the team's goals.
2. The **communicator role** includes behaviors that are focused on collaboration such as practicing good listening skills and using humor appropriately to diffuse tense situations. Good communicators help the team the team to feel more open to sharing ideas.
3. The **calibrator role** serves to keep the team on track and suggests needed changes to the team's process. This role includes starting discussions about potential team problems such as power struggles or other tensions.[17]

Team Norms

Norms Expectations about behavior that are shared by members of a team.

Norms are expectations about behavior that are shared by members of a team. They are the often unwritten rules that determine what is socially acceptable and what behavior is appropriate. Norms are developed and agreed to as a team interacts. Norms point out the boundaries between acceptable and unacceptable behavior and have a powerful influence on team behavior.[18]

Norms are broader than roles. They tend to be enforced by peer pressure from other members. Norms tend to be enforced for the following four reasons: (1) they help the group to survive. (2) They clarify role expectations, (3) they help individuals avoid embarrassing situations and (4) they emphasize the team's important values and identity.[19]

Conformity

Because people want to be accepted by the groups to which they belong, they are subject to pressure to conform. Early experiments by Solomon Asch showed the impact conformity has on individual judgment and attitudes. In these studies, groups of seven or eight people were asked to compare two cards held up by the researcher.

Conformity is a powerful force in groups and teams.

One card had three lines of varying lengths and the other had one line that was equal length to one of the lines on the other card. Each group member would announce out loud which of the three lines matched the single line. The experiment was fixed so that all of the members but one was told ahead of time to give incorrect answers after a few rounds. The result? In about one-third of the cases, the unsuspecting subject conformed to the incorrect answer.

While subsequent research suggest that conformity levels have declined since Asch's studies, managers can't ignore that conformity can still be a powerful force in groups. Group members often want to be seen as one of the group and avoid being observably different. In these cases, the group often exerts intense pressure on the individual to align is or her opinion to conform with others. In the extreme, this can result in group-think, Groupthink occurs when individuals want to preserve and protect their group from what they perceive as a collective threat to the group's image.[20]

Group cohesiveness The degree to which members are attracted to or loyal to the group

Cohesiveness

Another important characteristic of teams that affects team performance is group cohesiveness. Group cohesiveness is the degree to which members are attracted to or loyal to the group. When cohesiveness is high, individuals value their membership in the team and have a strong desire to remain as part of the group. When cohesiveness is low, members don't find their participation appealing and have little desire to remain in the group. Research suggests that managers should strive for moderate levels of cohesiveness because that is most likely to contribute to the organization.

Teams perform best when cohesiveness is high.

© Jacob Lund/Shutterstock.com

There are three major consequences of cohesiveness in teams. First, as cohesiveness increases, the participation by members increases. Participation contributes to team effectiveness because active members share information and ensure that tasks are completed. In teams where cohesiveness is too high, teams may focus on non-work conversations and jokes and meet too often. Second, increasing levels of cohesiveness result in higher levels of conformity to group norms. When cohesiveness is too high, there may be a tendency for groupthink. Finally, when cohesiveness is high, there is an increased emphasis on meeting the team's goals. When cohesiveness is too high, teams may place their goals ahead of those of the organization.[21]

Five factors can increase team cohesiveness. The first and strongest is intergroup competition. When two or more groups are competing, each is likely to become more cohesive. Second, is the group's personal attraction to one another. Third, a favorable evaluation of the group by outsiders can increase cohesiveness. If a team agrees on their goals, cohesiveness is likely to increase and finally, the more frequently the team interacts with one another, the more likely they are to become cohesive.

The outcome of cohesiveness can fall into two different categories; morale and productivity. As a general rule, morale is higher on cohesive teams because of increased communication between team members, a friendly team climate, loyalty, trust, and member participation in discussions. High cohesiveness nearly uniformly causes improved satisfaction of and higher morale of team members.

With regard to productivity, research suggests that in the case of teams where members share strong positive feelings of connectedness and positive interactions[22] with others tend to perform better. A positive team environment can contribute greatly to productivity.

Team Building

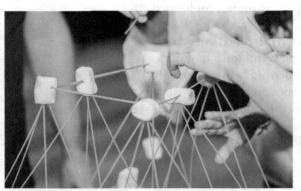

Team building activities may include experiential exercises that improve communication and decrease dysfunctional conflict.

Team building A set of planned activities aimed at improving the functioning of a team.

Team building is a set of planned activities aimed at improving the functioning of a team. They can be conducted by company trainers, outside consultants, or by managers. Team building workshops strive for greater cooperation, improved communication, and less dysfunctional conflict. Experiential learning exercises such as role-play sessions and competitive games are some of the active learning activities used by team building facilitators.

Research from Harvard Business School, the American Psychological Association (APA), and others suggest that team-building activities can help employees feel valued, and those that do are the most motivated to do great work. According to the APA's Psychologically Health Workplace Program, five simple teambuilding techniques have shown to be successful consistently over time:[23]

1. **Physical activities.** Sports make for great outings that allow employees to work together and while getting physical exercise. However, sports should be picked carefully: activities that could result in injury (like football) aren't as effective as noncontact options (like bowling or ice skating.)

2. **Field trips.** Casual simple trips such as visiting a park or museum or going to a baseball game can work wonders for a team.

3. **Professional development activities.** Workshops and retreats can give teams the opportunity to stay up to date with education and develop professional relationships in new settings.

4. **Shared meals.** Regular meals with the team allow for casual conversation in a comfortable environment and allows team members get to know each other outside of work.

5. **Volunteering.** The best activities are those where the whole team feels proud to participate. Research suggests that helping others makes people feel like they have more time on their hands! Volunteering can be an incredibly rewarding experience that encourages conversations outside the workspace.

Team Size

What's the best size for a team? Teams need to be large enough to include enough members with the diverse skill sets needed to complete a task, but small enough for members

Roman legions organized into squads of eight soldiers.

to feel like an intimate part of the team and foster effective communication. More than 30 years ago, psychologist Ivan Steiner studied team size and concluded that performance peaks at five members. He found that adding members beyond five decreased motivation, increased communication problems, and contributed to lower overall-performance. Since then, numerous studies have found that smaller teams perform better, although it's difficult to determine an optimum team size.[24]

The notion of smaller teams is not a new idea. In Roman times, a squad was composed of soldiers who could effectively hear their commander's orders during battle. The squad's size of eight, was defined by the number of soldiers who could share a standard tent.[25]

Jeff Bezos, founder and CEO of Amazon is a firm believer in the power of teams to promote innovation. At Amazon, teams have extensive autonomy to develop their ideas without intrusion from managers or other groups. Teams are kept deliberately small. According to Bezos, no team should be so big that it can't be fed by two pizzas.[26]

Is it a coincidence that Roman legion squads and Amazon's teams are of similar size? No. The very nature of the human brain, particularly our short-term memory, turns around what Harvard psychologist George Miller called "the magical number seven, plus or minus two." That is, human short-term memory is capable of capturing and briefly holding between five and nine pieces of information. Consider Zip codes or the way that phone numbers are chunked into a three-digit area code, a three-digit local prefix and a four-digit direct number at the end.

This means the optimum size of small teams is the same as the effective range of our short-term memory. Our minds seem to work best in the zone of seven, plus or minus two. Below that, the team often devolves into pairs or trios; beyond that, team communication begins to break down. But why, exactly, does it break down beyond the two-pizza-size team?

The answer comes from the mathematics of networks. Let's consider the smallest number of connections in a team and move forward:

2 members = 1 connection

3 members = 3 connections

4 members = 6 connections

5 members = 10 connections

16 members = 256 connections

32 members = 1,024 connections

Notice that he complexity of the network grows much faster than the number of team

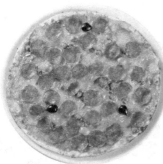

According to Amazon founder Jeff Bezos, the ideal sized team is one that can be fed by two pizzas.

Generally, small teams are have better interaction and are more cohesiveness than larger ones.

members does. And that creates a clear problem. Humans can only handle, much smaller numbers of connections. That's why, as the size of the team grows, relationships can degrade quickly.[27]

One more argument for small teams comes from Fred Brooks who coined the term Brooks Law in his book *The Mythical Man-Month*. Simply stated, Brooks' Law says that "adding manpower to a late software project makes it later." This has been proven in multiple studies. Legendary software developer Lawrence Putnam, made it his life's work to study how long things take to make and why. He examined 491 medium-sized projects at hundreds of different companies. When teams grew larger than eight, they took dramatically longer to get things done. Groups consisting of 3–7 people required about 25 percent of the effort of groups of 9–20 to get the same amount of work done. This result recurred over hundreds and hundreds of projects. That large teams accomplish less than small teams do seems to be an ironclad rule of human nature.

In a few words, Brook's law can be generalized to "Adding people to software development slows it down."[28]

Social loafing The tendency for an individual to expend less effort when working with a group than when working individually.

With social loafing, people are prone to exert less effort on a task if they are in a group versus when they work alone.

Social Loafing

Social loafing is an important research finding related to team size. Social loafing is the tendency for an individual to expend less effort when working with a group than when working individually. Social loafing may occur because people believe that others in the group aren't doing their fair share and therefore reduce their effort to make the workload equivalent. Also, it is sometimes difficult to see the direct efforts of an individual on a group. In these cases, people may free ride because they believe that their efforts can't be measured. Larger teams offer more opportunities for social loafers to hide their lack of effort as there is less interaction between individual team members.

Social loafing has significant implications for a team. Managers must find a way to identify individual efforts, otherwise group productivity and individual satisfaction may decrease.[29]

Social loafing can occur in all kinds of groups and teams in all kinds of organizations. It can result in lower team performance and may even prevent the team from reaching its goals. Managers can take three active steps to reduce social loafing:

1. **Identify individual contributions**. Some people engage in social loafing when they think that they can hide in the crowd. Other people avoid putting in high levels of effort because they think that their contributions won't be noticed. Managers can reduce social loafing by assigning specific tasks to individuals and holding them accountable for their completion.

2. **Emphasize the value of individual contributions**. Another reason for social loafing is that people sometimes think that their efforts aren't significant to the group. Managers can reduce this feeling by clearly communicating how each person's contributions contribute to the team as a whole.

3. **Keep the team at an appropriate size**. As a group's size increases, members are increasingly likely to think that their individual contributions aren't important. Managers should form teams with no more people than are needed to accomplish the group's goals and perform at a high level.

Building Effective Teams

Current research suggests five attributes of high-performing teams.[30]

1. **Collaboration**. Collaboration is the act of sharing information and coordinating efforts to achieve a collective result. Teams are more effective when they collaborate. For example, Whole Foods reinforces teamwork by structuring rewards for team rather than individual performance.

2. **Trust**. Trust is reciprocal faith in others intentions and behaviors. Trust is based on credibility. Research suggests a strong relationship between team performance and trust.

3. **Performance goals and feedback**. Teams need feedback on their performance just like individuals. The team's collective purpose should be defined in terms of measurable performance goals and feedback on how members are meeting those goals.

4. **Mutual accountability and interdependence**. Being mutually accountable to other members of the team makes members feel mutual trust and commitment. Mutual accountability is enhanced when members share accountability for their work.

5. **Team composition**. Team composition reflects the collection of people, jobs, personalities, skills, values, and experiences of team members. Diverse teams generally produce more creative results than homogenous ones.

Conflict

An important part of the group process is how a group manages conflict. Conflict is a disagreement over issues resulting in some form of interference or opposition. When conflict is constructive, it can add to creativity and reduces the likelihood of groupthink. But when conflict is destructive, it can break down the team and hurt performance.

Conflict A disagreement over issues resulting in some form of interference or opposition.

At its core, conflict is a disagreement between people. Conflict can be substantive, where it involves disagreements over issues such as goals, tasks, resource allocation, reward distribution, policies, and job assignments. Emotional conflict results from feelings of anger, mistrust, dislike, fear, and resentment.

Conflict is a necessary part of team work. However, it's essential that teams have some degree of conflict. If a team has too little conflict, it is likely to be plagued by apathy, lack of creativity, indecisiveness, and missed deadlines. As a result, the performance of the organization suffers.

One of the primary causes of conflict is completion for resources such as money, information, materials, or supplies. When individuals and teams must compete for scarce or declining resources, conflict is almost a certainty. In addition, conflict also occurs when people are pursuing different goals. Goal differences are a natural part of organizational life. For example, a sales department's goals may conflict with those of manufacturing.

Conflicts can also come from communication breakdowns. Poor communication can occur in any team, but for virtual and global teams, this is a particular problem. Trust issues can result as a source of conflict on virtual teams if members feel that they are excluded from important communication interactions and the lack of nonverbal cues in virtual settings can lead to more misunderstandings.

However, when there is excessive conflict, performance declines because of political infighting, dissatisfaction, lack of teamwork, and turnover. Workplace aggression and violence are manifestations of too much conflict.[31]

Over time, three different views of conflict have evolved. The **traditional view of conflict** argues that conflict should be avoided and if present indicates a problem with the group. The **human relations view of conflict** argues that conflict is natural and inevitable with groups and may contribute positively to the group's performance. Finally, the **interactionist view of conflict** proposes that conflict is necessary for a group to perform effectively.

The interactionist view doesn't suggest that all conflict is positive. **Functional conflict** is constructive and support the group's goals and performance. **Dysfunctional conflict**, on the other hand, is destructive and prevents the group from achieving its goals.[32] Figure 2 outlines the relationship between group performance and conflict.

FIGURE 2 CONFLICT AND GROUP PERFORMANCE.

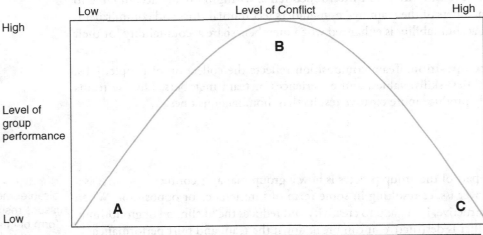

Situation	A	B	C
Level of Conflict	Low or none	Optimal	High
Type of Conflict	Dysfunctional	Functional	Dysfunctional
Group's Internal Characteristics	Apathetic Stagnant Unresponsive to change Lack of creativity	Viable Self-Critical Innovative	Disruptive Chaotic Uncooperative
Level of group performance		High	Low

Source: Jeffrey Anderson

Conflict Resolution

Researchers Thomas and Kilmann developed a model that organizes five conflict management styles based on two dimensions: assertiveness and cooperativeness. These two basic dimensions of behavior define the following five different modes for responding to conflict situations:

1. **Competing** is high in assertiveness and low in cooperation. With this style, an individual pursues his or her own concerns at the other party's expense. This is a power-oriented mode where one uses whatever power that seems appropriate to win such as position, ability to argue, rank, or economic sanctions.

   The advantage of competition is speed. It can get results quickly. The disadvantage is that it doesn't resolve personal conflict and can produce hurt feelings and resentment.

2. **Accommodating** is low in assertiveness and high in cooperation. It is the opposite of competing. When accommodating, the individual neglects his or her own concerns to satisfy the concerns of the other party; there is a degree of self-sacrifice in this mode. Accommodating can take the form of generosity or charity, obeying another person's order, or yielding to another's point of view.

   The advantage of accommodating is that it facilitates cooperation. The weakness is that often it is only a temporary fix that fails to confront the underlying problem.

3. **Avoiding** is low in both assertiveness and cooperation. With this style, the person neither pursues his or her own concerns nor those of the other party. The individual does not deal with the conflict. Avoiding may take the form of diplomatically sidestepping an issue, postponing an issue until a better time, or simply withdrawing from a threatening situation.

   The benefit of this approach is that it buys time in developing or ambiguous situations. The weakness is that it is only a temporary fix that sidesteps the real problem.

4. **Collaborating** is high in both assertive and cooperative. Collaborating is the complete opposite of avoiding. Collaborating involves an attempt to work with others to find a solution that fully satisfies their concerns. It means diving into an issue to understand the underlying needs and wants of both parties. Collaborating between two people might take the form of exploring a disagreement to learn from each other's insights or trying to find a creative solution to an interpersonal problem.

   The strength of collaborating is that it produces a long-lasting impact because it deals with the underlying problem, not just the symptoms. The weakness is that collaboration is very time consuming. Nonetheless, collaboration is usually the best approach for dealing with conflict in groups or teams.

5. **Compromising** is moderate in both assertiveness and cooperativeness. The objective is to find some convenient, mutually acceptable solution that partially satisfies both parties. Compromising falls intermediate between competing and accommodating. With compromising, one gives up more than with competing but less than with accommodating. Similarly, compromising addresses an issue more directly than avoiding, but does not explore it in as much depth as collaborating. In some situations, compromising may mean splitting the difference between the two positions, exchanging concessions, or seeking a quick middle-ground solution.

FIGURE 3 CONFLICT RESOLUTION TECHNIQUES.

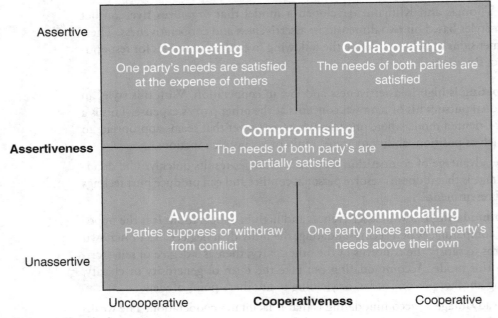

Source: Jeffrey Anderson

The benefit of compromise is that it is democratic and seems to have no losers. However, since many people approach compromise situations with a win–lose attitude, they may feel disappointed in the results.

Each of us is capable of using all five conflict-handling modes. No one can be characterized as having a single style of dealing with conflict, but certain people use some styles better than others and, therefore, tend to rely on those styles more heavily than others—whether because of temperament or practice.[33]

Table 4 suggests the most appropriate style for different situations.

TABLE 4 FIVE CONFLICT RESOLUTION STRATEGIES.

Resolution Strategy	Best Situational Uses
Collaborating	Use for true conflict resolution when time and cost permit
Competing	Use for quick decisions or when unpopular actions must be taken
Avoiding	Use when the issue is minor or when a "cooling off" period is needed
Accommodating	Use when other issues are more important or to build credit for future use
Compromise	Use as a temporary fix for complex issues or when time is limited

How to Stimulate Constructive Conflict

As a manager, your job is not only to manage conflict but also to create some. When it's appropriate and constructive, conflict can stimulate performance. Constructive conflict, if carefully monitored, can stimulate increased productivity in a number of situations; when the team seems afflicted with apathy and inertia resulting in poor performance, when there is a lack of creativity and new ideas, when there are symptoms of groupthink or when managers seemed unduly concerned with peace, cooperation, and compromise. The following four tactics can help to stimulate constructive conflict:[34]

1. **Spur competition**. Competition is a form of conflict but can be positive as it can motivate people to produce at higher levels. For example, a company might put sales people in a competition with one another by offering a bonus or an award such as a trip to a resort to the top performer.

2. **Change the culture**. Competition may result from deliberately changing the organizational culture. For example, a company might announce to employees that it is seeking innovative solutions, reward original thinking, and unorthodox ideas.

3. **Bring in outsiders**. Organizations can become stagnant and inbred without infusions of new people. This is why managers often bring in outsiders, people from other units in the organization or new hires or consultants. With different backgrounds and attitudes, outsiders can bring new perspectives.

4. **Use programmed conflict**. Programmed conflict is designed to provoke different opinions without inciting people's personal feelings. The idea is to get people, through role playing, to defend or criticize ideas based on facts rather than feelings or preferences.

There are two proven methods to engage people in a debate of new ideas:

1. Devil's advocacy—role playing criticism to test whether an idea is workable. A Devil's advocate is assigned to play the role of a critic and voice as many objections as possible to a proposal and thereby generate critical thinking.

2. The dialectic method—role playing two sides of a proposal to test if it is workable. The dialectic method uses two people or groups to play opposing roles in a debate. After the structured debate, managers are more equipped to make intelligent choices.

The Interest-Based Relational Approach

In times of conflict, it's easy for people to get entrenched in their positions and for tempers to flare, voices to rise, and posture to become defensive or aggressive. This can be avoided using the Interest-Based Relational (IBR) approach.

Roger Fisher and William Ury developed the IBR approach in their 1981 book, "Getting to Yes." They argue that one should resolve conflicts by separating people and

Interest-Based Relational (IBR) approach A conflict resolution style that focuses on building mutual respect and understanding, encouraging people to resolve conflict in a united, cooperative way.

their emotions from the problem. Their approach also focuses on building mutual respect and understanding, encouraging people to resolve conflict in a united, cooperative way.

IBR is based on the notion that your role as a manager is not simply to resolve conflict but to ensure that team members feel respected and understood, and that you appreciate their differences. In essence, it helps you to resolve conflict in a civil and "grown up" way.

During the process, the focus should be on behaving courteously and consensually, and on insisting that others do the same. The priority is to help each side develop an understanding of the other's position, and to encourage both to reach a consensus—even if that means agreeing to disagree.

To use the IBR approach effectively, everyone involved should listen actively and empathetically, recognize body language, be emotionally intelligent, and be able to use different anger management techniques. In particular, you and the conflicting parties need to follow these six steps:

1. **Make sure that good relationships are a priority.** Treat others with respect. Do your best to be courteous and constructive

2. **Separate people from problems.** Recognize that, in many cases, the other party is not "being difficult." Real and valid differences can lie behind conflicting positions. By separating the problem from the person, you can discuss issues without harming relationships.

3. **Listen carefully to different interests.** You'll get a better understanding of why people have adopted /their position if you try to understand their point of view.

4. **Listen first, talk second.** You should listen to what the other person is saying before defending your position. They might say something that changes your mind.

5. **Set out the "facts."** Mutually decide on the observable facts that might impact your decision.

6. **Explore options together.** Be open to the idea that a third position may exist, and that you might reach it together.

You can often prevent contentious discussions from turning bad by following these guidelines, and they can help you avoid the resentment and dislike that can cause conflict to spiral out of control.

However, bear in mind that the IBR approach may not work for all situations. For example, you may not be able to resolve differences in such a consensual, collaborative way during a crisis. On these occasions, you may have to "pull rank" as a leader and make quick decisions about disputes and conflicts.[35]

Summary of Learning Outcomes and Key Points

☐ **Understand the differences between groups and teams**

A group is two or more two or more freely acting individuals who share collective norms, collective goals, and have a common identity. A team is a small group of people with complementary skills who are committed to a common purpose, performance goals, and approach for which they hold themselves mutually accountable.

Work groups often interact to share information and make decisions to help each member perform their job more effectively or efficiently. Work teams by contrast have members that are work intensively on a common goal. Members of group teams have complementary skills and hold each other mutually accountable.

❒ **Remember and understand different types of teams**

Formal groups are those that are established to achieve to achieve organizational goals. Informal groups are formed for the individual needs of the members, for example, the need for social interaction.

Work teams have a clear purpose that all members share. Work teams work collectively on a specific common goal. Project teams are work teams that are assembled to solve a particular problem or complete a specific task. Cross-functional teams are set up to include members from different functional areas of the organization, such as finance, sales, and operations.

Self-managed teams are groups of workers who are empowered and have responsibility for administrative oversight of their tasks. On a day-to-day basis, team members decide what the team will do, how it will do it, and what specific tasks each team member will perform. A virtual team is a team whose members rarely meet face-to-face but instead interact using various forms of information technology such as e-mail, computer networks, telephone, fax, and video conference. An agile team is a cross-functional group of people that have the personnel and resources needed to produce a working, tested incremental version of a product. Scrum is an agile methodology to manage a project.

❒ **Understand the team development life cycle and team member roles**

Each team, as it develops, passes through distinct stages. First is the forming stage, which is a period of orientation where team members get to know one another. Next is the storming phase which is marked by conflict over team roles, goals, or methods. During the norming phase, the team agrees on roles, methods and goals, and norms are formed. Next is the performing stage where the team works together and finally the adjourning phase where the team disbands.

Roles are socially determined expectations of how team members should act in a specific position. A role is a tendency to behave, contribute, and interrelate with others in a particular. Teams tend to have two categories of roles; task and maintenance. Task roles are those behaviors that concentrate on completing the team's tasks. Maintenance roles are those behaviors that foster constructive relationships between team members.

❒ **Describe how factors such as conformity, cohesiveness, and team size influence team effectiveness**

Norms are expectations about behavior that are shared by members of a team. They are the often unwritten rules that determine what is socially acceptable and what behavior is appropriate. Because people want to be accepted by the groups to which they belong, they are subject to pressure to conform. Group members often want to be seen as one of the group and avoid being observably different. In these cases, the group often exerts intense pressure on the individual to align is or her opinion to conform with others. In the extreme, this can result in groupthink.

Group cohesiveness is the degree to which members are attracted to or loyal to the group. When cohesiveness is high, individuals value their membership in the team and have a strong desire to remain as part of the group. When cohesiveness is low, members don't find their participation appealing and have little desire to remain in the group. Team is a set of planned activities aimed at improving the functioning of a team. They can be conducted by company trainers, outside consultants, or by managers.

Teams need to be large enough to include enough members with the diverse skill sets needed to complete a task, but small enough for members to feel like an intimate part of the team and foster effective communication. Most effective teams are kept relatively small in size. The preferred number for most teams is seven, plus or minus two.

Social loafing is the tendency for an individual to expend less effort when working with a group than when working individually. Social loafing may occur because people believe that others in the group aren't doing their fair share and therefore reduce their effort to make the workload equivalent.

❏ **Understand the nature of conflict in teams and methods to resolve conflict**

Conflict is a disagreement over issues resulting in some form of interference or opposition. When conflict is constructive, it can add to creativity and reduces the likelihood of groupthink. But when conflict is destructive, it can break down the team and hurt performance. One conflict resolution model organizes five conflict management styles based on two dimensions: assertiveness and cooperativeness. These two basic dimensions of behavior define the following five different modes for responding to conflict situations: competing, accommodating, avoiding, collaborating, and compromising.

The Interest-Based Relational (IBR) approach to conflict resolution focuses on building mutual respect and understanding, encouraging people to resolve conflict in a united, cooperative way.

End Notes

1. http://www.bizjournals.com/bizjournals/how-to/growth-strategies/2013/06/the-difference-between-a-group-and-a.html, retrieved 5/17/17.

2. Bateman, T., Snell, S., and Konopaske, R., Management, 5th edition, McGraw-Hill, New York, NY, 2018, p. 273.

3. https://www.economist.com/news/business-and-finance/21694962-managing-them-hard-businesses-are-embracing-idea-working-teams, retrieved 11/16/17.

4. https://www.forbes.com/sites/jeffboss/2016/11/15/leverage-the-power-of-teams-for-better-business-performance/#cd4aeda1c6af, retrieved 11/21/17.

5. Jones, George, J., Essentials of Contemporary Management, 6th edition, McGraw-Hill, New York, NY, 2015, p. 363.

6. Kinicki, A. and Williams, B., Management, A Practical Introduction, 8th edition, McGraw-Hill, New York, NY, 2018, p. 439.

7. Schermerhorn, J. and Bachrach, D. Management, 13th edition, Wiley, Hoboken, NJ, 2015, p. 394.

8. Kinicki, A. amd Williams, B. p. 439.

9. Kinicki A. and Fugate, M., Organizational Behavior, 5th edition, McGraw-Hill, New York, NY, pp. 275–276.

10. Kinicki, A. and Williams, B., p. 440.

11. Williams, C., Effective Management, 7th edition, Cengage, Boston, MA, 2016, p. 277.

12. https://www.forbes.com/sites/stevedenning/2016/08/13/what-is-agile/#36dd318a26e3, retrieved 8.8.18.

13. https://www.leadingagile.com/2015/02/what-is-an-agile-team-and-how-do-you-form-them/, retrieved 9/19/18.

14. https://www.mountaingoatsoftware.com/agile/scrum, retrieved 10/9/18.

15. http://managementhelp.org/groups/dynamics-theories.htm#stages, 5/17/17.

16. Kinicki, A. and Williams, B., p. 448.

17. https://open.lib.umn.edu/principlesmanagement/chapter/13-4-understanding-team-design-characteristics/, retrieved 8.24.18.

18. Lussier, R., Management Fundamentals, 8th edition, Sage, Thousand Oaks, CA, 2019, p. 249.

19. Kinicki, A. and Williams, B., p. 449.

20. Robbins, S. and Coulter, M., Management, 13th edition, Pearson, Boston, 2016, p. 378.

21. Ibid, p. 485.

22. Daft, R. and Marcic, D., Understanding Management, 10th edition, Cengage, Boston, MA, 2017, p. 601.

23. https://www.inc.com/jeff-haden/10-scientifically-proven-ways-to-build-and-manage-great-teams-wed.html, retrieved 9/4/18.

24. Daft, R. and Marcic, D., p. 611.

25. https://www.forbes.com/sites/richkarlgaard/2015/04/01/think-really-small/#5dc5f8c28102, retrieved 8.8/2018.

26. Jones, G. and George , J., p. 361.

27. https://www.forbes.com/sites/richkarlgaard/2015/04/01/think-really-small/#5dc5f8c28102 retrieved 8.8/2018.

28. https://www.scrum.org/forum/scrum-forum/7460/scrum-dev-team-size, retrieved 8/8/2018.

29. Robbins, S. and Coulter, M., Management, p. 379.

30. Kinicki, A. and Williams, B., Management, p. 445.

31. Ibid, p. 453.

32. Robbins, S. and Coulter, M., p. 381.

33. http://www.kilmanndiagnostics.com/overview-thomas-kilmann-conflict-mode-instrument-tki, retrieved 8/27/2018.

34. Kinicki, A. and Williams, B., p. 456.

35. https://www.mindtools.com/pages/article/newLDR_81.htm, retrieved 8/27/2018.

CHAPTER 11 LEADERSHIP

Key Terms

Authentic leadership
Autocratic style
Charismatic leaders
Coercive power
Consideration
Contingency theory
Democratic style
Employee-centered leader
Expert power
Job-centered leader

Initiating structure
Leader
Leader–member relations
Leadership
Least-preferred co-worker (LPC)
  questionnaire
Legitimate power
Level 5 leadership
Managerial grid
Path-goal theory

Position power
Readiness
Referent power
Reward power
Servant leadership
Situational leadership theory (SLT)
Substitutes for leadership
Task structure
Transactional leadership
Transformational leadership

Introduction

In previous chapters of this book, we have discussed the management functions of planning and organizing. In this chapter, we explore the leadership function. Leadership is about influencing others to take those actions that are necessary for the organization to achieve its goals. In this chapter, I will define leadership. I will discuss power, which is the ability to influence others. I will compare leaders and managers and explore traits of effective leaders. Finally, I will outline behavioral, contingency, and contemporary theories on leadership effectiveness.

© Shutterstock.com

Learning Outcomes

After reading this chapter, you should be able to:

❑ Define leader and leadership

❑ Identify five sources of leader power

❑ Describe the differences and similarities between leaders and managers

❑ Compare and contrast early and behavioral leadership theories

❑ Describe three major contingency theories of leadership

❑ Compare modern leadership theories

What is Leadership?

Leadership is the ability to influence others toward the attainment of goals. A leader's influence is not passive but rather, actively focused on achieving organizational goals.[1]

Leadership is both a process and a property. It is a process because leaders help shape the group's goals, motivate group behavior toward achieving those goals, and help to define the organization's culture. Leadership is a property because it is a set of characteristics that are attributed toward people who are perceived as leaders. Leaders are thus (1) people who influence behaviors of others without using force and (2) people whom others accept as leaders.[2]

At its core, leadership is about influence. For our purposes, we will define a leader as someone who influences others and leadership as the process of influencing a group of people to achieve goals.

Leader Someone who can influence others

Leadership The process of influencing a group of people to achieve a goal

Management vs. Leadership

Leadership and management go together. While they are not the same thing, they are linked and complement one another. Still, many scholars have delineated the differences between leadership and management. The manager's job is to plan and organize, while the leader's job is to inspire and motivate. In his 1989 book "*On Becoming a Leader*," Warren Bennis composed a list of differences. Some of these differences are highlighted in Table 1.

Perhaps there was a time when the functions of manager and leader could be separated, a supervisor in an industrial-era factory might not give much thought to what he or she was producing, or to the people who were producing it. The job was to follow orders, organize and assign work, coordinate results, and ensure that the job got done as required. Efficiency was the focus.

In today's economy, where value comes increasingly from the knowledge of people, and where workers are no longer cogs in an industrial machine, management and leadership are not as easily separated. Employees look to their managers, not just to assign them a task, but to also define for them a purpose. Today, managers must organize workers, not just to maximize efficiency, but to develop and nurture their skills and talents.

TABLE 1 MANAGERS VS. LEADERS

The Manager	The Leader
Administrates	Innovates
Is rational	Is visionary
Maintains	Develops
Focuses on systems and structure	Focuses on people
Has a short-range view	Has a long-range perspective
Organizes	Nurtures
Asks how and when	Asks what and why
Looks at the bottom line	Looks at the horizon
Uses position power	Uses personal power

Position power The ability of a leader to control subordinates through reward and punishment.

Peter Drucker was one of the first to recognize this idea. He identified the emergence of the "knowledge worker," and the profound differences in how business was to be organized. With the rise of the knowledge worker, "one does not 'manage' people," said Drucker. Rather, "The task is to lead people. And the goal is to make productive the specific strengths and knowledge of every individual."[3]

Many viewed Apple CEO Steve Jobs as a leader because of his ability to influence his followers to make great products, but he was not considered a good manager. Chief Operating Officer (COO) Tim Cook did most of the managing at Apple and today, as CEO, he is viewed as both a good manager and leader.[4]

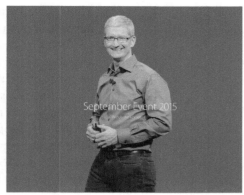
September Event 2015

Apple CEO Tim Cook is viewed by many as both an effective leader and manager.

Power

Sometimes the terms influence and power are used as synonyms, but there are distinct differences between the two. Power is the potential ability to influence the behavior of other people. Influence is the effect that a leader's actions have on the behavior, values, attitudes, and beliefs of others.[5]

Leadership theorists have generally agreed on the following five types of powers:

1. **Legitimate** or **position power** derives from the leader's position in the organizational hierarchy. A leader with legitimate power has the authority or right to tell others what to do. This power includes possession of information, veto power, and the power to set policy.

2. **Coercive power** comes from the follower's fear of punishment and the leader's power to inflict it. A leader with coercive power has control over punishments, people comply to avoid those punishments.

3. **Reward power** is based on the follower's expectations of positive rewards and the leader's ability to provide them. Because these leaders control rewards, people comply in order to receive those rewards.

4. **Expert power** comes from a leader's specialized knowledge or skill. Leaders with expert power possess certain knowledge or expertise. People comply because they believe that they can learn or otherwise gain from the leader's expertise.

5. **Referent power** is based on follower's identification with the leader's personal characteristics or traits. A leader with referent power has personal characteristics that others find appealing. People comply because they admire, respect, or desire to be like those leaders.[6]

Legitimate power The power a leader has as a result of his or her position in the organization

Coercive power The power a leader has to control followers through punishment

Expert power Power based on expertise, knowledge, or specialized skills

Referent power Power based on the leader's personal characteristics

Reward power The power a leader has to provide positive rewards

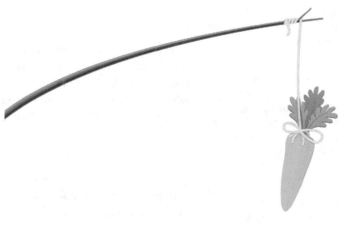

The ability to deliver rewards and punishments are two types of leader power.

All of these sources of power are potentially important. Generally, first-line managers have less legitimate, coercive and reward power than do middle and top managers.

While it's easy to assume that most powerful leaders have high legitimate power and control rewards and punishments, it's important not to underestimate the more personal referent and expert powers.[7] In many cases, these personal powers may be more effective, at least in the long term.

People will follow a leader, just because he or she is the boss. But only so far and for so long. Substantive change, in most cases, comes from leaders who have expertise and personal appeal rather than ones who allocate punishments and rewards. To be sure, most effective leaders use a combination of each of these five types of power. Consider Steve Jobs, presented in the closing case of this chapter.

Early Leadership Theories

Trait Theory

How can we identify effective leaders? Trait theory represents the earliest research attempt to answer that question. Researchers attempted to identify leader traits and qualities by examining leaders who had achieved greatness. Since the majority of great leaders in these studies were men, this approach has also been called by some, the "great man theory."[8]

The categories of leadership traits identified in these studies included a wide variety of physiological, demographic and personality characteristics.[9]

Early leadership research focused on studying the traits and characteristics of effective leaders

Trait theory lost its appeal as a result of research conducted in the 1940s and because there was a lack of consensus on the definitive traits that set leaders apart from non-leaders.[10] The general key positive traits of leaders, identified by this research, are listed in Figure 1.

Leadership Behavior Theories

Given the limitations of the trait approach, researchers looked for other ways to understand leadership. Three major university studies started to look at leader behaviors. Rather than looking at the traits a leader possesses, these behavioral theories examined what good leaders do. The three major studies in this field were conducted at the University of Iowa, Ohio State University, and Michigan University.

The University of Iowa Studies

The University of Iowa studies explored three leadership styles in order to determine which was the most effective. The autocratic style describes a leader who dictates work methods, makes unilateral decisions, and limits employee participation. A democratic style describes a leader who involves employees in decision making, delegates authority, and uses feedback as a means to coach employees. Finally, a laissez-faire style describes

Autocratic style
A leader who dictates work methods and limits employee participation

Democratic style A leader who involves employees in decision making, delegates authority, and uses feedback as a means to coach employees.

Laissez-faire style Describes a leader who lets the group make decisions and complete work as they see fit

FIGURE 1 SEVEN TRAITS ASSOCIATED WITH EFFECTIVE LEADERSHIP

1. **Drive**—Leaders demonstrate a high level of effort. They're ambitious, persistent, and have a high desire for achievement. They have high levels of energy and constantly strive for improvement.

2. **Desire to lead**—Leaders have a strong desire to lead.

3. **Honesty Integrity**—Leaders build trusting relationships with followers by being truthful and honest. They show integrity with a high consistency between words and deeds.

4. **Self-confidence**—A self-confident leader overcomes obstacles, makes decisions despite uncertainty and instills confidence in others.

5. **Intelligence**—Leaders must be intelligent enough to gather, synthesize, and interpret lots of data and information. They need intelligence to create visions, solve problems, and make decisions.

6. **Job Knowledge**—Effective leaders have a high degree of job specific knowledge. They understand their business and use their knowledge to make well-informed decisions.

7. **Extraversion**—Leaders are energetic, outgoing people. They're comfortable in social situations and assertive.

(Adapted from Robbins and Coulter, Management, 13 edition, p. 493)

a leader who lets the group make decisions and complete work as they see fit.[11] The results of the Iowa studies suggested that a democratic style was the most effective, but as later research discovered, it's not that simple.

The Michigan Studies

In the 1940s, researchers at the University of Michigan developed what became known as the University of Michigan Leadership Model by studying the effects of leader behavior on job performance. They identified two types of leader behavior or styles.

A leader who is primarily concerned with issues like production efficiency and meeting work schedules is characterized as a job-centered leader. A leader whose behavior focuses on subordinate's satisfaction and work group cohesion is defined as employee-centered leader.[12] These two different types of leader behavior are outlined in Table 2.

The Ohio State Studies

At about the same time as the Michigan studies, a team of Ohio State University researchers identified two similar types of leader behavior. Leaders who rated high on initiating structure engaged in behaviors that focused on task and productivity. Consideration was the term Ohio State researchers

TABLE 2 UNIVERSITY OF MICHIGAN LEADER BEHAVIORS

Job Centered Behaviors	Employee Centered Behaviors
❏ Emphasis on the technical or task aspects of the job	❏ Emphasis on interpersonal relationships
❏ Mainly concerned with accomplishing the group's goal	❏ Personal interest in needs of employees
❏ Regard members as a means to an end	❏ Accepts individual differences among group members

Source: Adapted from http://business.nmsu.edu/~dboje/teaching/338/behaviors.htm (retrieved 9/30/16)

used to characterize leader behavior that was focused on leader–follower relationships.[13] Table 3 describes the leadership behaviors for each of these styles.

> "My job is not to be easy on people. My job is to take these great people we have and to push them and make them even better."—*Steve Jobs*

The behaviors identified by Ohio State researchers were very similar to those described at Michigan but there are some important differences. One major difference is that Ohio State researchers interpreted each behavior to be independent of the other. Thus, a leader could exhibit varying levels of initiating structure at the same time as varying levels of consideration.

At first, Ohio State researchers thought that leaders who exhibit high levels of both behaviors would be more effective than other leaders. However, research at International Harvester (now Navistar International) suggested a more complicated pattern. Researchers found that employees of supervisors who ranked high on initiating structure where high performers but had low levels of satisfaction and higher levels of absenteeism from work. Employees of supervisors with high consideration behaviors were satisfied with their jobs and had low absenteeism but were low performers.[14]

TABLE 3 OHIO STATE LEADERSHIP BEHAVIORS

Initiating Structure	Consideration
1. Makes sure work-unit members know what is expected of them	1. Treats all work-unit members as equals
2. Schedules the work to be done	2. Is approachable and friendly
3. Encourages the use of standardized work procedures	3. Does little things to make work pleasant
4. Assigns particular tasks to work-unit members	4. Puts suggestions made by the work unit into operation
5. Plans tasks for work-unit members	5. Is concerned for personal welfare of work unit members
6. Makes his or her attitudes clear to the work unit	6. Creates a supportive socioemotional work atmosphere
7. Clarifies work roles	7. Maintains high morale
8. Expects and asks for results	8. Creates a collaborative work atmosphere

Source: Adapted from https://www.boundless.com/management/textbooks/boundless-management-textbook/leadership-9/behavioral-approach-70/leadership-model-the-ohio-state-university-350-3483/ (retrieved 10/2/16)

The Managerial Grid

After the Ohio and Michigan studies were published, it became popular to talk about leaders as people who are always performance and maintenance oriented. The best known leadership training model to follow that philosophy is Blake and Mouton's managerial grid.[15] In this model, Robert Blake and Jane Mouton identified two behavior dimensions; a concern for production and a concern for people. Using each behavior as an axis, they plotted five leadership styles as illustrated in Figure 2.

According to the Blake Mouton model, the team management is the best leadership style. Team management leaders stress production needs and the needs of the people in equally high proportions. Their premise is that employees understand the organization's purpose and are involved in determining production needs. When employees are committed and have a stake in the organization's success, their needs and production needs coincide. This creates a team environment based on trust and respect, which leads to high satisfaction and motivation and, as a result, high production.[16]

For a number of years, grid theory was highly regarded by U.S. businesses and industry but its popularity has faded. Critics regard the theory as too simplistic, a "one-size-fits-all" approach that ignores the possibility that a 9, 9 style might not be best in all circumstances. Regardless, a team management style is effective in many circumstances and is probably the best default style for a manager who is new or unfamiliar with situational variables.[17]

The managerial grid, as well as findings from Ohio State University and the University of Michigan led researchers to believe that leadership is more complex than

Managerial grid A two-dimensional grid for assessing leadership styles

FIGURE 2 BLAKE AND MOUTON'S MANAGERIAL GRID

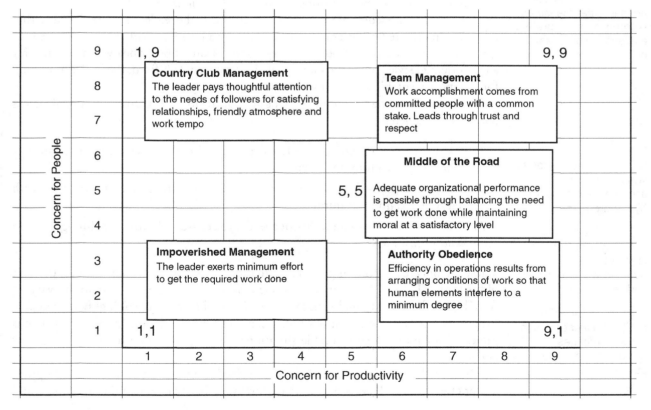

isolating leader traits or preferred behaviors. Researchers began to look at other situational influences on leadership effectiveness. Specifically, they sought to define various situations and the appropriate leadership style for those situations.

Contingency Theories of Leadership

In this next section we will examine three contingency theories; Fiedler's contingency theory, Hersey and Blanchard's situational leadership theory, and path-goal theory. Each seeks to define the relationship between leader styles and the situation. Each seeks to answer the *if-then* question of which leadership style is appropriate for which situation.

Fiedler's Contingency Theory

Fiedler's contingency theory of leadership is regarded by many as the first situational theory of leadership. He proposed that effective leadership is a function of the match or fit between a leader's style and the demands of the situation. Fiedler viewed leadership style as part of a person's personality and thus difficult to change. Instead, he theorized that the key to success was to use existing leadership styles in the situations to where they are best suited. In order to achieve the match between style and situation, a leader must understand his or her personal styles and the strengths and weaknesses of those styles.[18]

The first step in Fiedler's model is to identify the leader's preferred style. Fiedler believed that one's leadership style is fixed, and can be measured using an assessment he developed called least-preferred co-worker (LPC) questionnaire. The LPC questionnaire asks the individual to describe his or her least preferred co-worker in terms of bipolar adjectives. These questions are presented in Figure 3.

The sum of the scores of these questions indicates the leader's preferred style; either relationship oriented or task oriented. According to Fiedler, a score of 73 or above suggests a preferred relationship-oriented style and a score of 64 or below a preference for a task-oriented style. Since the individual's leadership style is fixed, the leader must look for the most favorable situation to match his or her style.

To understand the situation, Fiedler said that the following three situational factors had to be considered:

1. Leader–member relations—The degree to which a leader is accepted and supported by the group members.
2. Task structure—The extent to which the task is structured and defined, with clear goals and procedures.
3. Position power—The ability of a leader to control subordinates through reward and punishment.

These factors create either high or low situational control or favorableness on the part of the leader. The combination of these factors creates eight possible situations, varying from highly favorable to highly unfavorable. For highly favorable or highly unfavorable situations, Fiedler recommends a task-oriented style. A relationship-oriented style is preferred for moderately favorable situations. See Figure 3 for a matrix of situations and styles.

Because Fiedler viewed a leader's style as fixed, there are only two ways to improve leader effectiveness. First, a new leader whose style better matched the situation could

Path-goal theory A leadership theory that says the leader's job is to assist followers in reaching their goals using directive or supportive leader behaviors to ensure that the follower goals are compatible with organizational goals

Contingency theory A leadership theory that defines effective leadership as a match between the leader's preferred style and the situation

Least-preferred co-worker (LPC) questionnaire A questionnaire that measures whether a leader prefers a relationship- or task-oriented style

Leader–member relations The degree to which a leader is accepted and supported by the group members

Task structure The extent to which the task is structured and defined, with clear goals and procedures

Position power The ability of a leader to control subordinates through reward and punishment.

FIGURE 3 FIEDLER'S ANALYSIS OF SITUATIONS AND STYLES

Leader–Member Relations	Good				Poor			
Task Structure	Structured		Unstructured		Structured		Unstructured	
Leader Position Power	High	Low	High	Low	High	Low	High	Low
Favorable	_____→							Unfavorable
Most Effective Type of Leader	Task-Oriented	Task-Oriented	Task-Oriented	Relationship-Oriented	Relationship-Oriented	Relationship-Oriented	Relationship-Oriented	Task-Oriented

be brought in. Or the situation could be changed by restructuring tasks, increasing the leader's power, or improving the relations between the leader and members. While research that tests the validity of Fiedler's model shows evidence in support, the model isn't without criticism.

Situational Leadership Theory

One of the biggest criticisms of Fiedler's model is its lack of flexibility. Fiedler believed that because our natural leadership style is fixed, the most effective way to handle situations is to change the leader. He didn't allow for flexibility in leaders.

Paul Hersey and Kenneth Blanchard, creators of the leadership model they called situational leadership theory (SLT), suggest that a leader can and should adapt his or style to match the situation. The Hersey-Blanchard situational leadership model focuses on the fit of leadership style and follower maturity or readiness, and suggests that in order to be effective, leaders must respond with a degree of flexibility that allows the leader to adjust his or her leadership style as the follower(s) mature and are capable of tackling the task at hand.[20]

Leadership style in the situational model is classified according to the relative amount of task and relationship behavior in which the leader engages. This differentiation is similar to initiating structure and consideration as defined by the Ohio State studies. Task behavior is the extent to which the leader spells out the duties and responsibilities of an individual or group. It includes giving directions and setting goals. Relationship behavior is the extent to which the leader engages in two-way or multiway communication. It includes such activities as listening, providing encouragement, and coaching.

The situational model places combinations of task and relationship behaviors into four quadrants. Each quadrant calls for a different leadership style. Four styles are identified in the SLT model, often depicted in a 2 × 2 matrix, resulting in four quadrants as illustrated in Figure 5.[21]

Situational leadership theory (SLT) A leadership theory that matches the leader's style to the readiness of the followers

"Before you are a leader, success is all about growing yourself. When you become a leader, success is all about growing others."—*Jack Welch*

Each style is defined by the degree of task behavior and relationship behavior the leader is required to engage in with the follower. As such, each quadrant requires a different response approach by the leader

Employee **readiness** is a key component of this model. Readiness in situational leadership is defined as the extent to which a group member has the ability and willingness or confidence to accomplish a specific task. The concept of readiness is therefore not a characteristic, trait, or motive—it relates to a specific task.

Readiness has two components, ability and willingness. Ability is the knowledge, experience, and skill an individual or group brings to a particular task or activity. Willingness is the extent to which an individual or group has the confidence, commitment, and motivation to accomplish a specific task.

For the least ready followers, those who are unable, unwilling, and not confident in their ability, SLT advises a *Telling* style. Leaders using this style provide high amounts of task behavior and low amounts of relationship behavior. This style emphasizes giving instructions as follower readiness is low and requires a "hands on" approach. This can also be seen as an autocratic style since most decisions are made for the follower since the leader tells the employees the what, how, when, and where of assigned tasks. This leadership style is clearly autocratic in nature.

Followers with the next highest level of readiness are those who lack ability, but are willing and confident. The best style for this level of readiness is a *Selling* style, one that is high in both task and relationship behaviors. This style emphasizes explanation of decisions made by the leader. Task guidance by the leader is designed to facilitate performance through persuasive explanation. This leader style is very directive in nature but in a more persuasive and guiding manner. The leader provides a great deal of input into the task but also works to establish important relational aspects as well.

A *Participating* style is high in relationship behaviors and low in task behaviors. This style is preferred for followers who are able, but are unwilling and not confident about their abilities about tasks. This style emphasizes shared ideas and participative decisions on task directions. This style requires a higher degree of leadership intervention to help foster an improved sense of task understanding and confidence

Employees with the highest degree of readiness should be led with a *Delegating* style that is low in both task and relationship behaviors. This leader would allow the group to take responsibility for task decisions. Employees with high readiness require minimal leadership intervention. This leader style is considered Laissez-Faire.

Situational leadership theory has an intuitive appeal. The theory acknowledges the importance of followers. However, research that tests the validity of the theory has been disappointing. Nonetheless, hundreds of Fortune 500 companies have trained tens of

Readiness The extent to which people have the ability, confidence, and willingness to perform a task

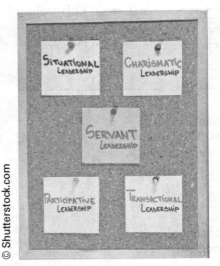

© Shutterstock.com

FIGURE 4 FOLLOWER READINESS

High	Moderate		Low
R4	R3	R2	R1
Able, Willing, and Confident	Able but Unwilling or Insecure	Unable but Willing or Confident	Unable and Unwilling or Insecure

(source: Hersey, P., The Situational Leader, Center for Leadership Studies, Escondido, CA, 1997, p. 63)

FIGURE 5 SITUATIONAL LEADERSHIP THEORY

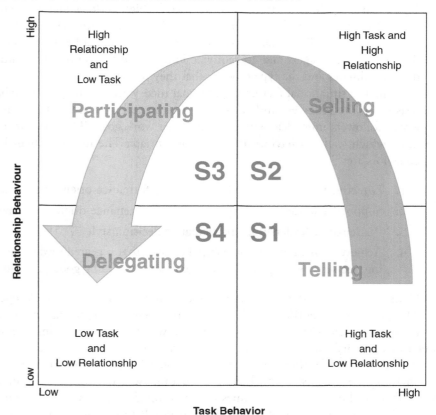

Source: The Situational Leader, by Paul Hersey. Center for Leadership Studies, 1984, p. 33.

FIGURE 6 THE PATH-GOAL MODEL

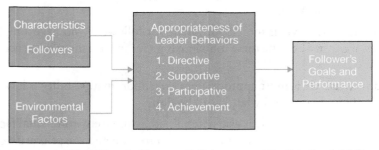

Source: *Management*, 11th Edition, by Thomas S. Bateman and Scott A. Snell. McGraw-Hill Education, 2015, p. 422.

thousands of employees in situational leadership and it remains a favorite approach of many leaders.

House's Path-Goal Theory

In what he called path-goal theory, researcher Robert House studied how leaders can motivate their subordinates to achieve group and organizational goals. The idea behind path-goal theory is that effective leaders motivate followers to achieve goals by (1) clearly

U2's leader Bono uses the supportive and participative approaches of path-goal theory.

identifying outcomes that subordinates are trying to achieve from the workplace (2) reward subordinates with these outcomes for high performance and achievement of work goals, and (3) clarify for subordinates the path that leads to work goal achievement. Path-goal theory is a contingency model because it suggests that the steps managers take to motivate followers depends upon the nature of the subordinates and the type of work that they perform.[22]

The key situational factors in path-goal theory are (1) the personal characteristics of the followers and (2) the environmental pressure and demands to which followers must deal with to attain their work goals. These factors determine which leader behaviors are most appropriate. The four pertinent leader behaviors are:[23]

1. Directive leadership, a version of task performance-oriented behavior
2. Supportive leadership, a type of group maintenance-oriented behavior
3. Participative leadership, a participative decision style
4. Achievement-oriented leadership, behavior that is geared toward motivating people by setting challenging goals and rewarding good performance.

Figure 6 shows how these situational factors and leader behaviors work together: The theory also identifies which follower and environmental characteristics are important. *Authoritarianism* is the degree to which individuals admire, respect, and defer to authority. Locus of control is the extent to which individuals see the environment as responsible for their own behavior. People with an internal locus of control believe that they are responsible for their own outcomes where as people with an external locus of control believe that outcomes are based on chance. Finally, ability reflects people's beliefs about their own ability to do their job. Path-goal theory states that the personal characteristics of the followers determine the appropriateness of various leadership styles. For example, the theory makes the following proposals.[24]

❒ A directive style is more appropriate for highly authoritarian followers because they respect authority.

❒ A participative style is more appropriate for followers who have a high internal locus of control because these individuals prefer to have more influence over their lives.

❒ A directive style is most appropriate when subordinate's ability is low because it helps them understand what has to be done.

The appropriate leadership style is also determined by three environmental factors; people's tasks, the formal authority system of the organization and the primary work group.

❒ Directive leadership is inappropriate if the tasks are well structured.

❒ If the task and the rule system are dissatisfying, directive leadership will create more dissatisfaction.

❒ Supportive leadership is most appropriate in dissatisfying situations as it offers positive gratification in an otherwise negative situation.

❒ If the primary work group provides social support, a supportive style is less necessary.

Path-goal theory offers many more suggestions. The best way for leaders to be effective is to analyze the situation and adopt the appropriate style.[25]

Contemporary Leadership Theories

Charismatic Leadership

Many of history's most effective leaders, Martin Luther King Jr., John F. Kennedy, Gandhi, and Winston Churchill, were charismatic leaders. Charismatic leaders are very skilled communicators. They are verbally eloquent, but also able to communicate to followers on a deep, emotional level. They can articulate a compelling or captivating vision and arouse strong emotions in followers.

Charisma is a process, an interaction between the qualities of the leader, the followers and their identification with the leader and a situation that requires charismatic leadership, such as a crisis or need for change. But at their core, charismatic leaders are able to communicate with followers to gain their trust and persuade them to follow. Many national politicians have developed their ability to be charismatic, to make speeches and "work a room" of potential donors and supporters.[26]

Charismatic have exceptionally high self-confidence and they dominate others. They have a strong conviction in the morality of their beliefs. They create an aura of competence and success and they communicate high expectations for their followers. The charismatic leader articulates ideological goals and makes sacrifices in the pursuit of those goals.

Consider Martin Luther King Jr. He had a dream for a better world. John F. Kennedy spoke of landing a man on the moon. These leaders had a compelling vision and they aroused a sense of excitement in others. Jeff Bezos, founder and CEO of Amazon.com is a charismatic leader who exudes energy, enthusiasm, and drive. Bezos's charismatic personality has enabled him to drive Amazon through the ups and downs of a rapidly expanding company.[27]

Charismatic leaders Leaders who are self-confident, enthusiastic, and whose personality influences people to behave in certain ways

President John F. Kennedy was a charismatic leader who inspired many followers.

Transformational and Transactional Leadership

Transformational leadership causes change in individuals and social systems. In its purest form, it creates positive, valuable changes in followers. Transformational leadership develops followers into leaders and enhances the motivation, morale, and performance of followers. Transformational leaders are able to connect followers to the collective identity of the organization.

James M. Burns first introduced the concept of transformative leadership in 1978 with his research on political leaders, but this term is now used in management theory as well. According to Burns, transformative leadership is a process in which "leaders and followers help each other to advance to a higher level of morale and motivation."[28] Transformational leaders create excitement with their followers in the following ways:[29]

Transformational leadership Leaders who inspire and cause change in individuals and social systems

- ❐ They are charismatic.
- ❐ They give their followers individualized attention. They develop people by delegating challenging work and providing one-on-one mentoring.
- ❐ They are intellectually stimulating. They arouse an awareness of potential problems and solutions with their followers. They stir imaginations and generate insights.

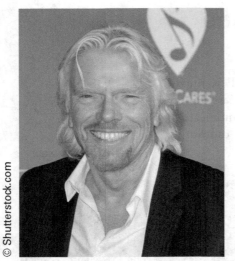

Virgin Group CEO Sir Richard Branson is a charismatic and transformational leader.

Pope Francis is a transformational leader.

Transactional leadership Leaders who exchange rewards and punishment based on follower performance

Level 5 leadership Leaders who blend extreme personal humility with intense professional will

Pope Francis is a contemporary example of a transformational leader. Since his election in 2013, Pope Francis has electrified the church and attracted legions of non-Catholic admirers by energetically setting a new direction for the church. He refused to live in the palatial papal apartments, he washed the feet of a female Muslim prisoner, he has driven around Rome in a Ford Focus, and famously asked "Who am I to judge?" with regard to the church's view of gay members. He created an advisory group of eight cardinals to council him on reform, which one church historian calls the "most important step in the history of the church for the past ten centuries."

Pope Francis asked the world to stop the rock-star treatment. He knows that while revolutionary, his actions so far have reflected a new tone and intentions. His hardest work lies ahead. But signs of a "Francis effect" are starting to appear: In a recent poll, one in four Catholics said they'd increased their charitable giving to the poor. Of those, 77 percent reported that it was due in part to the Pope.[30]

Transformational leadership may be better understood in comparison to transactional leadership. For many managers, power stems from their ability to provide rewards and threaten reprimands in exchange for subordinates performing their work. This is transactional leadership, which focuses on clarifying employee's roles and task requirements and providing rewards or punishment depending on performance.[31]

> "Leadership is lifting a person's vision to high sights, the raising of a person's performance to a higher standard, the building of a personality beyond its normal limitations."—*Peter Drucker*

As transactional leaders are able to satisfy the needs of subordinates, they may improve productivity. Transactional leaders are typically hard working, tolerant, and fair-minded. Transactional leadership is important to all organizations, especially during stable periods, but leading change requires transformational leadership.[32]

Level 5 Leadership

The concept of Level 5 leadership was created by business consultant, Jim Collins in his well-respected 2001 Harvard Business Review article and his popular book "*From Good to Great.*"

Figure 7 illustrates the five different levels of leadership according to Collings. Level 5 leadership is considered by some executives to be the ultimate leadership style. Level 5 leadership combines strong professional will and determination with personal humility to build enduring greatness. A Level 5 leader is always focused on the organization's long-term success while behaving with modesty and directing attention to the organization. Some examples include John Chambers, CEO of Sysco Systems and

IBM's former CEO Louis Gerstner. Gerstner is credited for transforming IBM from a computer hardware company to a global services provider. After his retirement, Gerstner wrote a memoir detailing the IBM transformation but said little about himself. Level 5 leadership is a way to transform organizations and make them great using a combination of transformational and transactional styles.[33]

Leaders Coaching Others

Coaching is leadership that instructs followers on how to meet the challenges they face in the organization. Operating much like a coach in athletics, a coaching leader identifies inappropriate behavior in followers then suggests how they might correct that behavior. Coaching has become more important in organizations because of the increasing use of teams. [34]

A successful coaching leader displays many different types of behavior including the following:

❏ **Listens closely**—The coaching leader gathers facts and listens for the feelings and emotions behind what is said. The leader is careful to listen and not immediately rebut statements made by followers.

Baseball's Dusty Baker, pictured here while manager of the Cincinnati Reds, is a coaching leader who listens, offers encouragement and builds trust with his team.

FIGURE 7 LEVELS OF LEADERSHIP

Level 5: Great Leader
Builds enduring greatness through a blend of personal humility and professional will

Level 4: Effective Leader
Catalyzes committment to and vigorous pursuit of a clear and compelling vision

Level 3: Competent Manager
Organizes people and resources towards the effective and efficient pursuit of objectives

Level 2: Contributing Team Member
Contributes individual capabilities to the team and works effectively with others

Level 1: Highly Capable Individual
Makes productive contribututions through knowledge, skills and good work habits

(adapted from https://hbr.org/2005/07/level-5-leadership-the-triumph-of-humility-and-fierce-resolve)

- ❐ **Provides emotional support**—The coaching leader gives personal encouragement to followers in order to motivate them to do their best to meet the high demands of the organization.
- ❐ **Leads by example**—The coaching leader shows followers demonstrates expertise and build the trust and respect of followers.

Substitutes for Leadership

Substitutes for leadership A theory stating that different situational factors can enhance, neutralize, or substitute for leader behaviors

In some situations, leaders don't have to lead. Sometimes situations constrain their ability to lead effectively or leadership may be unnecessary. Substitutes for leadership can provide the same influence on employees as leaders would provide.[35]

> "A leader is best when people barely know he exists, when his work is done, his aim fulfilled, they will say: we did it ourselves."—*Lao Tzu*

The substitutes concept identifies situations where leadership is neutralized or replaced by characteristics of subordinates, the task, or the organization. For example, when a patient is delivered to the emergency room at the hospital, the professionals on duty don't need to be told what to do by a leader. Doctors, nurses, and staff take actions without waiting for directive or supportive leader behavior. [36]

Jobs designed with clarity, meaning, and intrinsic motivation should require little guidance and inspiration from a leader.

Servant Leadership

Servant leadership An approach to leading where leaders view their primary role as helping followers in their quest to satisfy personal needs, aspirations, and interests

Servant leadership is an approach to leading where leaders view their primary role as helping followers in their quest to satisfy personal needs, aspirations, and interests. Servant leaders view their own needs as secondary to the needs of their followers. Servant leaders place a high value on service to others, placing it ahead of their own self-interests.

Many consider Zappos CEO Tony Hsieh as a servant leader because his focus is on fulfilling the personal needs of those in the organization. Hsieh found, early in his career, that it was difficult for him to enjoy his work because people weren't engaged in their work. As a result, when he formed Zappos.com, he focused on building a work environment that made employees feel good about their contributions and career, so good that they enjoyed coming to work.[37]

Servant leaders possess several distinctive characteristics that better enable them to support follower's goals and aspirations. Servant leaders are:

- ❐ *Good listeners,* the ability to listen gives servant leaders the information to define the need to define follower aspirations
- ❐ *Persuasive,* servant leaders focus on persuasion, not authority
- ❐ *Empathetic,* servant leaders identify with their followers and are thus better equipped to support their needs
- ❐ *Stewards,* servant leaders see themselves as being entrusted to manage the human assets of the organization

© Shutterstock.com

Duke Basketball Coach Mike Krzyzewski is regarded by many as an authentic leader.

Authentic Leadership

Authentic leadership refers to individuals who know and understand themselves and empower others with their openness and authenticity. Authentic leadership is rooted in the ancient Greek philosophy "To thine own self be true." Authentic leaders care about the interests of organizational stakeholders. They are able to sacrifice their own self-interest for others and are trusted by their followers. Authentic leaders are ethically mature and they exhibit moral reasoning.[38]

Authentic leadership Refers to individuals who know and understand themselves and empower others with their openness and authenticity

Mike Krzyzewski, basketball coach at Duke University, is an example of an authentic leader. Krzyzewski relies on developing personal relationships and emphasizes teamwork over individual performances. He builds strong relationships with his players so that the team has a family feel. Leading a basketball team is like leading a business he believes. "I think you have to be trustworthy. You have to take the time to develop a relationship that's so strong with each individual player, and hopefully with the team, that they will trust you. They let you in, and if they let you in, you can teach. If they don't let you in, you're never going to get there."[39]

While there are varying interpretations of the theory, most theorists agree that authentic leaders are:[40]

- ❐ *Genuine and self-aware.* Authentic leaders are aware of their strengths, their limitations, and their emotions. They also show their true selves to their followers. They are consistent in their public and private actions and they don't hide mistakes or failures for fear of looking weak.

- ❐ *Mission driven and focused on results.* They are able to put the organization's mission and goals ahead of their own self-interest. They pursue results not power, money or ego.

- ❐ *Not afraid to show their emotions.* They lead with their hearts as well as their minds. They are direct with their communication but do so with empathy.

- ❐ *Focused on the long term.* Authentic leaders are focused on long-term shareholder value, not in just beating quarterly estimates. Like Jeff Bezos at Amazon, these leaders realize that nurturing a company is hard work that requires patience but pays big dividends over time.

Gender and Leadership

Leadership today in business is still like an old boy's club. In fact, women head only 21 of the companies on the Fortune 500 list.[41] That's about 4 percent. According to the Pew Research Foundation, uneven expectations and companies not being ready to elevate women are cited more than any other factor as a major reason that more women are not in top leadership roles in business.[42]

When women do advance to top management positions, special attention is often focused on them and the fact that they are women. Because there are so few, women CEOs like Meg Whitman of Hewlett-Packard and Indra Nooyi of Pepsico are rock stars.

Hewlett-Packard CEO Meg Whitman, one of the few women in top management roles.

© Shutterstock.com

One widespread stereotype of women is that they are more nurturing and support-ive than men. This suggests that women would have a relationship-oriented leadership style. Research suggests though that male and female leaders behave in similar ways.[43]

Recent progress in balanced gender leadership can't be underestimated though. The chancellor of Germany, the head of the International Monetary Fund, and the chair of the U.S. Federal Reserve are women. General Motors, IBM, and Lockheed Martin are headed by women. Nearly 60 percent of the world's university graduates are women, and women control most consumer goods buying decisions.

Smart leaders have known that gender balance brings better performance. The com-panies with more gender-balanced leaders perform better than those with less. So the shift is moving away from diagnosing why women don't make it to the top and toward analyz-ing what is right with companies and leaders that build gender balanced leadership teams.[44]

Summary of Learning Outcomes and Key Points

❏ **Define leader and leadership**

Leaders influence others toward the attainment of goals. Leadership is a process, influencing others to attain goals. Leadership is also a set of characteristics and behaviors shared by leaders.

❏ **Identify five sources of leader power**

Power is the ability to influence others. There are five sources of power. Legiti-mate power comes from one's position in the organizational hierarchy. Reward and coercive power come from a leader's ability to provide rewards or punish-ments. Expert power comes from a leader's deep knowledge and specialized expertise. Finally, referent power comes from followers who identify with a leader or that leader's personal characteristics.

❏ **Describe the differences and similarities between leaders and managers**

While often used as synonyms, leadership and management are different things. Managers are mostly about process, efficiencies and organization. Leaders are about vision, influence and change. In today's environment, individuals need to be both managers and leaders.

❏ **Compare and contrast early and behavioral leadership theories**

Early research in leadership was focused on studying the personal characteristics and traits of effective leaders. This trait theory reasoned that we could select and train leaders based on a set of shared traits.

In the 1900s, leadership research began to focus on the behavior or style of leaders. Studies at the University of Iowa, Ohio State University, and the Univer-sity of Michigan observed two separate leadership behaviors centered on (1) the job to be done and (2) interpersonal relationships between leaders and followers. However, these studies couldn't identify which leadership style, or combination of styles was most effective. Blake and Mouton's Managerial Grid focused on training leaders to practice high levels of both task and relationship behaviors.

❏ Describe three major contingency theories of leadership

Fiedler's Contingency Theory is considered the first contingency theory of leadership. Fiedler believed that a leader's style is fixed and effective leadership depends on matching a leader with the appropriate situation. He defined three situational variables; (1) position power of the leader (2) task structure, and (3) leader–member relations. Fiedler suggested that a task-oriented style was most effective for very favorable and very unfavorable situations while a relationship style is most effective for moderately favorable situations.

Paul Hersey and Ken Blanchard developed Situational Leadership Theory. They believed that a leader was capable of changing styles and that effective leadership was dependent on matching a leader's behavior to the readiness of the follower. Hersey and Blanchard presented four different leadership styles; telling, selling, participating, and delegating which used varying amounts of task- and relationship-oriented behaviors.

House's Path-Goal Theory proposes that effective leaders motivate followers to achieve goals by (1) clearly identifying outcomes that subordinates are trying to achieve from the workplace (2) reward subordinates with these outcomes for high performance and achievement of work goals, and (3) clarify for subordinates the path that leads to work goal achievement. Path-goal theory is a contingency model because it suggests that the steps managers take to motivate followers depend upon the nature of the subordinates and the type of work that they perform.

❏ Compare modern leadership theories

Early leadership theories focused on leader traits, behaviors, and situations. Modern leadership theories take a broader look at effective leadership. Charismatic leaders are effective communicators who can articulate a compelling or captivating vision and arouse strong emotions in followers.

Transformational leaders can cause significant changes in organizations and followers where transactional leaders influence others through a combination of rewards and punishments.

The substitutes model suggests that leadership isn't always required and under some circumstances teams may function without instructions from a leader. Coaching is an important part of leading and coaching leaders listen to followers and give them feedback to help them improve.

Finally, servant leaders and authentic leaders focus on honesty and transparency. These leaders put the goals of the organization ahead of their own personal interests.

Questions for Review

1. Describe leadership and why it's important for organizational success.
2. Identify the five types of power. Which ones are the most effective?
3. Describe the trait approach to leadership. Why did the trait approach fall out of favor?
4. Describe the two types of leadership styles as determined by the Ohio State and Michigan studies.
5. Compare and contrast the three contingency approaches to leadership.
6. Compare modern leadership theories.

Closing Case—Steve Jobs the Leader

Steve Jobs. His story is the stuff of legends. In 1976, at the age of 21, he cofounded Apple in his family's garage. A year later, the Apple II became one of the first highly successful mass produced personal computers. After a power struggle, Jobs was forced out of Apple in 1985. He returned as CEO in 1997 and rescued Apple from near bankruptcy. While away from Apple, Jobs bought Pixar, leading it to produce the first completely computer generated film, *Toy Story*.

With Job's return to leadership, Apple produced a series of products that would have significant cultural impact, among them, iTunes, the iPod, the iPhone, and the iPad. These products and others transformed entire industries including personal computing, music, telephony, mobile computing, and digital publishing. At the time of Job's death in 2011, the market value of Apple's shares was about $351 billion, making it one of the biggest publicly traded U.S. companies.

But Job's wasn't perfect, a point to which many could testify. His tirades and fits were as legendary as his vision. He was extremely blunt in his criticism. He called people who didn't impress him "bozos" and was described by some as a "high maintenance" coworker. He was relentless and never let up on staff members.

Jobs was a dictator not a consensus builder. He had an amazing aesthetic sense and single vision of how Apple products should look, feel and function. He never compromised on this vision and he never tolerated anything that threatened that vision.

One Apple insider describes a meeting in 2008 when Jobs called in the team that was creating the MobileMe e-mail system. "Can anyone tell me what MobileMe is supposed to do?" After an answer from the group he replied "So why the #### doesn't it do that?" He went on to scold the group for 30 minutes. "You've tarnished Apple's reputation," he said. "You should hate each other for having let each other down."

So much of what we study about leadership today revolves around authentic and supportive leadership. Leaders who listen to others and serve their organization. Steve Jobs was none of those things. He was as approachable as a Pitbull.

But despite Job's harsh leadership style, or maybe because of it, Apple flourished under his leadership. Turnover at Apple was extremely low and people stayed despite the tough environment, because they believed in the mission of the company. Jobs wanted to change the world, and he did. And while he wasn't a saint, he will be remembered as one of America's greatest innovators, along with Thomas Edison, Henry Ford, and Walt Disney, not because of his personality, but for his contribution to technology and business.

1. What type(s) of power did Steve Jobs use to influence his followers?
2. What were the leadership traits and characteristic of Jobs?
3. Describe the behaviors Jobs exhibited when interacting with his followers.
4. This style worked for Steve Jobs. Will it work for everyone? Why or why not?

(adapted from: https://hbr.org/2012/04/the-real-leadership-lessons-of-steve-jobs, http://www.forbes.com/sites/jackzenger/2013/08/22/the-big-lesson-about-leadership-from-steve-jobs/#5850273c6a94, http://www.executivestyle.com.au/steve-jobs-an-unconventional-leader-1lcmo

Notes

1. Daft, R. (2016). *Management* (12th ed.). Cengage, Boston, p. 514.

2. Griffin, R. (2016). *Fundamentals of Management* (8th ed.). Cengage Learning, Boston, p. 329.

3. http://guides.wsj.com/management/developing-a-leadership-style/what-is-the-difference-betweenmanagement-and-leadership/ (retrieved 9/19/16)

4. Lussier, R. (2017). *Management Fundamentals: Concepts, Applications and Skill Development* (7th ed.). Sage, Los Angeles, CA, p. 383.

5. Daft, R. (2016) *Management* (12th.ed.). Cengage, Boston, p. 536.

6. Lee, J. (1980) *Leader Power*, in *Perspectives in Leader Effectiveness*, Stinson, J. and Hersey, P. (eds.), The Center for Leadership Studies, p. 37.

7. Bateman, T. & Snell, S. (2013). *Management* (3rd ed.). McGraw-Hill, New York, p, 234.

8. Wynn, S. (2012, January 30). Trait Theory. Retrieved from Encyclopedia of Educational Leadership and Administration: http://www.sagepub.com/northouse6e/study/materials/reference/reference2.1.pdf

9. http://www.managementstudyguide.com/trait-theory-of-leadership.htm (retrieved 8/4/14)

10. Ibid.

11. Bateman, T. & Snell, S. (2015) *Management* (11th ed.). McGraw-Hill, New York, p. 493.

12. Kinicki, A. & Williams, B. (2013) *Management, A Practical Introduction* (6th ed.). McGraw-Hill, New York, p. 432.

13. Jones, G. & George, J. (2015) *Essentials of Contemporary Management* (6th ed.). McGraw-Hill, New York, p. 328.

14. Griffin, R. (2016) *Fundamentals of Management* (8th ed.). Cengage Learning, Boston, p. 333.

15. Bateman, T. & Snell, S. (2015) *Management* (11th ed.). McGraw-Hill, New York, 2015, p. 416.

16. http://www.mindtools.com/pages/article/newLDR_73.htm (retrieved 9/30/16)

17. Bateman, T. & Snell, S. (2015) *Management* (11th ed.). McGraw-Hill, New York, p. 417.

18. Schermerhorn J. & Bachrach, D. (2015). *Management* (13th ed.). John Wiley & Sons, New York, p. 325.

19. Adapted from https://www.mindtools.com/pages/article/fiedler.htm (retrieved 9/28/16)

20. Hersey, Paul. (1997). The Situational Leader, Center for Leadership Studies, Escondido, CA.

21. Hersey, Blanchard, & Johnson. (2007). *Management of Organizational Behavior: Utilizing Human Resources*.

22. Jones, G. & George, J. (2015) *Essentials of Contemporary Management* (6th ed.). McGraw-Hill, New York, p. 342.

23. Bateman, T. and Snell, S. (2015) *Management* (11th ed.). McGraw-Hill, New York, p. 420.

24. Ibid., p. 422.

25. Ibid.

26. https://www.psychologytoday.com/blog/cutting-edge-leadership/201210/what-is-charisma-andcharismatic-leadership (retrieved 10/1/16)

27. Robbins, S. & Coulter, M. (2016). *Management* (13th ed.). Pearson, Upper Saddle River, p. 500.

28. http://www.langston.edu/sites/default/files/basic-content-files/Transformational-Leadership.pdf (retrieved 9/19/16)

29. Kinicki, A. & Williams, B. (2013). *Management, A Practical Introduction* (6th ed.)., McGraw-Hill, New York, p. 460.

30. http://fortune.com/2014/03/20/worlds-50-greatest-leaders/ (retrieved 10/2/16)

31. Certo, S. & Certo, S. (2014) *Modern Management* (13th ed.). Pearson, Upper Saddle River, p. 353.

32. Daft, R. & Marcic, D. (2015). *Understanding Management* (9th ed.). Cengage, Stamford, CT, p. 532.

33. Bateman, T. & Snell, S. (2015). *Management* (11th ed.). McGraw-Hill, New York, p. 426.

34. Certo, S. & Certo, S. (2014). *Modern Management* (13th ed.). Pearson, Upper Saddle River, p. 351.

35. Bateman, T. & Snell, S. (2015). *Management* (11th ed.). McGraw-Hill, New York, 2015, p. 247.

36. Griffin, R., (2016). *Fundamentals of Management* (8th ed.). Cengage Learning, Boston, p. 344.

37. Certo, S. & Certo, S. (2014). *Modern Management* (13th ed.). Pearson, Upper Saddle River, p. 351.

38. Bateman, T. and Snell, S. (2015). *Management* (11th ed.). McGraw-Hill, New York, 2015, p. 427.

39. https://leadingwithtrust.com/2015/04/05/dukes-coach-ks-secret-to-leadership-success/ (retreived10/15/16)

40. http://www.forbes.com/sites/kevinkruse/2013/05/12/what-is-authentic-leadership/#4e603ca22ddd (retrieved 10/11/16)

41. http://fortune.com/2016/06/06/women-ceos-fortune-500-2016/ (retrieved 10/1/16)

42. http://www.pewsocialtrends.org/2015/01/14/chapter-3-obstacles-to-female-leadership/ (retrieved 10/1/16)

43. Jones, G. & George, J. (2015). *Essentials of Contemporary Management* (6th ed.). McGraw-Hill, New York, p. 348.

44. https://hbr.org/2014/03/its-time-for-a-new-discussion-on-women-in-leadership (retrieved 10/15/16)

Other Notes and Acknowledgments

All boxed quotes in this chapter are attributed to http://www.forbes.com/sites/kevinkruse/2012/10/16/quotes-on-leadership/ (retrieved 10/15/16)

The closing case is based on Frederick E. Allen's article in *Forbes*, 8/27/2011 http://www.forbes.com/sites/frederickallen/2011/08/27/steve-jobs-broke-every-leadership-rule-dont-try-that-yourself/#5dd90f313b27

CHAPTER 12 INFORMATION, COMMUNICATION AND TECHNOLOGY

Contributed by Martin van den Berg and Jeffrey Anderson. (c) Kendall Hunt Publishing Company.

Key Terms

Big data

Cloud

Communication

Customer relationship
  management (CRM)

Data analytics

Data mining

Enterprise resource
  planning (ERP)

IT infrastructure

Social media

Supply chain management (SCM)

Systems development life
  cycle (SDLC)

The Internet of things (IoT)

Introduction

Managers use information, communication, and technology daily. They monitor, collect, and process data that provide them with information to make better decisions. They communicate with others both inside and outside their organization, and managers use technology to improve their efficiency and effectiveness.

In this chapter, we'll explore the different types of information systems that managers use to process data. We'll outline the communication process and affirm the importance of communication. Finally, we'll look at ways that organizations can achieve a competitive advantage by organizing and interpreting vast amounts of data.

Learning Outcomes

After reading this chapter, you should be able to:

❑ Remember and understand how managers use information to make decisions

❑ Describe the communication process and outline how managers can listen and communicate effectively

❑ Recall how organization's use the system development life cycle (SDLC) to create software applications

❑ Describe the various enterprise information systems

❑ Differentiate between different implementations of on-premises and cloud computing

Information

We live in the information age, a period in human history characterized by the shift from traditional industries fueled by the industrial revolution to one based on information. Technological advancements in networking and computer hardware and software have given managers the ability to analyze large amounts of data to support managerial decision making. In this section, we will outline the concepts of big data and describe how managers organize and analyze large amounts of data.

Management involves a series of decisions and decision making is at the heart of executive activity in business. However, decisions must be made quickly, especially in today's environment where the most precious and least manageable commodity available to managers is time. Mintzberg identified the informational managerial roles. These roles include monitoring, filtering, and disseminating information as a common, if not a universal part of a manager's job. Mintzberg also observed that a manager's unique access to information, along with status and authority, places him or her at the central point in the system that makes significant and strategic organizational decisions.[1]

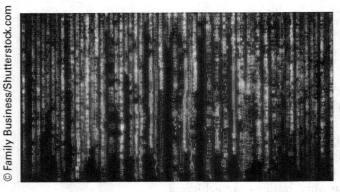

© Family Business/Shutterstock.com

Big Data

The term "big data" describes the large volume of data, both structured and unstructured, that are produced by the various information systems in an organization. The amount of data is often so large or complex that it floods a business on a day-to-day basis. The amount or complexity of data isn't particularly significant, it's what organizations can potentially do with that data that matters. Big data can be analyzed to help enable better decisions and strategic business changes.[2]

Big data a term that describes the large volume of data, both structured and unstructured, that are produced by the various information systems in an organization

Vast amount of data (big data) is being produced constantly. Every digital process, both inside and outside of an organization, generates data. Systems, sensors, mobile devices, social media, and so on produce and transmit data, which generates data sets that can be called "big data." Big data arrives from multiple sources at an alarming velocity, volume, and variety. In order to extract meaningful information from big data, organizations need optimal processing power, analytics capabilities, and skills.[3]

It's not the data that's important, it's what organizations do with the data that's important. Big data can be analyzed in order to make better business decision. The concept of big data gained momentum in the early 2000s thanks to industry analyst Doug Laney. Laney articulated the definition of big data as the three Vs.[4]

❏ **Volume.** Organizations collect data from multiple sources including business transactions, information from sensors, machine-to-machine data, and data from social media.

❏ **Velocity.** Data streams into the organization at tremendous speed and needs to be dealt with in a timely manner. RFID tags, sensors, and smart metering drive the need to deal with floods of data on a nearly real-time basis.

❏ **Variety.** Data comes in multiple formats, including structured, numeric data in databases, and unstructured data in the form of text documents, email, video, audio, stock ticker data, and financial transactions.

Data Mining

Data mining is the process of analyzing data to yield useful information for managers. With advances in computing power, statistics, and analytics, we are now able to collect and analyze more and more data. For example, UPS spends more than $1 billion per year on technology. One of their programs uses more than 1,000 pages of code to calculate optimum daily routes for drivers. By using this information, the company expects to save more than $50 million annually by eliminating excess driving miles.[5]

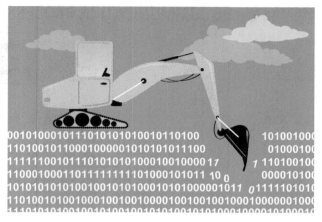

© Aleutie/Shutterstock.com

Data Analytics

Today's managers often think they are making informed decisions, only to find out later that a better decision could have been made if they had certain information at hand. With the large amounts of data stored and collected across an organization, the information to make better decisions can be made available to managers. This is where analytics comes in. Analytics, at a high level, is the discovery and interpretation of data and extracting information out of that.

There are several tools and software solutions available in today's market place that help organizations in the analytics space. Some of these solutions bring the power of analytics to the manager, where a manager can create his or her own information streams and dashboards.

Since analytics is something that is being done on data that is already available to an organization, much of the decision-making information is still hindsight. Originations that are really mature in analytics can start to discover patterns in their datasets, and potentially cross a boundary to "predictive analytics." Predictive analytics tries to predict what is going to happen next, based on standard patterns that are predefined and recognized in the datasets. Predictive analytics borders on artificial intelligence (AI) where systems start to mimic cognitive functions, such as learning or problem solving.

Data mining the process of analyzing data to yield useful information

Data analytics qualitative and quantitative techniques and processes used to extract, categorize, and identify behavioral data and patterns.

Communication

Communication is the transfer of information and understanding from one person to another. Managers spend a significant amount of time communicating. One study found that managers spend up to 80 percent of their time communicating in a typical workday.[6]

Communication the transfer of information and understanding from one person to another person

The Communication Process

The communication process is outlined in Figure 1. The process begins with a sender who encodes a message. When the sender encodes the message, he or she uses symbols such as words, numbers, visuals, or digital signals to relay meaning. The sender sends the encoded message through a communication channel where it is delivered to the receiver. The receiver decodes the message. It's important for the sender to anticipate

FIGURE 1 THE COMMUNICATION PROCESS. COURTESY OF JEFFREY ANDERSON.

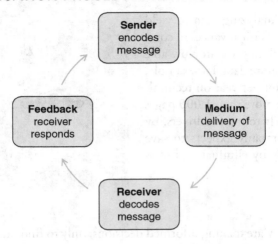

the decoding skills of the receiver. For example, when a businessperson from the Netherlands does business with someone from the United States, it's likely that all conversations and documents will be in English since most Americans don't speak Dutch and most businesspeople in the Netherlands speak English.[7]

Nonverbal Communication

According to author and consultant John Lund, the way we interpret verbal messages is based on the following three things:

- ❏ 55 percent is based on body language and facial expressions
- ❏ 37 percent is based on the tone of voice
- ❏ 8 percent is based on the spoken word

These numbers represent the averages for both men and women, but women alone would give greater weight to the facial expression and body language and less on the spoken word. Therefore, it's critical to be aware of our body language and tone when speaking to others.[8]

The Importance of Communication

Extensive research by the Gallup organization finds that employee engagement is highest when employees have some form of daily communication with their managers, whether it's face-to-face, by phone, or digitally. Managers who use a combination of different communication mediums are the most successful at engaging employees. Engaged employees report that managers return their calls or emails within 24 hours.[9]

Being an effective manager is largely dependent on good communication skills. This is nothing fancy, just being available to talk, provide guidance when needed, and return messages promptly and respectfully. Good communication builds rapport, rapport builds trust, trust shapes engagement, and engagement yields productivity.

As a manager, if you don't like communicating, you're probably in the wrong job.

Communicating Effectively

Effective communication isn't easy. Nearly all professionals can improve their communication skills. Here are some simple and direct keys to effective communication[10]:

- ❑ **Speak clearly and briefly**. Avoid flowery phrases or empty anecdotes. Trim your words to the essentials and let the power of simple phrases convey your message.
- ❑ **Back up your ideas with facts**. A little research can go a long way to prove your point and convince your audience.
- ❑ **Be positive**. Avoid being negative and talking down to your audience or bad-mouthing others.
- ❑ **Think before you speak**. In most speaking situations, it's ok to use notes. Stick to your script and avoid going off on unrelated tangents.
- ❑ **Don't interrupt**. There's no better way to tune people out than to cut them off.

Some great speakers are born, but others learn on the job. Using the right communication techniques helps. Most people have to speak in meetings or at organizational retreats; therefore, be prepared to use these techniques whether you're making a formal speech or having a personal conversation.

Communication Channels and Information Richness

The medium or channel is the method by which the sender communicates the message to the receiver. Written, verbal, and nonverbal communications have varying strengths and weaknesses. Channels vary in their information richness. Information-rich channels convey more nonverbal cues. Verbal communications are richer in information than written ones.[11] Figure 2 provides a hierarchy of channels with corresponding richness in information.

FIGURE 2 COMMUNICATION CHANNELS AND INFORMATION RICHNESS. COURTESY OF JEFFREY ANDERSON.

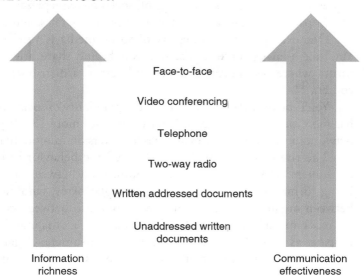

© goodluz/Shutterstock.com

Active Listening

Listening is one of the most important communication skills. How well you listen has a crucial impact on your job performance, and on the quality of your relationships with others both inside and outside of work. However, research suggests that we only remember between 25 percent and 50 percent of what we hear.[12]

We can all benefit from improving our listening skills. As a better listener, you will improve your productivity as well as your ability to influence others. Better listening helps us avoid conflict and misunderstandings.

One way to improve your listening skills is to practice "active listening." With active listening, you make a deliberate effort not only to hear the words that another person is saying but to try to understand the complete message being sent.

Here are five essential techniques for active listening:

1. **Pay attention**—Give your undivided attention and look for nonverbal cues.

2. **Show that you're listening**—Nod, smile, and use other facial expressions.

3. **Give feedback**—Use paraphrasing such as "What I'm hearing is," and "It sounds like you are saying," are great ways to reflect back.

4. **Defer judgment**—Allow the speaker to finish, don't interrupt.

5. **Respond appropriately**—Be candid and honest in your response.

Social Media

Social media electronic platforms, where users create, modify, share, and discuss Internet content

Social media includes electronic platforms such as content sharing sites, blogs, social networking, and wikis where users create, modify, share, and discuss Internet content. A presence on, as well as and usage of, social media represents a cultural phenomenon that impacts an organization's identity, reputation, sales, and even survival.[13]

One example of the ubiquity of social media is YouTube. Launched in 2005, YouTube allows people to discover, watch, and share original videos. It provides a forum where people can connect and acts as a distribution platform for original content.[14]

YouTube provides an example of the popularity of social media platforms. The site has more than a billion users. YouTube reaches more 18–49-year olds than any cable network in the United States and has local version in more than 88 countries.[15]

The rise of social media has changed the behavior of both organizations and consumers, and especially the communication between the two. Communities are being formed not only on social media platforms, who facilitate communication between organizations and consumers, but also between consumers. The concepts of "mass media" have been absorbed by a new "media mass" in which everyone participates as individual contributors and as consumers. Organizations can communicate instantly with consumers, but consumers can also communicate instantly with each other about a product or an organization. This creates an interesting dynamic, where an individual contributor can have just as much reach as a Fortune 50 conglomerate.

This web-based era is sometimes referred to as the Third Great Media Revolution, the invention of the printing press being the first and radio and TV being the second. In this media revolution, sometimes called the "Me-Media," personal and brand identities increasingly form the basis of the social and economic activities in which individuals, organizations, and government engage.[16]

Informal Communication Channels

Most organizations have an informal communication network often called the "grapevine." Usually this network thrives on negative information and speculation. It's important for managers to manage the grapevine to keep rumors from growing out of control. Here are some important issues regarding the grapevine[17]:

❑ **Grapevine communication often reveals boredom**—bored employees can create excitement by talking.

❑ **Poor communication fuels the grapevine**—communicating consistently and frequently keeps employees from depending on the grapevine.

❑ **The grapevine can alert you to important issues**—cultivating rapport with employees can keep you in touch with grapevine issues.

❑ **The grapevine can give you insight into other people's character**—you can learn a lot about employees by watching who feeds into the grapevine.

The best way to prevent major grapevine issues is to engage and inform employees regularly. Tell them where the organization is going and how their individual roles will help it to get there.

Technology

In the past few decades, information technology has brought about radical change across most industries in the form of software, social media, and more. These changes have created both opportunities and threats for organizations, and managers must have a foundational knowledge of technology in order to effectively perform their jobs.

In this section, we'll explore some of the various technologies and systems managers use to make decisions. We'll start with the systems development life cycle (SDLC), which describes the process used to create information systems. We'll examine IT infrastructure and cloud computing and describe various enterprise-wide systems including enterprise resource planning (ERP), supply chain management (SCM), and customer relationship management (CRM). Finally, we will discuss the Internet of things (IoT).

Application Development

When organizations have a need for a new information system, there are two routes they can take to implement that in their organization. They can go out and buy a software package, or they can custom develop their own application. Where there are pros and cons to both approaches, both need to be evaluated when the need for a new information system arises.

The benefit of buying a commercial of the shelf (COTS) information system is that it can usually be implemented relatively quickly. The functionality of the software package can be made available to users' right after installation in the IT infrastructure, and often there are manuals or even end-user training available on how to use the application. In most cases, "buy" is also more cost efficient than "build." There isn't always a COTS application available for the information system needs an organization has though, or when it's available, it doesn't always cover the required functionality.

The benefit of building a custom developed application is that it can be completely customized to the needs and requirements of the organization. Information systems can support unique business processes of an organization, which differ greatly from other organizations. There could also be a commercial advantage to custom developing applications, in that it can offer the organization with functionality or processes that their completion doesn't have access to.

Custom developing an application is often a lengthy and costly process, which starts with planning and analysis. The process most often used for developing custom applications is systems development life cycle (SDLC).

Systems Development Life Cycle

The systems development life cycle (SDLC) is the high-level process for developing information systems. The SDLC is the foundation for system development and can be organized into seven phases: planning, analysis, design, development, testing, implementation, and maintenance.[18]

Each of these phases is explained in more detail below[19]:

1. **Planning**—This phase presents a preliminary plan (or a feasibility study) for an organization's business initiative to acquire the resources to build on an infrastructure to modify or improve a service.

2. **Analysis**—Here teams consider the functional requirements of the project or solution. This includes system analysis that is analyzing the needs of the end users to ensure that the new system can meet their expectations. This is a vital step in determining an organization's needs, assigning responsibilities, and developing timelines.

3. **Design**—In this phase, the necessary specifications, features, and operations that will satisfy the functional requirements of the proposed system are outlined. During this phase, the essential components (hardware and/or software) structure (networking capabilities), processing, and procedures for the system are outlined.

4. **Development**—This phase signifies the start of production, when a programmer, network engineer, and/or database developer are brought on to do the major work on the project.

5. **Testing**—This phase is normally carried out by Quality Assurance (QA) professionals in order to determine if the proposed design meets the organization's business goals. Testing checks for errors, bugs, and interoperability.

6. **Implementation**—This phase involves the installation of the new system. This step sets the project into production, moves the data and components from the old system, and places them in the new system.

7. **Maintenance**—In this phase, end users can fine-tune the system, and if they wish, to boost performance, add new capabilities or meet additional user requirements.

Some organizations add two additional phases to SDLC: Evaluation and Disposal. Evaluation can be seen as an extension of the maintenance phase, where an information system is evaluated continuously to determine if it still serves the purpose it was originally developed for. If requirements for an information system change, functionality can be added or changed in a next release. Disposal is a phase in which an information system is phased out, often because the outcome of the evaluation phase indicated it no longer fits the purpose or because the platform it was built on is outdated. Often times the implementation of a new information system and the migration of data from the old information system are part of the disposal phase.

There are multiple other process models in use in IT organizations today, such as RAD—Rapid Application Development or Plan/Design/Run. All models aim for the same benefit: structure, control, and manageability of the process of information system development.

IT Infrastructure

IT infrastructure consists of the underlying, shared technology resources that serve as the platform for an organization's information systems, communication systems, and data. It includes hardware, software, and services that are shared across the organization. Major infrastructure components include computer hardware (both servers in the datacenter and workstations on the desktop), storage, operating systems, enterprise software, networking, security, telecommunications systems, database management systems, Internet platforms, consulting services, and systems integrators.[20]

With the trend of organizations using cloud computing, network and compute infrastructures are starting to expand more and more outside the traditional network boundaries.

IT infrastructure is the backbone of an organization's business operations, and they invest a significant amount of their IT budget to make sure this backbone operates efficiently and reliably. It needs to be up-and-running 24 hours a day to support the nonstop nature of most businesses. Many organizations have 24×7 Operations teams that monitor and manage the up-time and security of the IT infrastructure.

IT infrastructure the shared technology resources that serve as the platform for the organization's particular information system applications

Enterprise resource planning (ERP) an organization wide system that integrates all departments and functions throughout an organization into a single IT system or set of integrated IT systems

Enterprise Resource Planning

Enterprise resource planning (ERP) integrates all departments and functions throughout an organization into a single IT system or set of integrated IT systems enabling employees to make decisions by viewing information on enterprise-wide business operations.[21] An ERP helps organizations integrate and manage all financial, manufacturing, supply chain, human resources, and operational activities.[22]

© Wright Studio/Shutterstock.com

Consider ERP as the glue that binds the different systems in a large organization. Typically each division would have its own optimized system for that divisions' particular needs. With ERP, each division still has its own system but can also communicate and share information with other divisions more easily.

ERP functions much like a central nervous system for the organization. It collects information about different business activities and shares the information across the organization. Information from ERP systems is in realtime.[23]

An integrated ERP can provide the following benefits[24]:

❑ Financial management—Improves organizational control of assets, cash flows, and financial accounting.

❑ Supply chain and operations managements—Streamline organizational purchasing, manufacturing, inventory, and order processing.

❑ Customer relationship management—Improves customer service and increases cross-sell and upsell opportunities.

❑ Human resources management—Enables an organization to attract and retain talented employees with tools to help hiring, managing, and paying employees.

❑ Business intelligence—Allows organizations to make smarter decisions with easy-to-use reporting, analysis, and business intelligence tools.

Supply chain management (SCM) it is the active management of supply chain activities in order to maximize customer value and achieve a sustainable competitive advantage

After merging with MCI in 2006, Verizon needed to integrate hundreds of different financial systems spread across the world. Verizon has 24,000 users and operates in 140 countries, with 61 currencies and 23 languages. Their financial systems were extremely complex. After integrating with an ERP system, financial process at Verizon was streamlined, giving the company tighter control on financials. The resulting system offered managers the ability to get information in one place rather than searching multiple systems to get results.[25]

© Bakhtiar Zein/
Shutterstock.com

Supply chain management (SCM) is the active management of supply chain activities in order to maximize customer value and achieve a sustainable competitive advantage. SCM represents a deliberate effort to develop and run supply chains possibly in the most effective and efficient manner. Supply chain activities include activities ranging from new product development, through sourcing, production, and logistics. SCM includes the information systems needed to coordinate those activities.[26]

Retailing giant Walmart, with 2015 annual sales of $486 billion, has developed a powerful supply chain management system. Walmart's SCM funnels information such as point-of-sale data, warehouse inventory, and real-time sales into a centralized database. This information is shared with suppliers who ship more products as needed. SCM increases efficiencies for Walmart, yielding lower costs for product and inventory, better control over merchandise selection in stores, and ultimately lower process that can be passed on to consumers.[27]

Customer Relationship Management

Customer relationship management (CRM) a strategy for managing all of an organization's relationships and interactions with customers and prospective customers

Customer relationship management (CRM) is a strategy for managing all of an organization's relationships and interactions with customers and prospective customers. CRM helps organizations stay in contact with customers, streamline processes, and improve company profitability. Generally, when people talk about CRM, they are referring to a CRM system, a tool that helps with contact management, sales management, productivity, and other customer facing functions.

CRM enables the organization to focus on individual people—whether they be customers, service users, colleagues, or suppliers. CRM isn't just a tool for sales. Some of productivity gains have come from companies that have moved CRM as a sales and marketing tool and have imbedded into their business—from HR to customer services and supply chain management.[28]

Coca-Cola Enterprises (CCE) is one of the largest Coke bottlers in the world. It serves eight territories in Western Europe. CCE found that its sales representatives were spending too much time on administrative tasks and too little time dealing with customers and selling product. The company implemented salesforce, a customer relationship management system to transform its sales operations. The CRM enabled the company, its 12,500 employees to work smartly and more efficiently. As CCE's IT Vice President describes "We have reduced the time it takes to on-board a new customer by around 60 percent and decreased the administration overhead for service technicians by almost 50 percent."

The system is implemented across multiple geographic locations and business functions, from the call center agent to the service technician and sales representative. The CRM connects people and information to deliver a better customer experience. A new mobile app made it easier and quicker for service technicians to access their work schedules and log activity updates in real time, enabling them to respond to more customer requests in the same timeframe. The company

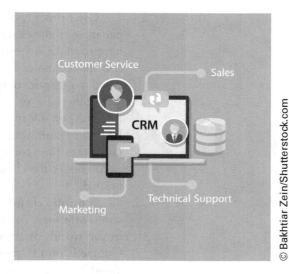

Coca-Cola Enterprises uses CRM software to manage customer relationships.

also developed an app to simplify the account creation and installation process for new customers, reducing lead time for installing new equipment by 50 percent and the onboarding process for new customers by 66 percent.[29]

The Cloud

"The cloud" is a popular tech term that many people use but can't clearly define. What is the cloud? When do you encounter it? How could it benefit a business? If you use any type of social media or access online data, then you're already using the cloud; although you may not realize it.

The cloud is a network of servers, each with a different function. Some servers use run applications or "deliver a service." Some servers provide an online service, such as Adobe Creative Cloud, and others allow you to store and access data, such as Instagram or Dropbox. You likely use the cloud every day when you use the services such as Google Drive, OneDrive, Evernote, or iCloud, anytime you're storing information without using your phone's internal storage, you're storing information on the cloud.[30]

Amazon Web Services (AWS) is one of the largest public cloud providers.

Cloud a network of servers that allow organizations to provide online services and store and access data

Oftentimes companies move to the cloud for financial reasons, whereas other companies go to the cloud for the increased agility and speed to market. Companies used to have to make large investments in hardware, the value of which depreciates every year and the technology might be outdated before it is fully amortized. However, with the cloud, companies only pay for what they use, and are always up-to-date with the latest technology. By using the cloud, organizations can reduce their capital expenditure (CAPEX) on information technology and exchange it for operating expenditure (OPEX). Not all organizations favors OPEX over CAPEX, but with the unpredictability of IT needs over time combined with technological advancements, more and more organizations choose the cloud model. The cloud model makes it easy to scale up or down as needed.[31]

A **public cloud** is a service offered to everyone. Gmail and Office 365 are public cloud offerings. Amazon Web Services (AWS), the largest cloud computing provider in the world, offers a portfolio of public cloud services, as do Microsoft Azure and Google Cloud. Dropbox is a public cloud service. Each of these examples is a public cloud because anyone can use these services, provided they pay for what they use. Some companies that have been started in the last decade rely heavily on public cloud services. Companies such as Airbnb and Uber almost exclusively use the public cloud for their information system needs, and are sometimes referred to as "born on the Internet."

A **private cloud** offers some of the same services as the public cloud, with the main difference being that those services are being delivered on IT infrastructure that is owned and managed by the organization itself. Private cloud often resides in an organization's own datacenter, and sometimes in a colocated facility. The cloud-like functionality on a private cloud is delivered by a software management layer that is installed on the IT infrastructure, such as VMware or OpenStack. The main benefit of private cloud is complete control over the IT infrastructure, and the ability to keep sensitive data within the network boundaries of the organization. These benefits are becoming less and less important as public cloud providers are offering more and more services and security offerings as part of their services portfolio. Private cloud also doesn't offer the same agility and speed to market as public cloud. In situations where users have similar requirements, they can institute a community cloud, under their combined control. Community clouds are a hybrid form of private clouds built and operated specifically for a targeted group.[32] **Figure 3** outlines the three different cloud deployment models.

FIGURE 3 CLOUD DEPLOYMENT MODELS. COURTESY OF JEFFREY ANDERSON.

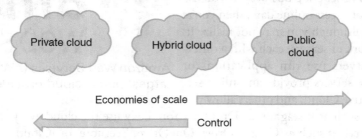

A **hybrid cloud** is the combination of public and private cloud services. Organizations can leverage some of the functionality offered by public cloud providers and integrate those with functionality that is available in their own private cloud environment. Hybrid cloud does not offer all the benefits that public cloud can offer from an agility, speed, and financial perspective, but it does offer more control and the ability to keep sensitive data within the network boundaries of an organization. There can also be practical reasons for organizations to implement a hybrid model, like in situations where large amounts of data are used by end-users and network bandwidth and latency become an issue.

Infrastructure as a service (IaaS) is an implementation of cloud computing where a vendor provides organizations with access to computing resources including servers, storage, and networking. Users use their own platforms and applications run on the service provider's infrastructure. Instead of buying hardware, users pay for IaaS on demand. The service is scalable depending on user needs.[33]

Platform as a service (PaaS) is a cloud computing service that provides organizations with a cloud environment in which they can develop, manage, and deliver applications. With PaaS, vendors deliver not only infrastructure but also middleware (databases, messaging engines, etc.) and solution stacks to build, develop, and deploy.[34] Service providers manage security, operating systems, server software, and backups. PaaS enables organizations to focus on development without having to worry about the underlying IT infrastructure.

Software as a service (SaaS) is a cloud computing service where the vendor provides access to cloud-based software. Instead of organizations installing applications on their own local devices, applications reside on a remote cloud network accessed through the web or an application program interface (API). In the SaaS model, vendors provide users with software and applications on a subscription model. Resources can be scaled depending on organizational needs. End-users can access applications from virtually any Internet connected device, anywhere in the world.[35]

The technology research leader Gartner predicts that by 2020, more computing power will be sold by infrastructure as a service (IaaS) and platform as a service (PaaS) cloud providers than sold and deployed into enterprise data centers.[36]

Figure 4 outlines the different types of cloud services and provides an analogy between cloud services and different methods of dining on pizza.

The Internet of Things

The Internet of things (IoT) refers to a network of sensors and actuators that are embedded in physical objects, everything from roads to pacemakers, which are linked together through networks, often using the Internet Protocol (IP), which connects the Internet.[37]

These networks produce huge volumes of data that provide opportunities for analysis. As IoT objects both sense the environment and communicate, they become tools to aid in understanding and responding swiftly to complex situations.

With the Internet of things, anything that can be connected will be connected. The real value of the Internet of things is that it creates a way to gather data and leverage it. Cloud-based applications are the key. The functionality IoT brings relies on

The Internet of things (IoT)
network sensors and actuators that are embedded in physical objects that are connected to the Internet

FIGURE 4 PIZZA AND CLOUD ANALOGY—A DESCRIPTION OF THE RESPONSIBILITIES OF AN ORGANIZATION IN THE DIFFERENT MODELS

Pizza

On Premises	Infrastructure as a Service (IaaS)	Platform as a Service (PaaS)	Software as a Service (SaaS)
Dining Table	Dining Table	Dining Table	Dining Table
Beverages	Beverages	Beverages	Beverages
Electric or Gas	Electric or Gas	Electric or Gas	Electric or Gas
Oven	Oven	Oven	Oven
Fire	Fire	Fire	Fire
Dough	Dough	Dough	Dough
Tomato Sauce	Tomato Sauce	Tomato Sauce	Tomato Sauce
Toppings	Toppings	Toppings	Toppings
Cheese	Cheese	Cheese	Cheese
Make at Home	*Take and Bake*	*Pizza Delivery*	*Restaurant*

Cloud Services

On Premises	Infrastructure as a Service (IaaS)	Platform as a Service (PaaS)	Software as a Service (SaaS)
Applications	Applications	Applications	Applications
Data	Data	Data	Data
Runtime	Runtime	Runtime	Runtime
Middleware	Middleware	Middleware	Middleware
O/S	O/S	O/S	O/S
Virtualization	Virtualization	Virtualization	Virtualization
Servers	Servers	Servers	Servers
Storage	Storage	Storage	Storage
Networking	Networking	Networking	Networking
	You manage		Vendor manages

the cloud based applications that interpret and transmit data to connected devices. The cloud is what enables apps to work for you anytime, anyplace.[38]

In the context of the Internet of things, technology leaders often will take the discussion to the Internet of everything (IoE). IoE is the integration of people, process, and the data generated by IoT devices. Without people and process, data doesn't have context, and adding that brings value and the possibility for action or activity based on that context. An example of IoE is that if you're on your way to a meeting, your car might access your calendar and advise on the best route. If traffic is heavy, your car might send a text message to the other party and let them know you may be late. On a broader scale, the IoE can be applied to create smart cities, helping us reduce waste and energy costs and improve how we work and live.[39]

© Alexandr III/Shutterstock.com

The Internet of things (IoT) is a network of sensors and actuators which are embedded in physical objects and are linked together through the internet.

Summary of Learning Outcomes and Key Points

❐ **Remember and understand how managers use information to make decisions**

We live in the information age and managers have unprecedented access to information. Managers use information to make decisions to help the organization reach its goals. Today's business systems produce vast amounts of data known as big data. Managers can arrange and analyze this information through data mining and business analytics.

❐ **Describe the communication process and outline how managers can listen and communicate effectively**

Communication is the process of transferring understanding. The communication process begins when a sender encodes a message. The message is sent through a medium where it is received by a receiver who decodes the message. The receiver then provides feedback, a response to let the sender know the message has been received.

Active listening is an important communication skill. With active listening, one makes a deliberate effort not only to hear the words that another person is saying but to try to understand the complete message being sent.

❐ **Recall how organization's use the System development life cycle (SDLC) create software applications**

When organizations have a need for a new information system, they can buy a software package or can custom develop their own application. There are pros and cons to both approaches, and both need to be evaluated when the need for a new information system arises.

The systems development life cycle (SDLC) is the high-level process for developing information systems. The SDLC is the foundation for system development and can be organized into seven phases: planning, analysis, design, development, testing, implementation, and maintenance.

❑ **Describe the various enterprise information systems**

Enterprise resource planning (ERP) integrates all departments and functions throughout an organization into a single IT system or set of integrated IT systems enabling employees to make decisions by viewing information on enterprise-wide business operations.

Supply chain management (SCM) is the active management of supply chain activities in order to maximize customer value and achieve a sustainable competitive advantage. SCM represents a deliberate effort to develop and run supply chains possibly in the most effective and efficient manner.

Customer relationship management (CRM) is a strategy for managing all of an organization's relationships and interactions with customers and prospective customers. CRM helps organizations stay in contact with customers, streamline processes, and improve company profitability.

❑ **Differentiate between different implementations of on-premises and cloud computing**

The cloud is a network of servers, each with a different function. Oftentimes companies move to the cloud for financial reasons, whereas other companies go to the cloud for the increased agility and speed to market. A public cloud is a service offered to everyone. A private cloud offers some of the same services as the public cloud, with the main difference being that those services are being delivered on IT infrastructure that is owned and managed by the organization itself. A hybrid cloud is the combination of public and private cloud services.

Infrastructure as a service (IaaS) is an implementation of cloud computing where a vendor provides organizations with access to computing resources including servers, storage, and networking. Platform as a service (PaaS) is a cloud computing service that provides organizations with a cloud environment in which they can develop, manage, and deliver applications. Software as a service (SaaS) is a cloud computing service where the vendor provides access to cloud-based software. Instead of organizations installing applications on their own local devices, applications reside on a remote cloud network accessed through the web or an application program interface (API).

End Notes

1. de Alwis, S. & Higgins, S.(2001). Information as a tool for management decision making: A case study of Singapore *Information Research*, 7(1).

2. Retrieved February 23, 2017, from https://www.sas.com/en_us/insights/big-data/what-is-big-data.html.

3. Retrieved February 23, 2017, from https://www.ibm.com/big-data/us/en/.

4. Retrieved March 12, 2017, from https://www.sas.com/en_us/insights/big-data/what-is-big-data.html.

5. Schermerhorn, J. & Bachrach, D. (2015). *Management* (13th ed.). Wiley, New York, NY, p. 149.

6. Kinicki, A. & Williams, C. (2013). *Management: A Practical Introduction* (6th ed.). McGraw-Hill, New York, NY, 2013, p. 476.

7. Gomes-Meja, L. & Balkin, D. (2012). *Management: People, Performance, and Change*, Prentice Hall, Upper Saddle River, NJ, p. 417.

8. Retrieved February 24, 2017, from https://www.forbes.com/sites/amyanderson/2013/05/28/successful-business-communication-it-starts-at-the-beginning/#699d49b21db5.

9. Retrieved March10, 2017, from https://www.forbes.com/sites/victorlipman/2016/01/18/the-best-managers-always-communicate/#513cf3b32a2c.

10. Retrieved March 13, 2017, from http://hiring.monster.com/hr/hr-best-practices/workforce-management/hr-management-skills/communication-in-the-workplace.aspx.

11. Retrieved March 10, 2017, from http://catalog.flatworldknowledge.com/bookhub/5?e=carpenter-ch12_s04.

12. Retrieved February 22, 2017, from https://www.mindtools.com/CommSkll/ActiveListening.htm.

13. Retrieved March 13, 2017, from http://www.sciencedirect.com/science/article/pii/S0007681311000061.

14. Retrieved March 13, 2017, from https://www.youtube.com/yt/about/.

15. Retrieved March 13, 2017, from https://www.youtube.com/yt/press/statistics.html.

16. Retrieved May 13, 2017, from https://www.ict-books.com/topics/me-the-media-pdf-lowres-en-1-info?download=3f1a143c22ae371b0bc96f296b65cf43.

17. Retrieved February 22, 2017, from http://www.forbes.com/sites/work-in-progress/2012/05/22/how-to-prune-your-organizational-grapevine/#473f51f47c72.

18. Baltzan, P. (2015). *Information Systems* (3rd ed.). McGraw-Hill, New York, NY, 2015, p. 210.

19. Retrieved March 13, 2017, from https://www.innovativearchitects.com/KnowledgeCenter/basic-IT-systems/system-development-life-cycle.aspx.

20. Retrieved March 13, 2017, from http://wps.pearsoned.ca/ca_ph_laudon_MIS_6/230/58989/15101256.cw/index.html.

21. Baltzan, P. (2015). *Information Systems* (3rd ed.). McGraw-Hill, New York, NY, p. 194.

22. Retrieved February 22, 2017, from https://www.microsoft.com/en-us/dynamics365/what-is-erp.

23. Retrieved March 3, 2017, from http://www.investopedia.com/terms/e/erp.asp.

24. Retrieved March 3, 2017, from https://www.microsoft.com/en-us/dynamics365/what-is-erp.

25. Retrieved March 12, 2017, from http://www.csc.com/cscworld/publications/75442/75654-sap_success_story.

26. Retrieved February 22, 2017, from https://scm.ncsu.edu/scm-articles/article/what-is-supply-chain-management.

27. Retrieved March 13, 2017, from https://www.usanfranonline.com/resources/supply-chain-management/walmart-keys-to-successful-supply-chain-management/#.

28. Retrieved February 22, 2017, from https://www.salesforce.com/crm/what-is-crm/.

29. Retrieved March 13, 2017, from https://www.salesforce.com/eu/customers/stories/coca-cola-enterprises.jsp.

30. Retrieved February 21, 2017, from http://mashable.com/2013/08/26/what-is-the-cloud/#6lvraCOxpgqB.

31. Retrieved February 21, 2017, from http://mashable.com/2013/08/26/what-is-the-cloud/#6lvraCOxpgqB.

32. Retrieved March 3, 2017, from https://www.sogeti.com/cloud.

33. Retrieved March 3, 2017, from https://www.ibm.com/cloud-computing/learn-more/iaas-paas-saas/.

34. Retrieved March 3, 2017, from https://www.ibm.com/blogs/cloud-computing/2014/02/cloud-computing-basics/.

35. Retrieved March 3, 2017, from https://www.ibm.com/cloud-computing/learn-more/iaas-paas-saas/.

36. Retrieved March 13, 2017, from http://www.gartner.com/smarterwithgartner/top-10-technology-trends-impacting-infrastructure-operations/.

37. Retrieved March 4, 2017, from http://www.mckinsey.com/industries/high-tech/our-insights/the-internet-of-things.

38. Retrieved March 10, 2017, from https://www.wired.com/insights/2014/11/the-internet-of-things-bigger/.

39. Retrieved March 10, 2017, from https://www.forbes.com/sites/jacobmorgan/2014/05/13/simple-explanation-internet-things-that-anyone-can-understand/#72f931ac1d09.

CHAPTER 13 CONTROLLING

Key Terms

Assets
Balance sheet
Balanced scorecard
Benchmarking
Breakeven analysis
Budget
Capital expenditure budgets
Concurrent control
Controlling
Economic order quantity

Expense budgets
Feedback control
Fixed budgets
Fixed budgets
Income statement
Inventory control
ISO 9000
Just-In-Time inventory
Lean Six Sigma
Liabilities

Operating budgets
PDCA cycle
Program Evaluation Review
    Technique (PERT)
Quality circle
Six Sigma
Stockholder's equity
Total quality management (TQM)
Variable budgets
Zero-based budgeting (ZBB)

Introduction

In Chapter one, we introduced the management process. The process begins with planning and closes with controlling. Planning and controlling are inextricably linked. We don't know the outcomes of our plans without the controlling function. Past performance, as evaluated by the controlling function, in term provides valuable information for future planning. In this chapter, we will explore the management controlling function and its purpose. We will examine various control mechanisms including financial measurements that managers use to monitor performance, compare that performance to planned goals, and take corrective action as needed.

© Shutterstock.com

Learning Outcomes

After reading this chapter, you should be able to:

❏ Remember and understand the purpose and types of managerial control

❏ Compare the balanced scorecard to traditional financial controls

❏ Describe total quality management concepts and approaches

❏ Apply quantitative control tools including breakeven analysis and inventory control

Controlling

Controlling is the management function of monitoring organizational performance, comparing performance to goals and taking corrective action as needed.[1] Thus, control involves regulating organizational activities to make sure they remain within accepted standards. Without control, organizations have no idea how well they are performing in relation to their goals.

The controlling function closes the loop on the management process. First, managers plan by setting goals and means to achieve those goals. Next, managers organize by arranging people and tasks. Managers lead by influencing and directing the activities of organizational members. The control function brings this process to a close by comparing actual performance to planned goals. Any differences between actual outcomes and plans are addressed with future planning; either taking corrective action to eliminate differences between goals and outcomes, reinforcing standards or adjusting future goals and plans.

Control Process

The control process involves four steps; (1) establish performance goals and standards; (2) measure performance; (3) compare actual performance to goals and standards; and (4) take corrective action if needed.[2] Establish performance goals and standards. As part of the planning process, managers establish goals and subgoals for the organization and its departments. These goals need to be defined in operational terms that include standards of performance that can be compared to actual outcomes.

1. Measure performance. Most organizations use a formal reporting mechanism that managers review regularly. These measurements must be related to the standards established as part of the planning process. For example, if an organization sets goals in terms of sales, it needs to have mechanisms in place to measure sales performance.

2. Compare actual performance to goals and standards. In this step, managers compare measured performance against planned goals. When managers view reports or walk around the workplace, they identify whether performance conforms to standards or falls short. Performance reports can simplify this process by comparing actual performance side-by-side with standards and calculating the difference.

3. When performance deviates from standards, managers need to determine what changes are needed and how to apply those changes. These changes can be prescribed by organizational policy or left to manager's judgment and initiative.[3]

4. Finally managers use performance results to plan new goals for the next cycle.

Types of Controls

Managers can control organizational activities before, during or after the activity has been completed. The most desirable type of control is feedforward control. **Feedforward control** is control that takes place before an activity is completed. Scheduled preventative maintenance on aircraft, performed by major airlines is an example of feedforward control. Concurrent control is control that takes place while an activity is in progress. Managers at Google monitor searches, tracking them by the hour, and fine-tune their advertising program based on current outcomes. Finally, feedback control is control that takes place after a work activity has been completed.

The major problem with feedback control is that it uncovers mistakes only after they have been made.[4] Feedforward is the best type of control to ensure that work is being done correctly. Through rules and training, feedforward control prevents problems before they occur. Concurrent control is really about managing by walking around the workplace and monitoring work. Concurrent control is not as efficient as feedforward control because resources are needed to correct problems as they happen. Feedback control is really a last resort as it takes place after a problem has occurred. Feedforward control is used to prevent problems from happening again. Feedforward control uses the most resources as compared to feedback and concurrent control.[5]

Feedback control
Control that takes place after a work activity has been completed

The Balanced Scorecard

The balanced scorecard is a control tool to give managers a comprehensive system to evaluate organizational performance through four indicators. With the balanced scorecard, managers set goals and measure performance in four areas; financial, customer, internal business and innovation, and learning. Developed by Robert Kaplan and David Norton, the balanced scorecard gives managers a dashboard like view of organizational performance. The balanced scorecard balances financial performance against these other performance measurements to give a more integrated evaluation of organizational performance.[6]

Balanced scorecard A control tool to give managers a comprehensive system to evaluate organizational performance through four indicators; financial, customer, internal business and innovation and learning

Financial performance has been the traditional measure of organizational success. Described later in this chapter, financial controls measure the organization's short and long term financial performance against goals. Traditional financial measures include net income and return on investment, among others. The financial performance indicators consider how the organization looks to its owners or shareholders.[7]

The second indicator of the balanced scorecard, customer service, considers the organization in terms of how it's viewed by customers. With this perspective, the organization sets goals and monitors performance with regard to customer satisfaction.

Internal process indicators focus on production and operating performance. In this perspective, managers answer the question "What must we excel at?" Managers set goals and measure performance for key organizational activities like time to process customer orders, producing products and delivering them to customers. Enterprise resource planning systems (ERP) can aid in this process.[8]

The final component of the balanced scorecard measures the organization's potential for learning and growth. Managers set goals and measure performance for learning and innovation, focusing on how well the organization's resources are being managed for the future. These measurements may include metrics like employee retention and the introduction of new products.[9]

The balance scorecard, if linked to a well-defined strategy and goals, is an effective tool for managing and

© Shutterstock.com

improving organizational performance. The balanced scorecard has become a core control system for many well-known companies such as Exxon Mobil, CIGNA (insurance), and Hilton Hotels.[10]

Total Quality Management

Total quality management (TQM) is an organizational-wide approach focused on continually improving product quality and value.[11] In the years following World War II, most products made in Japan were cheap and of poor quality. That changed thanks to the work of W. Edwards Deming and Joseph Juran. Desperate to rebuild its postwar economy, Japan listened to Deming's advice on good management. Deming, a mathematician, believed that quality focused on an organization's mission and used statistical measurements to reduce quality variation. Juran, another quality pioneer, described quality in terms of meeting customers real needs. The best way improve quality, according to Juran, was to listen to the real needs of customers.[12]

In his book Out of the Crisis, Deming offered 14 key principles for management to follow for significantly improving the effectiveness of a business or organization. Some of these principles are philosophical, others are more programmatic although all of them are transformative.[13] Table 1 outlines a condensed version of Deming's principles.

Total quality management (TQM) An organizational-wide approach focused on continually improving product quality and value.

TABLE 1 DEMING'S 14 PRINCIPLES

Deming's 14 Principles for Management

1. Create a constancy of purpose toward improvement.
2. Management must take leadership for change.
3. End dependence on inspection to achieve quality.
4. Move toward a single supplier for one item, based on a long-term relationship of loyalty and trust.
5. Constantly improve the system of production and service, to improve quality, productivity and decrease costs.
6. Institute on the job training.
7. The aim of managers should be to help people and machines to do a better job
8. Drive fear out of the process so that everyone may work effectively.
9. Break down barriers between departments.
10. Eliminate slogans.
11. Remove barriers that rob workers of pride in their workmanship.
12. Remove barriers that rob managers and engineers of pride in their workmanship.
13. Institute a vigorous program of self-improvement and education
14. Put everyone in the organization to work towards accomplishing the transformation.

Adapted from https://www.deming.org/theman/theories/fourteenpoints

Quality Circles

A quality circle is a participatory management technique where employees work together to solve quality problems. Quality circles are typically made up of volunteers that meet regularly to design solutions for improvements. Quality circles were first introduced in Japan, inspired by the lectures of W. Edwards Deming. American interest began in the 1970s and by 1980, more than half Fortune 500 companies had implemented quality circles. As a result of rulings from the National Labor Relations Board and the advancement of other quality initiatives, the popularity of quality circles has faded significantly. [14]

The PDCA Cycle

Another of Deming's quality initiatives was the Deming Cycle, or PDCA Cycle. The PDCA cycle is a continuous quality improvement model with four repetitive steps for continuous improvement and learning: Plan, Do, Study (Check), and Act. The PDSA cycle (or PDCA). The origin of the cycle can be traced back to statistics expert Walter Shewart, who introduced the concept of PLAN, DO and SEE in the 1920s. Deming modified the SHEWART cycle as: PLAN, DO, CHECK, and ACT.[15]

The PDCA cycle is an iterative process consisting of the following four steps:

- ❏ PLAN: for change. Analyze and predict the results.
- ❏ DO: execute the plan, taking small controlled steps.
- ❏ CHECK: check and study the results.
- ❏ ACT: on results to standardize the improvement.

Benchmarking

Benchmarking is a technique whereby an organization measures its performance against the performance of best in class organizations. Through benchmarking an organization determines how those best in class organizations achieve those performance levels. Organizations use this information to improve their own performance in areas like strategy, operations, and process. Benchmarking involves measuring processes, services and products against industry leaders. Through that measurement, an organization knows how it compares to similar organizations, even if those organizations operate in a different business segment or have different groups of customers. Benchmarking can be classified into two distinctive types; technical and competitive. Technical benchmarking is performed by design staff to compare products or services. Competitive benchmarking compares how well an organization performs with the performance of leading companies.[16]

Continuous Improvement

Six Sigma quality principles, first introduced by Motorola in the 1980s, were popularized by General Electric CEO Jack Welsh. Six Sigma is an ambitious quality standard that targets a goal of no more than 3.4 defects per million parts. This translates to

Quality circle A participatory management technique where employees work together to solve quality problems.

PDCA cycle A continuous quality improvement model with four repetitive steps for continuous improvement and learning: Plan, Do, Study (Check) and Act.

Benchmarking A technique where by an organization measures its performance against the performance of best in class organizations

Six Sigma Quality standard that targets a goal of no more than 3.4 defects per million parts

© Shutterstock.com

99.99997 percent defect free. Six Sigma has evolved from its original definition to become a general term for a quality control approach that takes nothing for granted and emphasizes higher quality and lower costs. Cardinal Health, a distributor of health care products initiated a Six Sigma program and experienced a 30 percent drop in order errors over three years.[17]

More recently, companies are using an approach called Lean Six Sigma. Lean Six Sigma focuses on problem solving and performance improvement with the goal of speed with excellence.[18] Like Six Sigma, lean is a tool that businesses use to streamline their manufacturing and production processes. The primary emphasis on Lean Six Sigma is to cut out wasteful steps in product creation so that steps directly related to adding value to the product are taken. A step is considered to have value only if a customer would be willing to pay for it. Any part of the process that doesn't add value is removed, leaving a streamlined, efficient, and profitable process. Six Sigma and Lean Six Sigma have the same goal. Both seek to eliminate waste and create the most efficient system possible. The main difference is that Lean practitioners believe that waste comes from unnecessary steps in the production process, while Six Sigma proponents believe that waste results from variation in the process.[19]

One reason for the TQM movement in the United States is the increasing significance of the global economy. Many countries have adopted a universal benchmark for quality management. ISO 9000 standards represent an international consensus on what constitutes quality management. The standard is outlined by the Organization for Standardization (ISO) in Geneva, Switzerland. Hundreds of thousands of companies in more than 150 countries have been certified against ISO 9000 standards to demonstrate their commitment to quality. ISO certification has become the standard for evaluating and comparing countries on a global basis and many U.S. companies must participate to remain competitive in global markets. In some cases, countries won't do business with an organization unless they meet ISO standards.[20]

Financial Controls

Breakeven Analysis

Breakeven analysis is a technique for identifying the point where total revenue equals total costs. When a project breaks even, it neither produces profits or losses. This analysis is a valuable tool that helps managers realize the relationship between revenues, costs, and profits (or losses). To compute the breakeven point (BE) a manager needs to know the selling price (P), the variable costs per unit (VC), and the total fixed costs (FC). An organization breaks even when revenues equal total costs. Cost has two components. Variable costs vary with output and include items like raw materials, labor, and energy costs. Fixed costs don't change with volume. Examples of fixed costs include rent, insurance, and taxes.[21]

The formula for the breakeven point in units is:

$$BE = \frac{FC}{P - VC}$$

Consider the following example; John is planning on opening a micro-brewery. He estimates his fixed costs; rent, utilities, insurance, equipment, and salaries to total $45,000 per year. His variable costs include mostly materials and ingredients estimated at $35 per keg and he can sell keg of beer for $100. Let's plug those numbers into the breakeven formula:

$$BE = \frac{\$45,000}{(\$100 - \$35)}$$

Solving the equation, the break-even point is 695 kegs of beer. At that volume, he will be able to cover his fixed costs of $45,000. If he sells less than 695 kegs he will suffer a loss. If he sells more than 700, he will make a profit. Figure 1 below illustrates graphically John's break-even point. His total costs, represented by the blue line include fixed costs of $20,000 and variable costs of $35 per keg. His sales revenue, represented by the green line, are $100 per keg. At $69,500 of revenue (695 units), revenue equals total expenses and John neither makes a profit or loss. Beyond $69,500 in sales, John makes a profit of $65 per keg sold. Of course John wants to make a profit, but a break-even analysis gives John an idea of how much he will need to sell to avoid a loss.

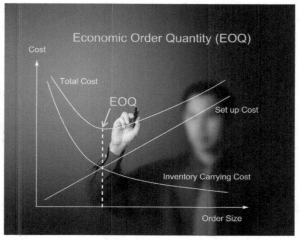

Inventory Control

Cost control is always an important management concern. Controlling inventory costs is one way managers can control organizational costs. Inventory control seeks to maintain inventory levels that are just big enough to meet immediate needs. This minimizes the carrying costs associated with holding inventory. The economic order quantity is a form of inventory control that determines a fixed number of items to be ordered when an inventory level falls to a predetermined point. Inventory orders are mathematically calculated to minimize total inventory costs.[22]

Inventory control
Maintaining just the right amount of inventory to meet the organization's needs.

Economic order quantity
A form of inventory control that seeks to minimize the costs of ordering and holding inventory.

FIGURE 1 BREAK EVEN ANALYSIS. IMAGE COURTESY OF JEFFREY ANDERSON.

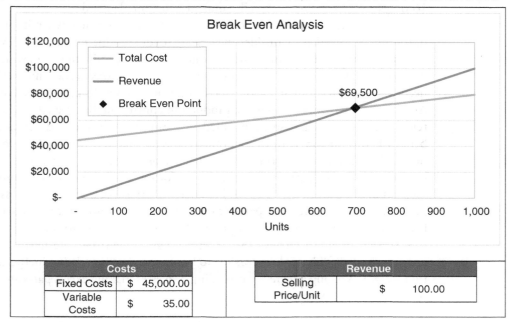

The formula for the economic order quantity is illustrated below:

$$EOC = \sqrt{\frac{2DO}{H}}$$

Where D equals the overall demand for a product, O equals the cost to place each order and H equals the cost to hold an item in inventory. For example, John needs to have an inventory of kegs on hand for output from his micro-brewery. He estimates demand for the year at 700 kegs. It costs John $100 to place an order and his cost to hold a keg in inventory is $10. Let's input these numbers into the formula below:

$$EOC = \sqrt{\frac{2(700)(100)}{H}}$$

Solving the equation, EOC = 167. Therefore, John should order 167 kegs each time he places an order. Given that he will need 700 kegs in a year, we can calculate his daily usage as:

$$\text{daily usage} = \frac{700}{365}$$

John uses 1.9 kegs per day. Therefore, he should order kegs in 167 quantity orders approximately every 88 days (167 kegs/2 kegs per day).

The EOQ formula attempts to minimize holding and ordering costs. The just-in-time inventory approach seeks to set inventory levels to zero. Just-in-time inventory (JIT) is an inventory system where component parts arrive from suppliers just as they are needed for production. When parts arrive just in time, inventories and holding costs are reduced to nearly zero. To have just the right amount of inventory arrive at just the right time requires significant coordination with suppliers. One way to do this is to use suppliers in close proximity. Most suppliers for Toyota's Georgetown, Kentucky plant are located within 200 miles of the facility. Some of these suppliers deliver as many as 16 times a day in order to meet Toyota's just-in-time demand.[23]

Just-in-time effectively means making "only what is needed, when it is needed, and in the amount needed." Consider the case of Toyota producing automobiles which can consist of nearly 30,000 parts. Toyota created a detailed production plan which included parts procurement, supplying what was needed, when it was needed and in the amount needed. This plan eliminates waste, inconsistencies and results in improved productivity. At the heart of Toyota's plan was a production control method called the "kanban system." This system has also been called the "Supermarket method" because the idea behind it was borrowed from supermarkets. Supermarkets use product control cards upon which product-related information, such as a product's name, code, and storage location. As Toyota employed kanban signs for use in their production processes, the method became known as the "kanban system." At Toyota, when a process refers to a preceding process to retrieve parts, it uses a kanban to communicate which parts have been used. In this system the next process (the customer) goes to the preceding process (the supermarket) to retrieve the necessary parts when they are needed and in the amount needed. This made it possible to improve upon the existing inefficient production system. No longer were the preceding processes making excess parts and delivering them to the next process.[24]

Just-In-Time inventory
An inventory system where component parts arrive from suppliers just as they are needed for production

Project Planning

Gantt Chart

During the scientific management era, Henry Gantt developed a tool for displaying the progress made on a project in a visual chart. One early application was tracking the progress of building a ship. Today's Gantt chart is a scheduling tool that takes the form of a horizontal bar graph as illustrated in Table 2 below:

The horizontal axis on Table 2 represents a time scale, expressed in absolute or relative time. The time interval, whether in days or months, depends on the project. Bars in the chart represent the beginning and ending time of individual tasks in the project. In this case each task begins when the preceding task is completed although there may be overlap in the case of projects where tasks can be performed in a parallel fashion. The strength of a Gantt chart is its ability to display the status of each activity or task at a glance. Gantt charts can be created by scheduling software or simply prepared in a spreadsheet like Excel.[25]

PERT Chart

More complex projects involve a series of activities, some which must be performed sequentially and others which can be performed in parallel with other activities. The Program Evaluation Review Technique (PERT) is a network model that accounts for randomness in activity completions times. In a project, an activity is a task and an event is a milestone that marks the completion of one or more activities. The milestones are numbered sequentially. Here are the steps in the PERT planning process: Identify specific activities and milestones.[26]

Program Evaluation Review Technique (PERT) A network model that accounts for randomness in activity completions times

1. Determine the sequence of these activities
2. Construct the network diagram
3. Estimate the time needed for each activity
4. Determine the critical path
5. Update the PERT chart as the project progresses

Table 2 below represents a simple network diagram, showing activities (A-F) and milestones (1-5). The estimated time for each activity is noted.

TABLE 2 SAMPLE GANTT CHART. COURTESY OF JEFFREY ANDERSON.

Task	Duration	Jan.	Feb.	Mar.	Apr.	May	Jun.	Jul.	Aug.	Sep.	Oct.	Nov.	Dec.
1	2 months	■	■										
2	1 month			■									
3	2 months				■	■							
4	3 months						■	■	■				
5	2 months									■	■		
6	1 month											■	

FIGURE 2 SIMPLE PERT NETWORK DIAGRAM. IMAGE COURTESY OF JEFFREY ANDERSON.

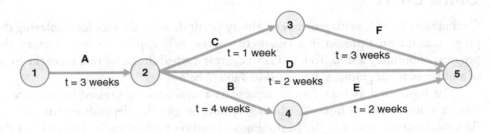

The critical path is determined by adding the time for each path through diagram. In this case, activities A-D take 5 weeks, A-C-F takes 7 weeks and A-B-E takes 9 weeks. The critical path is the longest set of activities in the diagram, in this case A-B-E. A delay in these activities will delay the overall project. A delay in other activities may not delay the project. Since A-B-E takes the longest amount of time, managers may devote extra resources to these activities to as a way to shorten the overall project time. PERT is a useful tool to determine the overall time needed for a project and the expected completion date. The limitation of PERT is that time estimates may be subjective and actual times may vary.

Budgets

A budget is a financial plan. It states an organization's plans for a given period in quantifiable terms such as dollars and hours. Budgets are prepared for the entire organization as well as for each individual unit and division of the organization. Budgets provide a yard stick by which managers can measure performance and make comparisons.[27]

Budgets typically cover a one-year period, broken down monthly. Recall from chapter one, the managerial role of resource allocator. Budgets are a tool that managers use to help them make decisions on resource allocation. In the context of this chapter, we'll focus on financial budgets but managers also use budgets to allocate other resources like machines, time, human resources, and more.[28]

There are many kinds of budgets and we will examine some in this chapter, but generally budgets fall into one of two types; fixed and variable. Fixed budgets are static and are based on a single estimate of costs. For example, an organization may budget $100,000 to buy new equipment during the year, and that amount may not be exceeded. With variable budgets, resources are allocated in proportion to organizational activity. For example, an organization may hire additional workers if sales exceed a certain level.[29]

Operating budgets include the revenue and expenses generated by an organization's daily operations. Revenue budgets forecast total annual income from all sources. Expense budgets forecast total operational spending for the year. Employee compensation is a major expense for most organizations. Capital expenditure budgets include all planned investments in major assets. These are assets that will be used, and paid for, over several years such as land, new buildings and some equipment.[30]

Zero-based budgeting (ZBB) is a practice where all expenses must be justified for each new period. Zero-based budgeting starts from a "zero-base" calling for each business function to be analyzed for its needs and costs. Budgets are then based upon what is needed for the next budget cycle, regardless of whether or not the budget is higher or lower than the previous one. Zero-based budgeting allows for strategic goals to be implemented in the budget process as it ties these goals to specific organizational functional areas, grouping costs and measuring them against previous results and current expectations.

Given the level of detail needed, zero-based budgeting may be a rolling process done over several years. In these cases, only a few functional areas reviewed at a time by managers or group leadership. ZBB can lower costs as it avoids blanket increases based on a prior period's budget. However, it is a time-consuming process that takes much longer than traditional cost-based budgeting. ZBB also favors areas with direct revenues or productions as their contributions are more easily justified than support services such as customer service or research and development.[31]

Financial Statements and Analysis

In addition to budgets, organizations commonly use other financial statements for control. Two financial statements that help managers control overall performance are the balance sheet and income statement.[32]

The balance sheet shows an organization's financial position at a given point in time. The balance sheet lists three elements:

1. **Assets** are items of value that the organization owns.
2. **Liabilities** are debts the organization owes to creditors.
3. **Stockholder's equity** is the amount accrued to the organization's owners.

The balance sheet outlines the basic accounting formula;

$$\text{ASSESTS} = \text{Liabilities} + \text{Stockholder's Equity}$$

Table 3 shows examples of these categories as typically included in a balance sheet:

Typically, current assets include cash and other assets that can be converted cash within one year of the date of the balance sheet. Examples include; cash and cash equivalents, short-term investments, accounts receivable, inventory and prepaid expenses. Investments included long-term investments in other companies, life insurance, bonds,

Zero-based budgeting (ZBB) A budget practice where all expenses must be justified for each new period.

Income statement A financial document that shows revenues and expenses, and the resulting profit or loss, over a period of time

Balance sheet Shows an organization's financial position at a given point in time

Assets Items of value that the organization owns

Liabilities Debts the organization owes to creditors

Stockholder's equity The amount of assets accrued to the organization's owners

TABLE 3 SAMPLE BALANCE SHEET. COURTESY OF JEFFREY ANDERSON.

Andy's Brewery Balance Sheet 12/31/2016			
Assets		**Liabilities**	
Current Assets		**Current Liabilities**	
Cash	$ 3,000	Accounts payable	$ 19,500
Accounts receivable	$ 16,500	Interest payable	$ 750
Inventory	$ 2,500	Taxes payable	$ 2,550
Total Current Assets	**$ 22,000**	**Total current Liabilities**	**$ 22,800**
Non-Current Assets		**Long-term liabilities**	
Land		Notes Payable	$ 27,200
Buildings	$ 36,000	**Total long-term liabilities**	**$ 27,200**
Equipment	$ 15,000		
Vehicles	$ 12,000	**Stockholder's Equity**	
Total Non-Current Assets	**$ 63,000**	Paid-in capital	$ 25,000
		Retained earnings	$ 10,000
		Total Stockholder's Equity	$ 35,000
Total Assets	**$ 85,000**	**Total Liabilities and Stockholder's Equity**	**$ 85,000**

and other investments. Property plant and equipment includes the cost of land, buildings, machinery, equipment, furniture, fixtures, and vehicles used in the operations of a business. Except for land, these assets will be depreciated over their useful life. Intangible assets include goodwill, trademarks, patents, copyrights, and other non-physical assets that were acquired at a cost. Valuable trademarks and logos that were developed by a company are not reported because they were not purchased from another person or company. Other assets often includes costs that have been paid but are being expensed over a period greater than one year such as bond issue costs and some deferred income taxes.

Current liabilities are obligations of a company that are due and payable within one year of the date of the balance sheet. Current liabilities include loans payable that will be due within the year and the current portion of long-term debt, accounts payable, income taxes payable and liabilities for accrued expenses. Noncurrent liabilities are also

TABLE 4 PRESENTS A SAMPLE INCOME STATEMENT

Income Statement for Andy's Brewery		
for the period ending 12/31/2016		
Total Revenue		**$ 100,000**
Cost of Goods Sold		$ (20,000)
Gross Margin		$ 80,000
Selling and Administrative Expenses		
Salaries	$ 10,000	
Rent	$ 10,000	
Utilities	$ 5,000	
Insurance	$ 5,000	
Depreciation	$ 5,000	
Total Selling and Administrative Expenses		$ (35,000)
Earnings Before Tax		$ 45,000

referred to as long-term liabilities. These obligations will not be due within one year of the balance sheet date. Examples include portions of automobile loans, portions of mortgage loans, bonds payable, and deferred income taxes.

Stockholder's equity includes Paid-in capital or the amounts paid by investors, retained earnings, and treasury stock.[33]

The **income statement** shows revenues and expenses, and the resulting profit or loss, over a period of time. The income statement primarily covers a one year period although monthly and quarterly statements are also used to measure interim performance.[34]

The income statement illustrates the following equation.

$$Revenue - Expenses = Net\ Income$$

Managers must be able to evaluate financial reports that compare organizational performance to earlier periods or to industry norms. Comparisons allow managers to objectively see organizational performance and measure it against others in the industry. The most common type of financial analysis focuses on ratios or statistics that provide performance indicators. Ratios, stated as a fraction or proportion, measure indicators like profits, assets, sales, and inventory.[35] Table 5 summarizes some of the most commonly used ratios.

TABLE 5 SELECTED FINANCIAL RATIOS

Type of Ratio	Calculation	Purpose
Liquidity		
Current ratio	$= \dfrac{\text{Current Assests}}{\text{Current Liabilities}}$	Measures how easily an organization can meet its short-term debts from current assets
Quick ratio	$= \dfrac{(\text{Cash + Accounts Receivable})}{\text{Current Liabilities}}$	
Leverage		
Debt ratio	$= \dfrac{\text{Total Debt}}{\text{Total Assests}}$	Indicates the degree to which organizations can pay their long-term financial obligations
Activity		
Inventory turnover	$= \dfrac{\text{Total Sales}}{\text{Average Inventory}}$	Measures the number of times inventory was sold on average throughout the year, providing an indication of the liquidity of inventory
Gross Margin	$= \dfrac{\text{Gross Income}}{\text{Sales}}$	Indicates the profitability of markup
Receivables turnover	$= \dfrac{\text{Sales}}{\text{Average Accounts Receivable}}$	Measures the efficiency of collections.
Profitability		
Return on Assets (ROA)	$= \dfrac{\text{Net Income}}{\text{Total Assests}}$	Measures how much return an organization generates on its assets
Return on Equity	$= \dfrac{\text{Profit after taxes}}{\text{Average shareholder,s equity}}$	Measures the rate of return on assets provided by shareholders

Adapted from http://basiccollegeaccounting.com/2007/07/table-summary-of-financial-accounting-ratio-analysis/

Summary of Learning Outcomes and Key Points

❏ **Remember and understand the purpose and types of managerial control**

Control is the final step in the management process. In the control function, managers monitor current performance and compare performance to goals, taking corrective action when needed. There are three types of management control; (1) feedforward control prevents problems before they occur. (2) Concurrent control corrects problems as they occur and (3) feedback control detects problems after they occur.

❐ **Compare the balanced scorecard to traditional financial controls**

Traditionally, organizations have relied on financial measurements to determine performance. The balanced scorecard provides four measurements upon which managers can set goals and monitor performance. These four areas of control are: (1) financial perspective, (2) customer perspective, (3) internal process perspective, and innovation and learning perspective. Overall organizational performance is determined as measured against goals in these four areas.

Financial controls include budgets or financial plans. Managers need to be familiar with the balance sheet and income statement. Financial ratios, determined from the balance sheet and income statement, give managers tools to compare the organization's performance to historic measurements or industry averages.

❐ **Describe total quality management concepts and approaches**

Total quality management is an organizational approach to improving quality. Total quality management was first advanced by W. Edwards Deming and Joseph Juran. Total quality management involves continuous improvement as an iterative process illustrated by the PDCA process (plan, do, check and act).

❐ **Apply quantitative control tools including breakeven analysis and inventory control**

Quantitative control tools include scheduling tools like Gantt and PERT charts which present visual project plans and timelines. Through breakeven analysis, managers can predict the profitability of a future project and determine the quantity that must be sold to cover project costs. In order to improve efficiency and reduce costs, managers must maintain only those inventories necessary to meet demand. The Economic Order Quantity seeks to lower inventory costs. In Just-in-Time inventory, pioneered by Toyota, managers works closely with suppliers so that inventories are eliminated and parts arrive only when needed for production.

Questions for Review

1. Describe the steps in the control process.
2. List the four components of the balanced scorecard
3. Describe the breakeven formula. At what point does a project break-even?
4. List some of the types of financial rations and their purpose.

End Notes

1. Kinicki, A. & Williams, C. (2013). *Management: A Practical Approach* (6th ed.). New York, NY, p. 550.

2. Schermerhorn, J. & Bachrach, D. (2015). *Management* (13th ed.). Wiley, New York, NY, p. 199.

3. Tripathi, A., Retrieved May 26, 2016, https://www.linkedin.com/pulse/20140 722083633-185713104-the-organizational-control-process

4. Robbins, S. & Coulter, M. (2016). *Management* (13th ed.). Pearson, Upper Saddle River, NJ, pp. 533–534.

5. Retrieved on May 25, 2016, from http://ezinearticles. com/?Feed-Forward-Vs-Concurrent-Vs-Feedback-Control&id=5681190

6. Kinicki, A. & Williams, C. (2013). *Management: A Practical Approach* (6th ed.). New York, NY, p. 521.

7. Daft (12th ed.). p. 665.

8. Kinicki (6th ed.). p. 522.

9. Daft (12th ed.). p. 666.

10. Ibid.

11. Kinicki (6th ed.). p. 59.

12. Retrieved on May 25, 2016, from https://www.deming.org/theman/theories/ fourteenpoints

13. Retrieved on May 26, 2016, from http://www.inc.com/encyclopedia/quality-cir-cles.html

14. Retrieved on May 24, 2016, from https://www.isixsigma.com/dictionary/ deming-cycle-pdca/

15. Retrieved on May 25, 2016, from http://asq.org/learn-about-quality/benchmark-ing/overview/overview.html,

16. Daft (12th ed.). p. 674.

17. Kinicki (6th ed.). p. 538.

18. Retrieved on May 27, 2016, from http://www.villanovau.com/resources/six-sigma/six-sigma-vs-lean-six-sigma/#.V0MIfPkrKUk

19. Daft, pp. 684–685.

20. Robbins & Coulter (13th ed.). p. 561.

21. Schermerhorn, J. & Bachrach, D. pp. 205–206.

22. Williams, C. (2016). *MGMT Principles of Management* (8th ed.). Cengage, Boston, MA, p. 393.

23. Retrieved on May 21, 2016, from http://www.toyota-global.com/company/ vision_philosophy/toyota_production_system/just-in-time.html

24. Retrieved on May 22, 2016, from http://www.netmba.com/operations/project/ gantt/

25. Retrieved on May 20, 2016, from http://www.netmba.com/operations/project/ pert/

26. Kinicki, p. 526.

27. Lussier, R. (2017). *Management Fundamentals: Concepts, Applications and Skill Development* (7th ed.). Sage, Los Angeles, CA, p. 458.

28. Kinicki, p. 526.

29. Lussier, p. 458.

30. Retrieved on May 23, 2016, from http://www.investopedia.com/terms/z/zbb. asp?layout=infini&v=5D&orig=1&adtest=5D

31. Bateman, T. & Snell, S. (2015). *Management* (11th ed.). McGraw-Hill, New York, NY, p. 337.

32. Retrieved on May 25, 2016, from http://www.accountingcoach.com/bookkeeping/explanation/11

33. Daft, p. 459.

34. Daft, p. 682.

GLOSSARY

Chapter 1

Administrative management An approach to management which describes what managers do and what constitutes good management practice.

Bureaucracy An organization on authority structures and relationships.

Conceptual skills The ability to think analytically and analyze abstract and complex situations.

Contingency approach A management approach that managerial situations are unique and require different methods depending on the situation.

Controlling Monitoring performance, comparing to goals, and taking corrective action if necessary.

Decisional roles Those roles and behaviors where managers make decisions to solve problems or take advantage of opportunities.

Effectiveness Doing the right things that will result in achieving organizational goals.

Efficiency Getting the most output from the least amount of resources.

First-line manager A manager who directs the daily activities of non-managers and focuses on short-term daily objectives of the organization.

Functional managers A manager who is responsible for one job function.

General manager A manager who is responsible for multiple job functions.

Hawthorne effect A phenomena where workers worked harder because they received added attention from management.

Human relations approach A management perspective that emphasizes the importance of understanding human behavior and motivation.

Informational roles Those roles and behaviors where managers collect and share information with others both inside and outside the organization.

Interpersonal roles Those roles and behaviors where managers interact with others both inside and outside the organization.

Interpersonal skills The ability to work well with others, individually or in groups.

Leading Directing, motivating, and influencing people to work toward organizational goals.

Manager Someone who coordinates the work of others to achieve organizational goals.

Managerial roles Specific actions or behaviors of managers.

Middle manager A manager who implements the policies and strategies developed by top managers and coordinates the work of front-line managers.

Operations management A management approach that is concerned with helping the organization produce its product or service more quickly and efficiently.

Organization A group of people who work together in a structured and coordinated way to achieve a set of goals.

Organizing Arranging tasks, people, and other resources to accomplish organizational goals.

Planning The process of setting goals and determining a means to achieve those goals.

Quantitative approach An approach uses quantitative tools to improve managerial decision-making.

Scientific management Uses the scientific method to find the "one best way" to perform a job.

Systems theory An approach that views the organization as a system with inputs, transformational process, outputs, and feedback.

Technical skills Job specific knowledge and expertise needed to do well at work tasks.

Theory X Managers who believe that workers dislike work, have little ambition, resist change, and prefer to be led.

Theory Y Managers who believe that employees enjoy work, accept responsibility, and are capable of self-control and self-direction.

Top managers A manager who makes long-term decisions about the overall direction of the organization.

Chapter 2

Board of directors A group whose members are elected by the stockholders (owners) of the organization to represent their interests.

Economic forces General environmental forces concerning the economy including interest rates, inflation, consumer spending, and numerous other economic indicators.

Employees People who make the organization's products or services.

Ethical dilemmas A complex decision that involves a choice between competing values or stakeholders.

Ethics Standards of right and wrong that guide human decisions and behavior.

General environment Also known as the macro environment, external forces that create opportunities or threats.

Government regulators Government bodies that have the potential to control, legislate, and otherwise influence an organization's operations and policies.

Instrumental values Preferences on how to reach desired ends, such as ambition and self-discipline.

Internal environment Those stakeholder groups that are directly impacted by an organization, includes owners, employees, and the board of directors.

Managerial ethics Standards of right and wrong that guide managers decisions and behavior in the workplace.

Owners People or institutions that have legal ownership of an organization.

Political and legal forces Forces in the general environment regarding laws and the political climate.

Sarbanes-Oxley Act of 2002 Also known as SarBox or Sox, provisions of this act require CEO's and CFO's to personally verify financial disclosers.

Sociocultural forces General environmental forces related to society's values, characteristics, and trends in society.

Special interest groups Are groups whose members try to exert influence on particular issues.

Specific environment Those stakeholders that are unique to a specific industry, including customers, competitors, suppliers, distributors, local communities, interest groups and government regulators.

Stakeholders People or groups whose interests are affected by an organization's activities.

Strategic allies Companies that join together to gain a strategic advantage.

Technological forces General environmental forces surrounding new developments in transforming resources into goods or services.

Terminal values Desired end states such as self-respect, family security, and others.

Values Underlying, relatively permanent, beliefs and attitudes that influence human behavior.

Chapter 3

Contract manufacturing A situation where a company has another company manufacture its products

Culture shock Feelings of disorientation experienced by someone who is suddenly subjected to an unfamiliar culture, way of life, or set of attitudes

Embargo A complete ban on imports from a particular country

Ethnocentrism A natural tendency of people to regard their own native country, culture, language, and behavior as superior to all others

Euro a single European currency

European Union (EU) An agreement between 27 European countries to create a unified trade and economic entity

Exporting Making products domestically and selling them abroad

Foreign subsidiary It is a local operation that is partially or completely owned and controlled by a foreign company

Franchising A form of licensing where a company allows a foreign company to use its brand name and operating methods for a fee

Geocentric managers A believe that there are differences and similarities between domestic and foreign practices and that managers should use the techniques that are the most effective

Global mindset The ability of managers to appreciate and influence individuals, groups, organizations, and systems that include different social, cultural, political, intellectual, and psychological characteristics

Global sourcing Also known as offshoring, is the practice of purchasing materials or labor from around the world

Globalization Refers to the extent to which trade, investments, information, cultural and social ideas, and political cooperation flow between countries

Greenfield venture Establishing a new wholly owned subsidiary in a foreign country by building its facilities from the start

High-context culture A culture where the written and spoken word may only convey a part of the message

Importing Acquiring products made overseas and selling them domestically

Joint venture A type of strategic alliance where a company partners with another company in a foreign location to form a separate independent company

Licensing An organization authorizes another organization the right to make or sell its products

Low-context culture A culture where most communication takes place through the written or spoken word

Monochromic cultures A culture where time is perceived as being limited, precisely segmented, and driven by schedules

Multinational corporations Businesses with extensive international operations in multiple foreign countries

Non-tariff barriers Rules and regulations which make trade more difficult

North American Free Trade Agreement (NAFTA) An agreement between the Mexican, Canadian, and U.S. governments that eliminates trade barriers

Political risk The risk of loss of assets, earning power, or managerial control due to political events or actions of a host country.

Polycentric managers They believe that native managers best understands local personnel and practices

Polychromic cultures A culture where time is viewed as being more flexible and multi-dimensional

Quotas Limits placed on the number of imports

Subsidies When government gives a domestic company a subsidy, creating a competitive advantage for that company.

Tariff barriers Taxes on certain imports which raise the price of goods making imports less competitive

World Trade Organization (WTO) A global organization of 159 countries that deals with the rules of trade between nations

Chapter 4

Competitive advantage Having the ability to transform inputs into goods and services at a maximum profit on a sustained basis, better than one's competitors.

Competitor analysis An examination of the strengths and weaknesses of a firm's competitors.

Cooptation Including members of an outside group within the organization to secure their compliance and assistance.

Core capability Unique resources that provide an organization with a distinctive competence or unique competitive advantage.

Core competency The unique skills and resources that give an organization a competitive edge.

Cost leadership A competitive strategy that depends on being able to sell more products because they are less expensive.

Culture The system of shared values and beliefs in an organization that influence the attitudes and behaviors of members and make each organization unique.

Differentiation A competitive strategy that depends on selling higher-priced products that are distinguished by such things as higher quality.

Domain The sectors or sub-environments surrounding each organization that impact how it interacts with its environment.

Environmental complexity Refers to the number of external organizations an organization is required to interact with, and the nature of these interactions.

Environmental scanning Examining the conditions in the external environment that might have an impact on the economic success of the firm, such as economic conditions, the supply of labor, and governmental regulations.

Environmental stability Refers to how much change occurs in a firm's products and the stability of its suppliers and buyers.

Five-forces model A model that is used to examine a firm's competitive advantage within its industry by examining suppliers, buyers, rival firms, substitutes, new entrants.

Focus strategy A competitive strategy that depends on selling a unique product within a segmented niche of the market.

Imperfect competition An economic condition that allows an organization to achieve a competitive advantage because there are few competitors, numerous suppliers and buyers, asymmetric information, heterogeneous products, and barriers to entry.

Industrial organization model A strategy theory that focuses on identifying the competitive advantage of each organization within its industry.

Mission statement A statement that explains what an organization is trying to accomplish and why it exists.

Offshoring The practice of moving jobs from one country to another country where they can be performed less expensively.

Processes The interactions among members of an organization, especially the communication, leadership, decision making, and power.

Resource-based theory of the firm A strategy theory that focuses on examining the resources of a firm, rather than on the external environment, to find a competitive advantage.

Strategy The set of goals and policies designed to achieve competitive advantage in a particular marketplace.

Structure The fixed relationships in an organization that describe which jobs are assigned to which departments, who has authority to make decisions, who reports to whom, and how many people each leader supervises.

SWOT method of strategy development A method of developing a firm's strategy by examining its strengths, weaknesses, opportunities, and threats.

Systems The patterned activities of the various subsystems in an organization that keep it functioning.

Chapter 5

Bounded rationality The idea that rationality in decision-making in individuals is limited by the information they have, the cognitive limitations of their minds, and the finite amount of time they have to make a decision

Brainstorming A group creativity technique by which efforts are made to find a conclusion for a specific problem by gathering a list of ideas spontaneously contributed by its members.

Certainty A decision situation where decision maker has complete information on possible alternatives and outcomes

Creativity A way of thinking that produces new ideas to solve problems or exploit opportunities

Decision tree A choice among alternative courses of action

Decision tree A decision support tool that uses a tree-like graph to model alternatives and their possible consequences.

Delphi technique A method of group decision-making and forecasting that involves successively collating the judgments of experts

Expected value A probability weighted average of all possible outcomes for each decision alternative.

Groupthink A psychological phenomenon that occurs within a group of people in which the desire for harmony or conformity in the group results in an irrational or dysfunctional decision-making outcome.

Heuristics A strategy to simplify the process of making decisions

Innovation The implementation of a new idea

Mind map A diagram used to visually organize information into a hierarchy showing relationships among pieces of the whole

Nominal Group Technique (NGT) A group process involving problem identification, solution generation, and decision-making

Nonprogrammed decision A decision regarding an unique and unstructured problem

Programmed decisions A routine or repetitive decision that can be handled by established business rules or procedures

Risk A decision situation where the decision maker has incomplete information about available alternatives but has a good idea of the probability of outcomes for each alternative

Satisficing model A decision-making strategy or cognitive heuristic that entails searching through the available alternatives until an acceptability threshold is met

Uncertainty A decision situation where the decision maker cannot list all possible outcomes and/or cannot assign probabilities to the various outcomes

Chapter 6

Bureaucracy An organizational structure that is characterized by an elaborate division of labor based on functional specialization, a hierarchy of authority assigned to different offices, a system of rules explaining how everyone is to perform, and impersonal relationships.

Centralized authority Where the authority to make organizational decisions is retained by top managers in the central office.

Contingency design theories Organizational design theories that claim that the ideal structure depends on the organization's requirements.

Cultural artifacts The visible symbols and objects that are unique to an organization and that suggest the kinds of shared beliefs and expectations of members.

Cultural values The social values that are shared among the members of an organization and tend to regulate their individual behaviors and induce collective conformity.

Customer departmentalization Creating departments by assigning all the jobs that serve a particular group of customers to the same department.

Decentralized authority Where the authority to make organizational decisions is delegated to lower-level managers and supervisors.

Departmentalization The process of assigning jobs to units or departments according to one of these common criteria: function, product, geographical area, or clientele.

Differentiation The degree of segmentation or division of labor into specialized jobs. It includes the behavioral attributes brought about by creating a narrow, department-oriented focus in the minds of individuals.

Division of labor The process of dividing work into specialized jobs that are performed by separate individuals.

External adaptation How the organization responds to the external environment and the changes that occur in it.

Formalization the degree to which employee behaviors are guided by formal rules and procedures.

Functional departmentalization Creating departments by grouping jobs that all perform similar functions.

Geographic departmentalization Creating departments by assigning all the jobs in the same geographical region to the same department.

Individualism versus collectivism The degree to which people are willing to act individually as a unique person versus as a uniform member of a group.

Integration The coordinating activity that is used to achieve a unity of effort among various subsystems within an organization. The five major methods of integration include direct supervision, standardization of work processes, standardization of outputs, standardization of skills, or mutual adjustment.

Internal integration How the organization coordinates its internal systems and processes.

Linking pins People who link different organizational units by being a member of one group and the leader of the group below.

Masculinity versus femininity The degree to which gender role differences are emphasized in terms of valuing assertive and aggressive male roles over more tender feminine attributes.

Matrix organizational structure A combination of two different forms of departmentalization, usually functional and product departmentalization.

Means-ends inversion Where the means of accomplishing a goal become so important that people focus on that activity rather than what the activity is intended to accomplish.

Mechanistic organizational structure A formal organizational structure characterized by highly specialized tasks that are carefully and rigidly defined, with a strict hierarchy of authority to control them. Bureaucracy is a type of mechanistic structure.

Mutual adjustment A means of achieving organizational coordination by allowing people to coordinate their work through informal processes, mutually adjusting to each others' needs.

Organic organizational structure A type of organization structure characterized by people who work together in an informal arrangement, sharing ideas and information, and performing a variety of tasks based on whatever is needed to accomplish the group's task.

Organizational climate The characteristics describing an organization that are relatively visible and stable, but amenable to change.

Organizational culture The shared beliefs and expectations among the members of an organization that are relatively enduring and resistant to change.

Organizational design The process of deciding on the type of structure appropriate for an organization, particularly regarding its division of labor, departmentalization, span of control, delegation of authority, and coordinating mechanism.

Organizational myths Significant stories that are told about an organization's earlier years that impact the way members think about its history even if they are not true.

Organizational myths Significant stories that are told about an organization's earlier years that impact the way members think about its history even if they are not true.

Organizational structure The arrangement of jobs and the relationships among the jobs in an organization.

Peter Principle A satirical explanation for incompetence in bureaucracies, suggesting that people rise to their level of incompetence.

Power distance The acceptability of status differentials between members of a society.

Principle of supportive relationships A universal principle that suggests that every interaction between superiors and subordinates should be transacted in a way that builds and encourages each in the performance of their respective duties.

Product departmentalization When departments are created by assigning all jobs that produce the same product to a department.

Rites and ceremonies The special events in organizations that recognize individuals and the ways they are treated.

Shared assumptions The foundation beliefs that impact how people think about and respond to organizational events, but which are mostly subconscious.

Shared norms The common expectations that guide the behavior of organizational members.

Span of control The number of subordinates assigned to a supervisor.

Suboptimizing Where one department pursues its self-interest at the expense of the larger organization.

System Four A type of organizational structure that is characterized by responsibility and initiative on the part of members, widely shared decision-making authority, decentralized decision making, and goal setting by employees.

Technology The knowledge, tools, techniques, and actions that are used to transform organizational inputs into outputs. Essentially, technology is the organization's transformation process.

Uncertainty avoidance The degree of ambiguity and uncertainty people are willing to tolerate.

Universal theories of organizational design Theories of organizational design that purport to be universally appropriate for every organization. Two widely contrasting universal design theories are bureaucracy and System Four.

Virtual workplace A flexible workplace where people work at any time and anyplace in informal relationships, usually with computer technologies.

Chapter 7

Base compensation The salary or hourly wages paid to employees.

Collective bargaining The negotiation process that results in a contract between employees and management concerning working conditions.

Development Ongoing education, designed to improve the skills employees need for future jobs.

Equal employment opportunity Requires that employment decisions are made without regard to sex, race, color, religion, national origin or religion.

External recruiting Involves attracting job applicants from outside the organization.

Human capital Refers to the knowledge, skills, and abilities of employees that add economic value to an organization.

Human resource management Includes all organizational activities managers perform to attract, develop and maintain a talented workforce.

Human resource planning Includes all of the activities that managers use in order to project current and future human resource needs

Human resource management process Includes those activities aimed at attracting, developing, and retaining a qualified workforce.

Internal recruiting The process of making those already employed by the organization aware of job openings.

Job analysis A systematic study to determine the basic elements of a job.

Job description Summarizes the duties of a job.

Job specification Lists the minimum qualifications a person must have to perform the job successfully.

Labor unions Organizations of employees that are formed to protect and advance the interests of their members through collective bargaining on job-related issues.

Onboarding The process of introducing a new employee to the organization and the job.

Orientation Same as onboarding.

Performance appraisal A formal assessment of how well an employee is performing in his or her job.

Realistic job preview Applicants are given complete, undistorted information before being selected.

Recruiting The process of locating and attracting qualified applicants for open jobs.

Reliability Means that a selection method delivers consistent results with regard to what it measures.

Selection The process of choosing the most qualified applicants among those recruited for a given job.

Sexual harassment Is a form of workplace discrimination against individuals because of their sex.

Socialization The process by which new members learn and adapt to the ways of the organization.

Training The set of activities that provide learning opportunities for employees to acquire and improve job-related skills.

Validity Means that there is a clear and direct relationship between what the method measures and future job performance.

Chapter 8

Attitude A learned predisposition towards and a given object.

Burnout A state of chronic stress that leads to physical and emotional exhaustion, cynicism and detachment and feelings of ineffectiveness and lack of accomplishment.

Causal attribution The process of trying to determine the causes of people's behavior.

Diversity The range of human differences, including but not limited to race, ethnicity, gender, gender identity, sexual orientation, age, social class, physical ability or attributes, religious or ethical values system, national origin, and political beliefs.

Emotional intelligence One's ability to notice and manage emotional signals and cues.

Emotional Stability The extent to which people feel secure and unworried and how they are to experience negative emotions during stressful situations.

Employee engagement A strong sense of belonging and connection to one's work and employer.

Fundamental attribution error The tendency to overestimate the effect of personality and underestimate the effect of the situation in explaining a person's behavior

Halo effect An impression that is formed based on a single trait

Job satisfaction The extent to which an individual feels positively about a job and work experiences.

Locus of control Is the degree to which people believe that they control their outcomes through their own efforts

Machiavellianism A personality type which tends to deceive and manipulate others.

Organizational commitment Psychological attachment that an employee has with their organization.

Perception The analysis of sensory information within the brain

Personality The unique combination of an individual's emotional, thought, and behavior patterns.

Recency effect The tendency to remember recent information more than earlier information

Selective perception Tendency to focus on aspects of a situation or person that are consistent with and reinforce our existing beliefs and ignore those that are inconsistent with those beliefs

Self-efficacy The personal belief that one has in their ability to perform a task

Self-esteem A person's overall opinion of themselves

Self-fulfilling prophecy A belief that comes true because one acts as if it is already true.

Self-serving bias The tendency of people to attribute positive events to their own character but attribute negative events to external factors.

Stereotyping The tendency to attribute characteristics of a group to an individual that belongs in that group.

Stress A state of tension experienced by people who face situations that require change or some type of response.

Values Global beliefs and feelings that are directed toward objects, people or events

Chapter 9

Content theories Motivation theories that emphasize the needs that motivate people.

Continuous reinforcement A consequence follows every occurrence of the behavior

Distributive justice The perceived fairness of the amount and allocation of rewards between individuals

Esteem needs The need for a positive self-image and to receive attention, recognition, appreciation and respect from others

Expectancy An individual's perception of his or her ability to accomplish an objective

Extinction Withholding reinforcement when undesired behavior occurs

Extrinsic rewards Tangible rewards given to employees by managers, and include pay raises, bonuses, and benefits.

Flexible working hours The practice of allowing employees some choice in their daily work schedules

Hygiene factors Factors that do not provide satisfaction or motivation though dissatisfaction results from their absence

Inputs Factors that an employee contributes to his or her job including education, skill, experience, work ethic and training

Instrumentality The perception of the relationship between performance and the likelihood of receiving a desired outcome or reward

Intermittent reinforcement Consequences are delivered after so many occurrences of the behavior

Interval reinforcement Consequences follow behavior after different times, some shorter and some longer, varying around a specified average time

Intrinsic rewards The psychological rewards that employees get from performing important work and doing it well.

Job enlargement Increasing the scope of a job through extending the range of its job duties

Job enrichment The vertical expansion of a job's scope by adding planning and evaluation responsibilities

Job rotation The practice of moving employees between different tasks to promote experience and variety.

Motivation The psychological processes that stimulate and direct goal-directed behavior

Motivators Factors that provide positive satisfaction, arising from intrinsic conditions of the job itself

Need A physiological or psychological deficiency that arouses behavior

Negative reinforcement The withdrawal of a negative consequence for desired behavior

Outputs Factors that an employee receives from his or her job including salary, perks, bonus, and recognitions in the form of awards

Physiological needs The most basic human physical needs

Positive reinforcement The use of positive consequences to strengthen a desired behavior

Procedural justice The idea of fairness in the processes that resolve disputes and allocate resources

Punishment Negative consequence undesired behavior

Safety needs The need for safety and freedom from threats

Self-actualization needs The need to develop to one's fullest potential

Social needs The need to be accepted by others, have friendships, be part of a group and be loved by others

Valence The importance that an individual places on the potential outcomes or rewards that can be achieved on the job

Chapter 10

Agile team A cross-functional group of people that have the personnel and resources needed to produce a working, tested incremental version of a product.

Conflict A disagreement over issues resulting in some form of interference or opposition.

Cross-functional teams Teams that include members from different functional areas of the organization, such as finance, sales and operations.

Group Two or more two or more freely acting individuals who share collective norms, collective goals, and have a common identity.

Group cohesiveness The degree to which members are attracted to or loyal to the group

Interest-Based Relational (IBR) approach A conflict resolution style that focuses on building mutual respect and understanding, encouraging people to resolve conflict in a united, cooperative way.

Norms Expectations about behavior that are shared by members of a team.

Scrum An agile methodology to manage a project.

Self-managed teams Groups of workers who are empowered and have responsibility for administrative oversight of their tasks.

Social loafing The tendency for an individual to expend less effort when working with a group than when working individually.

Team A small group of people with complementary skills who are committed to a common purpose, performance goals, and approach for which they hold themselves mutually accountable

Team building A set of planned activities aimed at improving the functioning of a team.

Virtual team A team whose members rarely meet face-to-face but instead interact by using various forms of information technology such as e-mail, computer networks, telephone, fax and video conference.

Chapter 11

Authentic leadership Refers to individuals who know and understand themselves and empower others with their openness and authenticity

Autocratic style A leader who dictates work methods and limits employee participation

Charismatic leaders Leaders who are self-confident, enthusiastic, and whose personality influences people to behave in certain ways

Coercive power The power a leader has to control followers through punishment

Consideration A leadership style based on mutual trust and respect for the group member's ideas and feelings

Contingency theory A leadership theory that defines effective leadership as a match between the leader's preferred style and the situation

Democratic style A leader who involves employees in decision making, delegates authority, and uses feedback as a means to coach employees.

Employee-centered leader A leaders whose behavior focuses on subordinate's satisfaction and work group cohesion

Expert power Power based on expertise, knowledge, or specialized skills

Job-centered leader A leader who is primarily concerned with issues like production efficiency and meeting work schedules

Initiating structure A leadership style where the leader defines the roles and work of the group

Laissez-faire style Describes a leader who lets the group make decisions and complete work as they see fit

Leader Someone who can influence others

Leader–member relations The degree to which a leader is accepted and supported by the group members

Leadership The process of influencing a group of people to achieve a goal

Least-preferred co-worker (LPC) questionnaire A questionnaire that measures whether a leader prefers a relationship- or task-oriented style

Legitimate power The power a leader has as a result of his or her position in the organization

Level 5 leadership Leaders who blend extreme personal humility with intense professional will

Managerial grid A two-dimensional grid for assessing leadership styles

Path-goal theory A leadership theory that says the leader's job is to assist followers in reaching their goals using directive or supportive leader behaviors to ensure that the follower goals are compatible with organizational goals

Position power The ability of a leader to control subordinates through reward and punishment.

Readiness The extent to which people have the ability, confidence, and willingness to perform a task

Referent power Power based on the leader's personal characteristics

Reward power The power a leader has to provide positive rewards

Servant leadership An approach to leading where leaders view their primary role as helping followers in their quest to satisfy personal needs, aspirations, and interests

Situational leadership theory (SLT) A leadership theory that matches the leader's style to the readiness of the followers

Substitutes for leadership A theory stating that different situational factors can enhance, neutralize, or substitute for leader behaviors

Task structure The extent to which the task is structured and defined, with clear goals and procedures

Transactional leadership Leaders who exchange rewards and punishment based on follower performance

Transformational leadership Leaders who inspire and cause change in individuals and social systems

Chapter 12

Big data a term that describes the large volume of data, both structured and unstructured, that are produced by the various information systems in an organization

Cloud a network of servers that allow organizations to provide online services and store and access data

Communication the transfer of information and understanding from one person to another person

Customer relationship management (CRM) a strategy for managing all of an organization's relationships and interactions with customers and prospective customers

Data analytics qualitative and quantitative techniques and processes used to extract, categorize, and identify behavioral data and patterns.

Data mining the process of analyzing data to yield useful information

Enterprise resource planning (ERP) an organization wide system that integrates all departments and functions throughout an organization into a single IT system or set of integrated IT systems

IT infrastructure the shared technology resources that serve as the platform for the organization's particular information system applications

Social media electronic platforms, where users create, modify, share, and discuss Internet content

Supply chain management (SCM) it is the active management of supply chain activities in order to maximize customer value and achieve a sustainable competitive advantage

Systems development life cycle (SDLC) the high-level process for developing information systems, which is organized into seven phases: planning, analysis, design, development, testing, implementation, and maintenance

The Internet of things (IoT) network sensors and actuators that are embedded in physical objects that are connected to the Internet

Chapter 13

Assets Items of value that the organization owns.

Balance sheet Shows an organization's financial position at a given point in time.

Balanced scorecard A control tool to give managers a comprehensive system to evaluate organizational performance through four indicators; financial, customer, internal business and innovation and learning.

Benchmarking A technique where by an organization measures its performance against the performance of best in class organizations.

Breakeven analysis A technique for identifying the point where total revenue equals total costs.

Budget A financial plan that states an organization's plans for a given period in quantifiable terms such as dollars and hours.

Capital expenditure budgets Budgets that include all planned investments in major assets.

Concurrent control Control that takes place while an activity is in progress.

Controlling The management function of monitoring organizational performance, comparing performance to goals and taking corrective action as needed.

Economic order quantity A form of inventory control that seeks to minimize the costs of ordering and holding inventory.

Expense budgets Budgets that forecast total operational spending for the year.

Feedback control Control that takes place after a work activity has been completed.

Fixed budgets Control that takes place before an activity is completed. (or) Static budgets that are based on a single estimate of costs.

Income statement A financial document that shows revenues and expenses, and the resulting profit or loss, over a period of time.

Inventory control Maintaining just the right amount of inventory to meet the organization's needs.

ISO 9000 International quality standards representing an universal standard on what constitutes quality management.

Just-In-Time inventory An inventory system where component parts arrive from suppliers just as they are needed for production.

Lean Six Sigma Focuses on problem solving and performance improvement with the goal of speed with excellence.

Liabilities Debts the organization owes to creditors.

Operating budgets Include the revenue and expenses generated by an organization's daily operations. Revenue budgets forecast total annual income from all sources.

PDCA cycle A continuous quality improvement model with four repetitive steps for continuous improvement and learning: Plan, Do, Study (Check) and Act.

Program Evaluation Review Technique (PERT) A network model that accounts for randomness in activity completions times.

Quality circle A participatory management technique where employees work together to solve quality problems.

Revenue budgets forecast total annual income from all sources.

Six Sigma Quality standard that targets a goal of no more than 3.4 defects per million parts.

Stockholder's equity The amount of assets accrued to the organization's owners.

Total quality management (TQM) An organizational-wide approach focused on continually improving product quality and value.

Variable budgets A budgeting system where resources are allocated in proportion to organizational activity.

Zero-based budgeting (ZBB) A budget practice where all expenses must be justified for each new period.

INDEX

liabilities, 263
licensing, 36
line authority, 110
liquidation, 67
local communities, 23
locus of control, 147–148
long-term *vs.* short-term
    orientation, 44–45
low-context culture, 47

M

machiavellianism, 149–150
maintenance, SDLC, 243
management
    Deming's 14 principles for, 256
    Fayol's principle, 9
    vs. leadership, 212–213
    managers, 2–7
    organization, 1–2
    study management, 7–10
management environments
    ethical, 25–28
    general, 20–22
    internal, 24
    specific, 22–24
managerial ethics, 25
managerial grid, 217–218
managerial roles, 4–5
managers
    definition, 2
    first-line, 3
    functional, 3
    general, 3
    geocentric, 43
    informational and decisional, 6
    interpersonal roles, 5
    vs. leaders, 212
    leading and controlling, 4
    management functions, 4
    managerial roles, 4–5
    middle, 3
    polycentric, 43
    skills, 6–7
    top, 2
    types of, 2–3
    viewpoint, culture and practice, 43
market culture, 107

Mary Parker Follett and the
    Hawthorne Studies, 10–11
masculinity *vs.* femininity, 44
Maslow's hierarchy of needs,
    170–172
matrix structure, 113
mechanist organizations, 117
middle managers, 3
mind mapping, 93
mission statement, 58
modular network, 115
monochronic cultures, 48
motivation
    acquired needs theory,
        173–174
    and compensation, 183–184
    content theories, 170
    definition, 170
    design of, 181–183
    equity theory, 175–177
    ERG theory, 172–173
    expectancy theory, 177–178
    extrinsic rewards, 170
    flexible working hours, 184
    goal-setting theory, 178–179
    Herzberg's two factor theory,
        174–175
    intrinsic rewards, 170
    Maslow's hierarchy of needs,
        170–172
    practical application, 181
    reinforcement schedules, 180
    reinforcement theory, 179–180
multinational corporations, 38
mutual-benefit originations, 109
Myers Briggs type indicator
    (MBTI), 144–145

N

National Labor Relations Act, 129
National Labor Relations Board
    (NLRB), 130, 137
negative reinforcement, 180
network organization, 115
neuroticism, 146
niche strategy, 68
nominal group technique, 91–92

nonprofit organizations, 109
nonprogrammed decisions, 82
nonverbal communication, 238
"norming," by groups, 194
norms, 196
North American Free Trade
    Agreement (NAFTA), 40

O

objective performance measures, 135
observable artifacts, 104, 105
Occupational Safety and Health
    Act (OSHA), 129
onboarding, 134
openness to experience, 145
operating budgets, 262
operational planning, 59
operations management, 12–13
organic organizations, 117
organizational charts, 109
organizational commitment,
    158–159
organizational culture
    collective commitment, 107
    competing values framework,
        106–108
    definitions, 104, 105
    high performing cultures, 108
    importance of, 107–108
    shapes behavior, 108
    social stability, 108
    three levels of, 104–106
organizational design
    differentiation *vs.* integration, 118
    link between strategy and
        structure, 119
    vs. mechanistic, 117–118
    organizational life cycle,
        118–119
organizational identity, 107
organizational life cycle
    birth stage, 118
    maturity stage, 119
    midlife stage, 118
    youth stage, 118
organizational structure, 109,
    111–117